Samuel Minton

The glory of Christ in the creation and reconciliation of all things

With special reference to the doctrine of eternal evil. Third Edition

Samuel Minton

The glory of Christ in the creation and reconciliation of all things
With special reference to the doctrine of eternal evil. Third Edition

ISBN/EAN: 9783337085988

Printed in Europe, USA, Canada, Australia, Japan

Cover: Foto ©Lupo / pixelio.de

More available books at **www.hansebooks.com**

SERMONS.

LONDON: PRINTED BY
SPOTTISWOODE AND CO., NEW-STREET SQUARE
AND PARLIAMENT STREET

THE

GLORY OF CHRIST

IN THE

CREATION AND RECONCILIATION OF ALL THINGS.

WITH SPECIAL REFERENCE TO

THE DOCTRINE OF ETERNAL EVIL.

A COURSE OF SERMONS

PREACHED AT EATON CHAPEL, EATON SQUARE,
LONDON.

BY

SAMUEL MINTON, M.A.

OF WORCESTER COLLEGE, OXFORD.

THIRD EDITION.

LONDON:
LONGMANS, GREEN, AND CO.
1871.

'Search the Scriptures; for in them ye think ye have eternal life: and they are they which testify of Me.'

JOHN v. 39.

'These were more noble than those in Thessalonica, in that they received the word with all readiness of mind, and searched the Scriptures daily, whether those things were so.' ACTS xvii. 11.

'Prove all things.' 1 THESS. v. 21.

'Follow on, to know the Lord.'

Hosea, vi. 3.

'It is owned that the whole scheme of Scripture is not yet understood; so, if it ever come to be understood before the restitution of all things, and without miraculous interpositions, it must be in the same way that natural knowledge is come at, by the continuance and progress of learning and liberty, and by particular persons attending to, comparing, and pursuing intimations scattered up and down it, which are overlooked and disregarded by the generality of the world. For this is the way in which all improvements are made, by thoughtful men tracing out obscure hints, as it were dropped us by nature accidentally, or which seem to come into our minds by chance. Nor is it at all incredible that a book which has been so long in the possession of mankind should contain many truths as yet undiscovered.'—*Bishop Butler.*

'If God reveal anything to you by any other instrument of His, be as ready to receive it as over you were to receive any truth by my ministry; for I am verily persuaded—I am very confident—*the Lord has more truth yet to break forth out of His holy word.* For my part, I cannot sufficiently bewail the condition of the Reformed Churches, who are come to a period in religion, and will go at present no further than the instruments of the first Reformation. The Lutherans cannot be drawn to go beyond what Luther saw; whatever part of His will our good God has imparted and revealed unto Calvin, they will rather die than embrace it. And the Calvinists, you see, stick fast where they were left by that great man of God, who yet saw not all things. This is a misery much to be lamented.'—*Robinson's Last Charge,* A.D. 1620.

'The Christian Church is even yet but very imperfectly freed from the unholy influence and the mischievous operation of human authority. The house requires to be more carefully swept than it was at the Reformation from Popery, and a more thorough search must be made for the old leaven, that it may be more completely cast out.'—*Dr. Brown.*

'Is God's purpose, though declared in Scripture, to be damned as false doctrine simply because the Church is blind to it? Is Israel's path to teach us nothing? Are men's traditions as to God's purpose to be preferred to His own unerring Word? When I see the Church's blindness at this day, almost unconscious of the judgment which is coming on it—when I see that if I bow to the decisions of its widest branch, I must receive not Transubstantiation only, but the Immaculate Conception also, I can only fall back upon that Word which, in prospect of coming apostasy, is commanded to the man of God, as the guide of his steps, and the means to perfect him. It is indeed a solemn thing to differ with the Church, or, like Paul, to find oneself in a "way which they call heresy," simply by "believing," not some, but " all the things which are written in the law and in the prophets." But the path is not a new one for the sons of God. All the prophets perished in Jerusalem. And, above all, the Lord of prophets was judged as a deceiver by those whom God had called to be His witnesses. The Church's judgment, therefore, cannot decide a point like this, especially if it be in opposition to Holy Scripture.'—*Andrew Jukes.*

' How important to the cause of our heavenly Master is the free discussion of religious topics, which we are naturally so anxious to repress when it goes against our faith. Yet we need not. We dislike being called to account for our more sacred opinions, especially those which we hold with an uncertain grasp; and we equally dislike to study the reasons advanced by our opponents, without which it must needs be impossible either to persuade or to be persuaded. " Prove all things" is a counsel of Christian perfection beyond most men's observance, though it is the only way to "holding *fast* that which is good."'—*J. P. Gell.*

' The hope of the millennial kingdom of Christ [and, we may add, the hope of "life and immortality" in Christ alone, with the ultimate " reconciliation of all things "] has naturally encountered the suspicions of those Christians whose faith has been crystallised and frozen down in artificial systems of theology. When the doctrines of the gospel have once been compacted together by a logical process, and the result is conceived to embody the whole counsel of God, every new truth drawn fresh from the Scriptures is an unwelcome guest or even a suspected enemy. It wears a strange and foreign aspect, and disturbs the symmetry of a laboriously-constructed system.'—*T. R. Birks.*

' It is not all truth that triumphs in the world, nor all good; but only truth and good up to a certain point. Let them once pass this point, and their progress pauses. Their followers in the main cannot keep up with them thus far. Fewer and fewer are those who still press on in their company; until at last even these fail, and there is a perfection at which they are deserted by all men, and are in the presence of God and of Christ alone.'—*Dr. Arnold.*

' Deliver me from the narrowing influence of human lessons, from human systems of theology; teach me directly out of the fulness and freeness of Thine own word. Hasten the time when, unfettered by sectarian intolerance, and unawed by the authority of men, the Bible shall make its rightful impression upon all; the simple and obedient readers thereof, calling no man Master, but Christ only.'—*Dr. Chalmers.*

' The truth has a vitality in it still; and many dry rudiments of it, which at present lie dull and uninteresting in our minds, are yet destined to expand and acquire a new significance. Let the mind be frankly open to any and every Truth, however unfamiliar to us the first view of it, which may turn out to be in accordance with the teaching of the Apostles.'—*Dr. Goulburn, Dean of Norwich.*

TRUTH AND LOVE.

Letter to a Clergyman.

I SHOULD not have troubled you with another letter, but for the avowal with which you conclude, that you feel bound to withdraw from Christian intercourse with any who 'cause to err'—i.e. who differ from you in any religious opinion, and venture to express their opinion; including, of course, all Baptists, Arminians, anti-Millennarians, and others, whom you must necessarily consider amongst those who 'cause to err.' This spirit, or principle if you prefer it, has been the bane of the Church in all ages; it was the life and soul of the Inquisition, it is the essential virus of the worst kind of schism, and is that which enables the world to say, 'See how these Christians hate one another.'

In this question of eternal suffering you have not even the excuse of its being a matter of *faith*; it is simply a matter of *opinion*. I do not say merely of *interpretation*, because a matter of faith, such as the Deity of Christ or the Atonement, may depend on interpretation; but this doctrine, however important in its practical bearings, and therefore however worthy of earnest discussion, is purely a matter of opinion.

I might have some excuse for elevating it into a matter of faith. For my enjoyment in looking forward to eternity depends in great measure on the assurance that God will be '*all in all*;' that sin and misery will come to an end.

I can rejoice even now, notwithstanding the existence of present evil, 'in hope of the glory of God;' in the prospect not merely of being myself delivered from the power of evil, but of forming part of God's glorious Universe, when evil has been banished from it for ever.

I should be sorry to be *able* to rejoice in the prospect of an eternity, throughout which the wailings of despair would be continually ringing in my ears, and the writhings of agony be ever before my eyes; and equally sorry to think that I could ever sink to such an unutterable depth of selfishness as to be able to spend an eternity of happiness in forgetfulness of the fact that such things were going on, even though they were put far away out of sight and out of sound.

Furthermore, my hope of personal immortality depends upon the plain natural meaning of those innumerable texts, which you are obliged to rationalise upon, and interpret in a non-natural sense, in order to maintain the traditional philosophy about man's inherent immortality.

But *you* have no such pretext. Your faith and hope cannot in the slightest degree depend upon your interpretation of those passages being correct. They centre in the salvation which Christ offers from sin and all its consequences. What those consequences will ultimately be to such as are not saved is a matter of opinion, and cannot possibly, in *your* view of it, touch the foundation at all. The eternal life, which we have in Him, is precisely the same thing, whatever be the alternative to those who refuse it. So too are the means by which He obtained it for us, and communicates it to us.

If, indeed, we believed your view to be taught in Scripture, and still denied its truth, the case would be different; for we should then be shaking the foundation of *all* faith. But you know that this is not the case. You may think that our judgment is biassed by our feelings, as we may think that yours is biassed by traditional opinion and party discipline. But when Christians of approved character and undoubted credibility on both sides solemnly declare their belief, that the view they hold is in accordance with the teaching of Scripture as a whole, then for either party to break fellowship with the other on such a matter as this, because they refuse to do violence to their own convictions, and to accept the dictum of those who take another view, is in the last degree unchristian in principle, and disastrous in its effects upon the Church and the world. 'Whereto we have already attained let us walk by the same rule, let us mind the same thing; and if in anything ye be otherwise minded, God shall reveal even this unto you.'

That the difference of opinion is a very serious and important one, as bearing upon the success of the Gospel, from a human point of view, I not only admit but strenuously maintain. I believe that your doctrine is the fruitful parent both of infidelity and of indifference; that it weakens the Gospel message, and in a variety of ways does incalculable mischief. You, on the other hand, think that my doctrine will make sinners less anxious to be converted, because less afraid of the ultimate consequences of sin. No doubt this difference of opinion, like *every* difference in a greater or less degree, must interpose *some* difficulty in our working together, and detract *somewhat* from the pleasure of mutual intercourse. But to refuse to hold communion with one another, to denounce one another, or to change countenance towards one another on that account would be a grievous sin—a sin of ignorance perhaps, but still a sin.

Do not they who are looking for the Lord's speedy coming believe that those who expect the world to be converted by missionary agency 'cause to err,' and weaken the force of the cry, 'Prepare to meet thy God?' And, on the other hand, do not they who believe that expectation to be scriptural, consider that you and other Millennarians 'cause to err?' Do they not believe that you will probably be the cause of many heathens spending an eternity in torment, by damping the missionary zeal of those whose enthusiasm would otherwise have been kindled at the prospect of converting the world? It is no doubt the duty of both, according to the strength of their convictions, to endeavour to spread their own opinions. But are they to excommunicate one another, or look coldly upon one another, on account of this difference? Is it to embitter their intercourse, or to debar them from all intercourse? Is the one to call the other 'heretic,' 'infidel,' and so forth, because he 'perverts' or 'corrupts' what appears to his opponent's eyes so 'plainly revealed,' so 'explicitly declared' in Scripture? Alas for our Master's seamless robe! Alas for the unity of the Spirit in the bond of peace! How long, O Lord, how long?

PREFACE

TO

THE SECOND EDITION.

It was easy to foresee that this book would receive little favour from the Religious Press.* The amount of hostile criticism that it has received is neither more nor less than I expected. The 'orthodox' have attacked it for its 'heresy' on one point; the 'Liberals' for its orthodoxy on other points. Besides, nearly all the organs of theological thought in this country are Platonist

---

* Since writing the above, I have received a letter from the editor of a religious newspaper in America, in which he says: 'I see by the *Rock* that you are making a brave fight for the truth, and have to endure some hardness; therefore may the Lord of Love sustain you in your efforts to vindicate His character from the aspersions of centuries of false theology. It is positively astounding that the dogma of the eternal torment of the wicked should have ever obtained in the Christian Church. I wonder at myself, when I think I once believed or accepted it. Most fatal consequences to the Churches are following in this country. The Spiritualists and other infidels make this doctrine their main fulcrum in their attacks upon Christianity; and a mighty power it gives them. Probably no other gives them so much success in their attacks upon Christianity and the Bible.'

in their belief that the human soul is indestructible. They differ widely amongst themselves as to the conditions of eternal life hereafter in certain cases; some following Origen in the belief that all will ultimately be restored to the favour of God,* others holding with Augustine that those who die impenitent will live for ever in a state of sin and misery. But they agree in rejecting the revealed truth, so humbling to human pride, namely, that man is mortal and fleeth away like a shadow, that the Creator Himself 'only hath immortality,' that in Christ alone can anything permanently consist, that only they who eat of the bread which He gives will live for ever, and that all moral creatures, on whom the wrath of God

* 'I entirely agree with your correspondent in regarding Universalism as unscriptural. But he is perhaps not so well aware as I am now beginning to be, how many Christians have been driven to adopt that view, as the only way of escape that presented itself to their minds from the popular doctrine of eternal torture. Your readers would be astonished if I were to mention the names of some revered fathers of the Evangelical party, living and dead, who have hoped against hope that all would eventually be saved, from feeling it utterly impossible that they could be kept alive for ever for the sole purpose of being tortured. And, in addition to the hundreds of believers, in and out of my own congregation, who are rejoicing, either in having their own previous views confirmed, or in being delivered from the dismal shadow of the popular delusion, I know of several Universalists who have abandoned that theory, on having the truth of God's Word put plainly before them. An aged Christian, who has spent a long life in his Master's service, and has been a Universalist for thirty-five years, said to me, after reading *The Glory of Christ*, " It is as clear as daylight." '—Letter to the *Rock*.

abideth with its whole force, must sooner or later 'fail before Him,' be crushed out of existence, and 'perish everlastingly.' Naturally, therefore, they join in condemning the doctrine here advocated.

It would be uncandid in me, however, not to say, that while agreeing with the Augustinians in almost all their other points of controversy with the Origenists, I feel infinitely greater sympathy with their opponents than with them, on this particular subject. The heart and soul of the whole matter is the question, whether Evil will ever cease, or not. Are sin and suffering to last for ever, or is the whole Universe to be reconciled to God? The Universalists accept the revealed truth, that every enemy shall be destroyed, and God be all in all. I firmly believe them to be partially mistaken as to the way in which this will be brought about. The reconciliation of all things does not necessitate the restoration of every individual form of life that has ever appeared; and, to my mind, Scripture plainly teaches that it will only be accomplished after the destruction of multitudes of creatures who were made capable of immortality.* And, believing this, I cannot, of course, doubt

---

* Hence the title of this book, which has been superficially criticised. 'Is destruction reconciliation?' No; but it may be a necessary preliminary to it. Individuals will be destroyed, that the universe may be reconciled. 'In no possible sense of the word,' says the editor of

that the denial of it, like every other error, must be to a certain extent injurious. But, compared with the error of believing that sentient creatures will be kept alive to all eternity, for the sole purpose of being tortured, and that without the slightest hope of their deriving one particle of good from it, in order to enhance the glory of God and the happiness of their fellow-creatures, the strongest objections that can possibly attach to the Universalist's creed sink into insignificance. That creed casts no dark shadow upon the justice and the love of God, it drives no thoughtful persons into infidelity, nor is it chargeable with any of the numerous evils that hang about the neck of the popular doctrine. This explains why it is so lightly touched upon in the following sermons. My war is against the belief in Eternal Evil: and that belief is not entertained by the disciples of Origen—it is entertained by those of Augustine.

Most of what had previously been written in defence

the *Christian Advocate,* 'can the destruction of personal existence be regarded as a reconciliation or restoration. Mr. Minton is compelled to exempt Hell from the range of things restored as much as we are.' Yes; but my argument is, that the reconciliation of the universe will be effected by *some* things being blotted out of it, and not 'restored' at all. 'Death and Hell' will be 'cast into the lake of fire,' to be destroyed for ever; and *then* 'God will be all in all.' With this argument, as far as I am aware, no one has attempted to grapple.

of endless torment being directed against Universalism, I felt some anxiety to see what could be said against the direct evidence from Scripture in favour of Destructionism. That anxiety has now been entirely removed. Several writers have applied their whole strength to the task, and they have all utterly failed to shake the evidence in any material point. They have detected a few mistakes in my conduct of the argument; but the chief result of their efforts has been to prove how impregnable is its main position. Some notice of these replies will be found in the Appendix. A few preliminary points may be considered here.

In the first place, as to the tone and spirit in which such a subject should be treated.

Mr. Grant rebukes me for using 'irony' in the discussion. But his rebuke falls quite as heavily upon Elijah, Isaiah, and Paul, not to add upon our Master Himself. Elijah was fully aware of the importance of his controversy with the priests of Baal, when he said, 'Peradventure he sleepeth, and must be awaked.' Isaiah was not forgetting the sinfulness of idolatry, when he showed its absurdity also. Paul was far from meaning to use lightness, when he asked the Corinthians to forgive him the wrong of ministering to them gratuitously. Nor did Jesus intend to represent unbelief and persecution as trifling matters, when, at one time, he likened his opponents to peevish children quarrelling over their games, and, at another time, told them that they were the children of their father in more ways than they thought of. Mr. Grant evidently mistakes irony for jesting or levity, and thereupon breaks forth into an exclamation about there being 'no subject in the illimitable universe of God' less suitable for it.

Other remarks, however, have been made, which are entitled to more serious consideration. And, in addition to what will be found in my letter to the *Christian Advocate*, at the end of this Preface, I would submit—1st, That in controversy it is not always easy to determine whether the probable advantage of answering a fool according to his folly, 'lest he be wise in his own conceit,' is great enough to counterbalance the danger of 'becoming like unto him;' and, 2ndly, That it is often quite as difficult to determine how far the sacredness or solemnity of any truth should be allowed to shield a grievous perversion of it from the treatment it deserves. Few Protestant controversialists scruple to handle the doctrine of Transubstantiation with the utmost freedom, and to describe it as a monstrous and absurd superstition. Yet the question relates to the bodily presence of the incarnate Son of God; and the fact of that presence, under the form of bread and wine, has been regarded by countless millions of Christians for many centuries as the central truth of their religion. So the doctrine of eternal torment is connected with the solemn subject of final judgment; and a still larger proportion of Christians firmly believe it to be a revealed truth. Yet, while earnestly desiring to approach it with all 'seriousness of mind,' I cannot feign 'more modesty of opinion,' or use 'more deference of language,' with respect to it; for nothing can exceed the clearness with which, to my own mind, the destruction of evildoers, and the reconciliation of all things, are revealed in Scripture; and no language can express my horror of the popular doctrine, or my amazement that any thoughtful person could ever heartily believe it. It may no doubt be 'more probable' in the abstract, that the majority should be right; but it has so often proved otherwise, that the test of numbers becomes very precarious indeed.* One of our Homilies, not content with express-

---

* There once sprang up within the Church of God a 'sect' which was 'everywhere spoken against,' and that not by the heathen, but by the Church itself. It appealed to 'the oracles of God;' but the people, to whom those oracles were 'committed,' and especially those who 'sat in Moses' seat' as its authorised expounders, rejected the appeal, and proing a modest opinion that the Reformed Faith may possibly be the true one, in spite of its being the faith of a 'minority,' boldly asserts that nearly all Christendom was for ages sunk in idolatry and superstition; and I verily believe that almost the last remnant of that widespread error, which Evangelical Christians have now to be delivered from, is the doctrine of Eternal Evil.

Those who think that 'the words of the living God' only convey 'general impressions of most just judgment,' must, of course, be 'humbly content' with such general impressions; they must be willing to 'wait,' and 'leave' all explanations for another world. But why should they blame others for speaking plainly what they see distinctly? Why should they charge them with seeking to be 'wise above what is written,' and 'yielding to the pride of intellect,' and not exercising 'simple faith,' and so forth? Secret things—namely, things not revealed—belong unto God; but those which *are* revealed, however obscurely, belong

---

nounced the appellants guilty of 'heresy.' Priests and Levites, Scribes and Pharisees, Sadducees and Herodians, Doctors and Lawyers, though differing on almost everything else, cordially agreed in condemning the new sect, root and branch. It was a tremendous *primâ facie* presumption against it, no doubt; but the sect was right, and the Church was wrong, notwithstanding.

to us and to our children. To cry after knowledge, and lift up our voice for understanding, to seek it as silver, and search for it as for hid treasure, so that we may become wise *up to* what is written, affords no proof of any desire to reach *above* it. 'The humble Christian,' says one reviewer, 'will believe as it is written.' No doubt; but the question remains, What *is* written?

The position here maintained is, that the utter destruction of those who finally remain out of Christ is positively revealed in God's word; but that all its details are purposely hidden from us. In some form or other, we are assured, each of them will receive his own separate desert, many or few stripes; but they will all be alike in this,—that, not having life, they must ultimately perish.

This position has been assailed both for its definiteness and its indefiniteness. The venerable Dean of Carlisle warns us against 'daring to define with the accuracy of critics, or the vain curiosity of philosophers, what that awful thing may be.' Mr. Garbett, on the other hand, pronounces that, 'if, indeed, Mr. Minton deliberately holds that an undefined period is to be spent by the wicked in torment before they cease to exist as such, the case is yet stronger against his system than we thought it to be.' And Mr. Grant adduces our acknowledged ignorance as to the duration of future suffering, supposing it to be temporary, as almost amounting to proof, that its duration will be eternal. 'There is another consideration which I have not met with in any books on the subject [very unlikely indeed that he should], but which weighs much with me in my belief of the eternity of future punishment. It is this, that those who repudiate the idea of the never-ending punishment of the ungodly cannot furnish us with any information as to the period during which future punishment will last. . . . If their views on this point are right, there is no resisting the conclusion that so far as regards the duration of future punishment, the Bible, which we otherwise regard as a revelation from God, is no revelation at all.' And so on, through two or three pages of such reasoning, which he considers 'almost amounts to proof,' and which 'anyone whose mind is unbiassed by preconceived opinions, and uninfluenced by particular theories, must admit.' In other words, because God has not thought it necessary to reveal how long or how short will be the process of destruction in the case of each lost soul, Mr. Grant refuses to believe what He *does* reveal, that they all *will* be destroyed eventually. He charges one of the views, against which he contends, with abolishing degrees of guilt and punishment. What would he say if its advocates retorted that there cannot possibly be degrees of punishment at all, or else God would certainly have revealed *what* degree of punishment each sinner was actually to receive? Surely, to borrow his own language, this is something very like the 'awful presumption' of 'setting up to be the judge of God,' of 'dictating to Him,' of 'arrogating to themselves the right of being wiser than God,' and, in short, indicates 'a fearful frame of mind.'

If we are right in our belief, that everlasting destruction is a clearly revealed truth, all objections grounded on the supposed 'danger' of promulgating it, and on the probability of its being misunderstood or abused, simply fall to the ground. A faithful ambassador will 'not shun to declare *all* the counsel of God,' so far as it has been made known to him. Whether men will hear or whether they will forbear, whether his message prove a savour of life or a savour of death, he is bound to speak what he believes, knowing, that whatever the results, he must, so far as he is a true witness, be 'a sweet savour of Christ.' But in this case I am quite unable to feel that any special exercise of such faith is required. I see so clearly the disastrous effects of the popular doctrine and feel so strongly how incomparably more effective a weapon for arresting the attention of the careless is God's truth than man's attempt to improve upon it, that no risk of weak believers being disturbed, or of the truth being misunderstood and turned into licentiousness, seems too great to incur for the sake of helping to disseminate that truth.* What doctrine has not been misunderstood and abused? Are the doctrines of justification by faith, and of election, always rightly understood by those who hear them? Does the offer of free and full forgiveness for the vilest sinner always produce its proper effect upon the minds of those who theoretically believe in it? Does it not most certainly soothe multitudes into a fatal slumber? Yet who proposes to suppress it, or to promulgate it only in books for the learned? Who doubts that it is to be proclaimed aloud to the men that sit on the wall? Did not our Lord tell His apostles that what He spoke to them in the ear they were to proclaim upon the housetops? And was not one of those sayings 'Fear Him who is able to destroy both soul and body in

---

* Mr. Grant appeals to converted persons, and asks whether it was not 'the conviction that punishments hereafter will be of endless duration that filled your souls with fear and trembling, and constrained you to cry out mentally, if not with an audible voice, "What must I do to be saved?"' Does he really suppose that any such conviction was present to the mind of the Philippian jailor, when he asked that question?

hell'? Are we to be told that this truth, of all others, is only to be confided to the initiated, or suggested in learned language for the consideration of scholars? Are we to be told, in the teeth of Christ's own words, that if it is proclaimed upon the housetops, it will cause men *not* to 'fear Him'?—that the love of life, long ago attributed to man, and talked so much about in every age, is all a delusion?—that destruction has no terrors for him, and that non-existence is the very thing he covets? What could have driven sensible men into anything so preposterous, but the unnatural state of mind engendered by the fiction of eternal torture? Destruction a 'boon'! Yes, in comparison with eternal torture. But that is comparing it with what has no existence. The alternative, the *only* alternative, is an endless life of perfect happiness. And what must be the horror of awaking to the consciousness that this magnificent inheritance is hopelessly lost!

There is a special reason, however, why this truth should be spoken directly to the people, rather than submitted to the consideration of them that sit in Moses' seat; namely, that in no other way will it ever reach them at all. The strength of the opposition lies in the teachers and their more devoted adherents. If this gigantic error is ever to be overturned, it will be by a popular movement amongst the religious portion of the masses. They will not be deterred by the fear of man, or by the fetters of tradition, from looking the question full in the face. And when they have once got a little help to set them on the right track, and prevent them being led astray by misunderstanding one or two familiar expressions, they will only wonder, as several pious and intelligent persons told me they did on hearing the following sermons, how anyone with the Bible in his hands could ever have believed that the wicked were to live for ever.

As to the deterrent effect of the common opinion upon the *irreligious* masses, in restraining them from open wickedness, I believe it is hardly appreciable. Whenever any fear of the future arises in their minds, it is a vague indefinite apprehension of something very terrible, which, however, can always be escaped by repenting, even at the last moment. Who can imagine that it would make the smallest practical difference to them, whether they understood the general belief of religious people to be, that the lost will live for ever in misery, or be destroyed body and soul in hell;—that they will be able to endure the wrath of God to all eternity, or be crushed to death by it? At all events, things could not be much worse than they are; and if we might be in any degree guided by experience, the disastrous failure of the common doctrine would make us only too ready to try anything else that could pretend to the slightest warrant from Holy Scripture.

But after all, the Gospel alone is the power of God unto salvation; and it is, quite unconsciously in most cases, a defective faith in its power that makes timid Christians so alarmed at the rapidly-spreading disbelief in endless suffering. Of the many astounding things which this controversy has elicited, none can exceed the statement of an excellent Evangelical clergyman, that 'the hand which takes away the doctrine of eternal punishment, takes the meaning, the object, the force, the life out of the entire Gospel scheme.' So that for the words, 'God so loved the world,' &c., to have any meaning or force, it is necessary that we should understand 'perish' to mean 'live for ever in misery,' and 'everlasting life' to mean 'everlasting happiness.' To say that the Gospel is the power of God unto salvation from everlasting destruction unto glory and honour and immortality; that it offers to guilty, perishing sinners, wisdom, righteousness, sanctification, and redemption; that, when received, it gives them eternal life, makes them partakers of the

Divine nature, and exalts them to be heirs of God and joint-heirs with Christ; to say that it is *merely this*, is to 'take the meaning, the object, the force, the life out of the entire Gospel scheme!' What must be the force of truth, when the recoil from it can drive a good and able man into such a position as that!

But he is not alone. A writer in the *Bible Treasury*, whom the editor describes as 'a valued servant of God,' though not so sweeping, is even more precise and dogmatic. 'Responsibility and the atonement are lost, and must be so, wherever it is received.' Therefore, if we believe that only they who eat of the bread which Christ gives will live for ever, that he who hath the Son of God hath life, while he who hath not the Son of God hath not life, we '*must*' give up the 'atonement,' nay, the very belief in human 'responsibility'! Was ever such a stab given to a doctrine in the house of its friends? What an illustration of the reckless way in which controversialists will sometimes fling about 'firebrands, arrows, and death,' when they are plunging in a quagmire and endeavouring to beat off an assailant who stands on firm ground! *

---

* The same writer pronounces the Destructionist theory to be 'simply a work of Satan; it is infidelity even as to what man is, for in this case we are beasts with a bigger brain.' So that if God creates a being in

Another proof of the same rashness is afforded by two contradictory representations that have been given of the doctrine here maintained,—the one of which is almost as great a caricature as the other. It has been described, on the one hand, as reducing future punishment to a mere trifle, and, on the other, as making it something even more horrible than endless torment.

One person thinks the loss of a glorious immortality, the being destroyed soul and body in hell, 'nothing worth talking of,' and says that the ungodly 'will thank me for my soothing words.' Another asks if 'virtual annihilation' is not the very thing the wicked desire. Another compares it to the 'hope of the infidel,' that there is no hereafter. The above-mentioned writer in the *Bible Treasury* considers that 'the passage which illustrates this doctrine is, "Let us eat and drink, for to-morrow we die."' A correspondent of the *Rock* regards it as 'making hell to be nothing so formidable

His own image, capable of immortality, capable of knowing and loving Him for ever, and then, because this being defaces that image by sin and refuses to have it renewed, destroys him utterly, we must infer that the being so created was only 'a beast with a bigger brain'! Anything above that must be absolutely indestructible, even by the Creator Himself!

And this is maintained, let it be observed, by the special champion selected by the editor of a religious magazine to combat my arguments —'a valued servant of God, who has seen much of the workings of this pernicious system.'

after all, little more than a painted fire.'* And the Editor himself argues, that it 'reduces the Divine threatenings to the extreme of absurdity,' for 'if Mr. Minton will persist in interpreting future punishment as non-existence, how could it have been better for Judas that he should never have been born?'

Mr. Grant, on the other hand, regards my view as 'the most awful and repulsive of any form in which the doctrine of Destruction has ever yet been presented to the human mind,' creating in him 'a revulsion of mind which no words that he could use would adequately express.'† On reading the first of those ex-

---

* How differently the doctrine strikes other minds may be seen by the following extract from a letter addressed by an Australian clergyman to the Rev. W. Ker: 'What a motive, too, to thrill through the hearts of believers in Jesus—making them in deepest earnest to win perishing souls for Him, and to communicate to all unsaved the knowledge of His blessed Gospel—is the fact that *Life* and *Immortality only* come to men through His blood. Ever since the Lord called me, a child of twelve years of age, now twenty-six years ago, I have always yearned over unconverted souls, and fervently desired their salvation, and been stirred up to speak, and write, and visit, and do anything I could think of to reach hearts in His name. *But I never felt so stirred up as since getting this idea from your book*—that if they *do* miss salvation by Christ, they are all dead men, doomed to complete destruction. Life, life, eternal life by the blood of Jesus! How can those who have it be absorbed in anything else but how they may communicate it to others?'

† Mr. Grant's horror of the Scripture doctrine of everlasting destruction knows no bounds. He tells us of one, who 'began his theological career both as author and preacher as a Unitarian, and, as many others holding the class of views indicated by that term have done since his

pressions I was quite at a loss to imagine what he meant, being unconscious of any material point in which my views differed from those of other Destructionists, and wondering greatly what there could be in *any* view of *limited* suffering so to horrify a believer in *unlimited* suffering. And what does the reader suppose it is? Why, simply the length of time which he imagines that I expect to elapse before the condemned are actually destroyed. 'Mr. Minton has embraced the doctrine of the complete and eternal destruction, both of body and soul, of the ungodly, after they have endured torment immeasurably more terrible than the mind can conceive, for, it may be, countless ages.'

Now, in the first place, I have embraced no such doctrine, and think it in the last degree unlikely. My doctrine is, that nothing whatever has been revealed with reference to the duration of future suffering,

day, he gradually descended in his religious belief, until he got to the low deep—than which there is no lower—of embracing the doctrine of Annihilation.' Therefore Mr. Grant regards the belief that 'the wages of sin is death' as *worse* than denying the Incarnation or the Atonement, and at least as bad as Atheism, Pantheism, Paganism, or any form of unbelief or superstition to which the human mind is capable of sinking! There is 'no lower'!

He also describes the doctrine as 'cold, cheerless, repulsive;' the inference being that he regards his own doctrine as warm, cheerful, and attractive.

except that it will, sooner or later, end in the destruction of the condemned. It is somewhat remarkable that a private correspondent wrote to me, 'You have evidently made up your mind that the destruction of the wicked will be instantaneous.' This was as far wrong on the other side. I hold that the process of destruction may be more prolonged, and will certainly be more terrible, in one case than another— answering to the 'many' or 'few stripes.' What will be the nature or duration of it in any case, I cannot guess.

But still, even supposing that *had* been my view, how could it appear so dreadful to one who holds something *infinitely*—yes, infinitely, in the fullest sense of the term—more 'awful' and 'appalling' (words which he elsewhere applies to his own doctrine) than any possible number of ages of 'the most appalling agonies of body and anguish of soul,' even though indicated by a line of figures reaching from this earth to the farthest star? Mr. Grant's 'revulsion of mind' is solely caused by this frightful torment *coming to an end!* Only let it go on *for ever*, and his mind can rest on it with entire satisfaction.

He seems to have felt the inconsistency of this; and has recourse to a stratagem that is but too familiar in controversy. He deliberately asserts, without a word of proof, as if it were a self-evident proposition, and that in two different parts of his book, that if God inflicts any *limited* amount of suffering upon the condemned, before destroying them, it must be done 'gratuitously,' without any moral necessity, because He 'is a vindictive Being,' 'actuated by a spirit of revenge,' and 'luxuriating in the frightful misery of millions of those whom He called into existence, without its being necessary that He should do so, *whereas*'—pray let the reader observe the quietness of the assumption—'the doctrine of eternal punishment is based on the belief that nothing less will satisfy the demand of Divine justice.' I thought it was supposed to be based upon two or three texts of Scripture. The doctrine of limited suffering is certainly based upon some hundreds. And those positive declarations of God's Word establish the 'belief,' which, from the moral nature that God has given us, we might 'even of ourselves judge to be right,'* that *some* penal suffering, how much or how little we cannot tell, *is* necessary 'to satisfy the de-

---

* Even Mr. Grant says: 'Let me now very briefly invite attention to what Reason says on the subject.' But when *we* invite attention to it, even though we 'feel a thorough persuasion that it speaks the same language as Inspiration,' we are stigmatised as 'Rationalists,' and are sharply rebuked for setting up our own judgment against the Word of God.

mands of Divine justice,' but that *endless* suffering would violently outrage that justice. The worst part of the matter is, that Mr. Grant puts this 'gratuitous' aspect of the case as if it were part of *our* doctrine. No one would gather a hint from his remarks that we could possibly believe in any necessity for *limited* suffering. 'As I have said, in dealing with Mr. Minton's arguments in his newly-published work, there is something so utterly unlike the character of God, and so awfully dishonouring to Him, in the belief that He will gratuitously subject His creatures,' &c. What is this but to represent it as *my* 'belief,' in defence of which I have adduced 'arguments,' that God will '*gratuitously*' inflict punishment upon His creatures?

The writer in the *Bible Treasury* adopts the same subterfuge. 'Pure vengeance for a lengthened period on what is to perish is gratuitous misery.' Then what must the 'vengeance' be that is inflicted for an *endless* period on what is *never* to perish!

So also Mr. Waller, Tutor of St. John's Hall, Highbury, thus represents my argument:—

'It is inconceivable that a God of love should keep any of His creatures in everlasting tortures, though they may still be of service in His dominion, as I shall presently show. But it is quite conceivable that *for no purpose whatever* (!) except mere vengeance and retribution, a God of love should keep some of His creatures in prolonged torment, simply to annihilate them when it is over. What should we think of a law which, having condemned a criminal to death, sentenced him to be first imprisoned and tortured to his utmost powers of endurance, as long as he could possibly be kept alive? Is this *more* merciful or *more* just than the doctrine which Mr. Minton condemns? To my mind it is most monstrous. It is like the old barbarous laws of disembowelling, burning alive, boiling, crucifying, impaling, starving, pressing to death those sentenced to die. The ultimate annihilation makes the previous torture hard indeed to justify!'

Most certainly, as compared with his own view, that the tortures will be continued *for ever*, and death *never* be allowed to release the sufferer from them, even the above monstrous caricature of the doctrine of Scripture would be tender mercy itself.

Strangest of all, even Mr. Garbett has endorsed this palpable fallacy.

'We most fully agree in the view so vividly expressed by Mr. Grant in his book, that this belief appears to the mind most horrible, and incalculably to exceed in horror the ordinary orthodox doctrine. For, in this case, God must be supposed to keep the wicked alive in order that He may torment them, lingering over the process of dissolution as if to crowd into it as much agony as possible; whereas, in the orthodox view the eternity of existence is but a part of that mystery of being with which God endowed His creatures at the beginning, and the endless suffering but a perversion of that lofty capacity of nature which was formed to be a vehicle of everlasting joy, and which human sin alone has changed into a vehicle of everlasting suffering.'*

Surely God can *withdraw* any nature with which He has 'endowed' any of 'His creatures at the beginning.' Every creature is dependent upon God for existence from one moment to another. 'In Him we live, and

---

* This is certainly not the view that was taken of 'endless suffering' by that profound and learned divine, Jonathan Edwards, if we may judge from the following passage in his writings, which describes something very much beyond 'a perversion' of man's 'lofty capacity of nature':—

'The world will probably be converted into a great lake or liquid globe of fire—a vast ocean of fire, in which the wicked shall be overwhelmed, which will always be in tempest, in which they shall be tossed to and fro, having no rest day or night, vast waves or billows of fire continually rolling over their heads, of which they shall for ever be full of a quick sense within and without; their heads, their eyes, their tongues, their hands, their feet, their loins, and their vitals shall for ever be full of a glowing, melting fire, enough to melt the very rocks and elements. Also they shall be full of the most quick and lively sense to feel the torments—not for one minute, not for one day, not for one age, nor for two ages, nor for a thousand ages, nor for ten thousand of millions of ages, one after another, but for ever and ever, without any end at all, and never, never be delivered!'

move, and have our being.' Therefore, when a moral creature like man has turned his 'lofty capacity of nature' into a curse, God may either deprive him of life altogether, or leave him to endure the consequences of his own sin. In the latter case, it is to all intents and purposes 'keeping him alive.' No creature can live an instant longer than God chooses. 'The mystery of his being' may affect the *mode* in which Divine power is exerted for its sustenance; but, practically, an Archangel is kept alive by God as much as an insect.* It is, therefore, a purely gratuitous, groundless assumption, to say that it *may* be necessary to keep fallen creatures alive *for ever* under punishment, but that it *cannot* be necessary to keep them alive under it *for a time*. The argument that no limited

* Since writing the above, I have met with the same argument in the *Rainbow*, March 1869 :—
'To our aspirations for eternity, Scripture answers by the promise of eternal life through Christ Jesus; but there it stops. An essential immortality of the soul it denies as explicitly as it denies it to the body. To one Being only—to God—does it allow to have 'Life in Himself:' of one Being only—God—does it allow immortality, *i.e.* the absolute incapacity of death (ἀθανασία), to be an attribute (John v. 26; 1 Tim. vi. 16). And here, as in everything else, Scripture is the book of the highest reason. That which has had a beginning may have an end. That on which God has bestowed life He may and can inflict death upon. The highest intelligences, as much as the lowest, must depend on Him for the continuance of their life. Let Him withdraw His sustaining power, and the mighty archangel becomes a thing of naught as completely as the insect which dances in the sunbeams for an hour and then passes away for ever.'

amount of punishment would be an adequate manifestation of the Divine wrath, however it may make one shudder, is at least based upon the exceeding sinfulness of sin. But to represent unlimited suffering as a righteous necessity, while the infliction of any limited number of stripes is represented as 'pure vengeance,' that cruelly 'lingers over the process of dissolution, as if to crowd into it as much agony as possible,' is simply to assume, that if a moral creature forfeits his life by sin, it *must* be taken away from him instantaneously and painlessly, or he is treated cruelly.

Besides, even if God had endowed man's soul at the beginning with an indestructible existence, his body was certainly not thus endowed; so that the raising of the *bodies* of the wicked, and keeping them for ever in torment, would be as much the direct act of God Himself, as Scripture represents their future temporary sufferings to be. The gift of immortality would be bestowed upon their mortal bodies, for the express purpose of aggravating the pain, which it is said that the soul, being indestructible and impenitent, must necessarily endure to all eternity.

Subjoined is a letter, which the Editor of the *Christian Advocate* was kind enough to insert after the appearance of his first article on the subject of these sermons, and which contains some remarks that would otherwise have been made here.

Several expressions that were found in the first edition of this volume have been withdrawn, as liable to give needless offence to honoured brethren who differ from me. I wish that I could conscientiously have withdrawn others.* But further reflection only confirms me in the belief, that this question demands the plainest possible dealing; and I must therefore take up the cross, which many of my friends will say that I have made for myself, and continue to speak what I believe. He Who has called me to this work knows my heart, and will not make me an offender for a word. There is no cause, I am confident, that any of His servants could undertake, in which He would be

* It has been suggested to me, for instance, in no unfriendly spirit, that the words 'God would suffer an eternal defeat' (p. 26) 'savour of irreverence.' But in what do they differ from the words, 'God is not unrighteous to forget your work of faith?' or 'It was impossible for God to lie?' or 'He cannot deny Himself?' The Apostle's argument is—God cannot act unrighteously, tell a lie, or deny Himself; under such and such circumstances He would be doing so; therefore such circumstances cannot possibly arise. My argument is—God cannot suffer an eternal defeat; under such and such circumstances He would be doing so; therefore such circumstances cannot arise. Where is the difference? What is there more irreverent in saying that it is impossible for God to suffer an eternal defeat than in saying that it is impossible for Him to lie? Does not our whole confidence in God, from first to last, rest upon such postulates? And St. Paul's example proves, if any proof be required, that there is no irreverence in appealing to them.

more ready to pardon any infirmities or imperfections, than that of endeavouring to wipe off the most terrible aspersion that has ever been cast upon His character. In such a cause, 'It is a very small matter that I should be judged of man's judgment: yea, I judge not mine own self; for I know nothing by myself, yet am I not hereby justified, but he that judgeth me is the Lord.'

May every reader join in the prayer, 'What I know not, teach Thou me.'

S. M.

April 1869.

To the Editor of the 'Christian Advocate.'

DEAR SIR,

I believe it is not customary for Magazines to admit replies to their own articles; but, under the exceptional circumstances of my case, perhaps you will allow me a few words.

First, let me thank you for the tone of brotherly kindness with which you speak of myself personally, as well as for the candour and moderation with which you express your dissent from my views. The 'pain' that has been caused by them to yourself and others can be as nothing compared with that which the knowledge of it inflicts upon me. It is not what they may say or do that I care about, but what I know that they think and feel. The bare thought of it would, but for Divine grace, have utterly unnerved me in attempting the task to which I feel imperatively called.

You complain of the 'temper' and 'spirit' of my book. It is only too probable that there may be much to complain of on that ground. But I must beg you to distinguish between the tone in which I speak of the doctrine and the tone in which I speak of its advocates. They are simply opposite extremes. Right or wrong, I felt that the only way to deal effectually with the doctrine was to smite it with all the power that God might give me. In the mode of doing so

I doubtless may have erred. I am not conscious of anything in the whole book that I ought not to have thought and felt, but there may be things in it that would have been better not said. It is the familiar difficulty in controversy—to know how far we ought to restrain the full expression of our own feelings out of deference to the feelings of our opponents. We are aware, for instance, how deeply a devout Romanist is shocked by what appears to him the blasphemy with which our Article speaks of the Mass. He regards the Mass as a sacred mystery: we as a superstitious fiction. Are we to pain him by giving full expression to our convictions? or, are we to say less than we feel, out of respect to his honest, though mistaken, belief? If I have not acted sufficiently on the latter principle, I exceedingly regret it; but as to the substance of my book, I feel compelled to say, with the outspoken Reformer whose change of views must have deeply grieved many of his former friends, and whose headlong zeal drew forth expostulations even from his sympathisers, 'Here I stand: I can do no otherwise. God help me. Amen.'

With regard, however, to multitudes of eminent saints, living and dead, who have held and defended that doctrine, I have not a hard thought, and trust that I have not uttered a hard word. That I could have no intention of doing so, must be sufficiently evident both from what I have said of them in several parts of my book, and from the fact that any censure of them would in some measure at least have fallen upon myself also. With reference to the injurious effects alleged to be produced upon Christian character by this doctrine, you adduce the names of men who, through believing it, have excelled in the very graces referred to. I fully admit it; but still, if you will allow me to quote my own words, 'However good these eminent saints may have been, they would have been better still if they had been free from this theoretical error.' And elsewhere I speak of them as 'far brighter saints, more thoroughly furnished divines, and more zealous evangelists' than myself. Indeed, were I to say all that I feel on this head, no one would believe me. So I will content myself with assuring you, that the only doubt I ever feel for a single moment arises entirely from thoughts about myself. The truth appears to me as clear as daylight: my sole difficulty is to believe that it is I who see it.

This leads me to remark further, that the appearance of presumption in denying the common doctrine is not nearly so great now as it would have been some years since. It is surely not correct to describe me in this matter as 'one solitary clergyman.' Mr. Grant himself admits that disbelief in it has spread, and is spreading, with marvellous rapidity even amongst Evangelical clergymen. He intimates that in one diocese there is scarcely a clergyman who believes it; and though this is no doubt an exaggeration, yet the incident he mentions proves that there must be a very wide-spread defection. I have been perfectly astonished to find the number, both of clergymen and laymen, who had previously arrived at the same conviction with myself; several in my own congregation, whom I never in the least suspected of doubting the common doctrine. It is true that Universalism is spreading still more rapidly than the belief in destruction, but you will be greatly surprised before long to find how many will openly range themselves on the side upon which I take my humble stand.

The only other point that I should like to touch on is that of 'Rationalism.' Here we are more unfairly treated than on any other part of the controversy. Even your candour has partially failed at this point, though, I am sure, quite unconsciously.*

---

* To show how recklessly the word 'Rationalism' is sometimes used as a mere term of reproach, without the slightest reference to its meaning, it may be worth mentioning that a leading article upon this subject in the *Rock* was headed 'Rationalism in the Pulpit;' while its chief ground of complaint against me was that I insisted upon a *too literal* interpretation of Scripture, without making sufficient allowance for its metaphorical language; in other words, that I would not consent to rationalise away such plain terms as 'life,' 'death,' and 'destruction.'

The following remonstrance was addressed to the editor:—

'First, as to the application of the term "Rationalism" to a belief in the "everlasting destruction" of the wicked. It is just as reasonable as was the application of the term "Irvingism" some time ago to a belief in the personal reign of Christ; when Dr. M'Neile and a few other Evangelical men were thought to have "lost their senses," and "got out of their depth," and been "led astray by the pride of intellect," and "fallen into a snare of the devil," and so forth, in presumptuously opposing the general opinion of the Evangelical world, and paralysing its missionary zeal, by "relaxing the motives and obligations" to preach the Gospel to the heathen. No; I am wrong. It is not nearly *so* reasonable; for the Irvingites did believe in the personal reign, while Rationalists do not in general believe in "everlasting destruction," but rather lean to universal salvation. I agree with them in denying the eternity of evil; but if that makes me a Rationalist, then to agree with Romanists in denying the claims of Mahomet must make us all Romanists. What is there in the doctrine of the nature of Rationalism? Absolutely nothing. I ground it entirely on the authority of Scripture, and maintain that it is the plain, direct, positive teaching of the whole Bible: there being only three or four expressions that are not manifestly and palpably in harmony with it, and every one of those, on careful consideration, admitting of such an interpretation as, in the language of our article, does not "so expound one place of Scripture, that it be contrary to another."'

It may be added, that although five leading articles, and several letters,

You speak of our agreeing with the Rationalists. We do no such thing. They are almost to a man Universalists. Our excellent friend Mr. Birks, who is still justly regarded as an oracle by the Evangelical party, goes more than half way with them in believing that all will ultimately be saved from sin, though not from suffering. We, on the contrary, believe that those who are sentenced to everlasting punishment will utterly perish, and be destroyed body and soul in hell. But even if we did agree with the Rationalists, why should that make us doubt the soundness of our position any more than your agreeing with the Sacerdotalists should make you doubt the soundness of your position? If on the merely negative side of our position we stand by Francis Newman and Professor Jowett, you stand, on the positive side of yours, by John Henry Newman and Dr. Pusey.

But my chief ground of complaint lies in the assumption, which nearly all the advocates on your side make, that we are biassed in our views by semi-rationalistic principles. Some may be so, but many are not. I entirely demur to your inference from my remarks about the way in which a practical unbeliever may be turned into a positive infidel by this doctrine. I know Christians who were first led to doubt it, not in the least by feeling its difficulty, but by being struck with the unnatural meaning it assigns to life and death

had appeared in the *Rock*, all endeavouring to show my 'unspeakable, folly' in believing that the finally impenitent will be 'destroyed soul and body in hell,' or, as the Athanasian Creed expresses it, 'perish everlastingly,' its readers were subsequently informed, in an article upon the writings of Origen, that he held, '*like Mr. Minton of modern times*, that all men, however bad, though dying without repentance, and that even devils, would be finally restored to God's favour.'

in Holy Scripture. But, granting that some do begin by seeing that it is highly improbable, have not many converts from Romanism begun by seeing the extreme difficulty of believing in transubstantiation? What matter is it how the investigation begins, if the enquirer becomes perfectly satisfied at last that the doctrine in question is unscriptural? We maintain with reference to eternal evil just the three positions that you maintain with reference to transubstantiation—that the texts adduced to prove it wholly fail to do so, that other texts disprove it, and that it is inherently impossible. You say that the incredibility which we allege lies only in our own minds, for that you do not feel it to be at all incredible. The Romanist would say the same to you. He would say that you first conjure up a supposed impossibility, and then wrest the plainest language of Scripture to make it fit your preconceived ideas about the properties of matter. Yet you do not refrain, for fear of being called a Rationalist, from pressing him with the impossibility of his doctrine. Neither shall we. And my firm conviction that, whatever may be made of my arguments, you will entirely fail to prove your position by Scripture, arises not only from twenty-three years' study of the subject, but also from my perfect confidence that the Bible is the Word of God, and therefore cannot possibly teach anything so utterly inconsistent with the character of its Author.

I am, yours faithfully,
SAMUEL MINTON.

PREFACE

TO

THE FIRST EDITION.

THE WIDE-SPREAD BELIEF in the Eternity of Evil is perhaps the most astounding phenomenon that has ever appeared in the history of the human mind. There is nothing at all to be compared to it, except the belief in Transubstantiation. No human ingenuity could invent a more absolute physical impossibility than the one, or a more absolute moral impossibility than the other. But there is this great difference between them: that the one only insults and degrades the human understanding; the other casts a fearful aspersion upon the moral character of God. And though it is no more possible to degrade man's intellect than to degrade his body, without demoralising him, yet the theory of Transubstantiation does not so directly blaspheme the Majesty of Heaven as the theory of Eternal Evil. The one charges God with performing a stupendous piece of jugglery, the other accuses Him of infinite cruelty.*

* In justification of this expression, let the language of St. Paul be remembered: 'God is *not unrighteous* to forget your work and labour of love.' Any doctrine, therefore, which taught that God did forget our good works would charge Him with *unrighteousness*. Just so, as God has told us that the wages of sin is death, a doctrine which teaches that He will inflict on sinners a punishment *infinitely greater* than He has Himself declared to be the just desert of sin, charges Him with infinite cruelty.

Some persons will doubtless be greatly shocked by the language in which this doctrine is stated in the following pages, just as many others are shocked by the abominations of the confessional being publicly exposed. They *ought* to be shocked, not by such things being *stated*, but by their being *believed* or *practised*. What kind of doctrine must that be which will not bear being stated in plain terms? And what kind of practice must that be which will not bear being brought to light?

The following extract from a letter of the Rev. Dr. Leask, editor of the *Rainbow*, to Mr. James Grant, will show that I am not alone in feeling it right to use great plainness of speech upon this subject:—

'With the greatest respect for you, I must decline inserting your letter, for which I hope you will pardon me, when I express my *profound sorrow* that you have written a book in vindication of the monstrous absurdity, the wicked blasphemy against the God of heaven, that any human creature is to suffer unending torments, literally everlasting agony. I am amazed how any man who has the slightest conception of the Divine character can *believe* that frightful and utterly unscriptural dogma. If there be one fact in the Word of God clearer than another, it is His settled purpose to destroy sin and sorrow out of His universe, and to make all things new. The "*destruction*" of every creature who is not united to Christ, "who *only* hath immortality," is the revealed law of action. It is settled that a time is coming when God will be all in all. No being destitute of the Divine nature will *exist* in the universe of God, when He shall have completed His most glorious purpose. Man, by nature, is mortal. In the entire Bible you will not find immortality predicated of man as such. *Death* is the wages of sin; *life* is the gift of God.

But why use such strong language? Because nothing less will open men's eyes to see what a monstrous doctrine they are at least professing to hold. The subject has generally been treated, except by infidels, far too apologetically. Men have stood trembling before this huge idol, and half apologising for venturing to express a doubt whether it is really possessed of any actual life, instead of taking the sword of the Spirit and hewing it in pieces before the Lord. This has resulted from two causes: First, from their not having sufficiently grappled with the whole teaching of Scripture upon the question to feel perfectly certain of its thorough consistency; and secondly, from the dread of party excommunication.*

The most wonderful thing connected with this doctrine is the tenacity with which it is, or has been until very recently, held almost universally by 'Evangelicals.' That

'Out of respect for you, I purposely avoided entering into particulars; otherwise I should have had to condemn the book *toto cœlo*. Sooner than advocate the atrocious calumny against God, that He will keep wretched beings in life for the purpose of tormenting them as long as He himself exists, I would rather be broken on the wheel.'

* 'In a free country parties will always be found; and party has its ties, its friendships, its antipathies. Join it, and you are welcome; stand aloof from it, and you are watched; desert it, and you are abused —all the more bitterly, the more nearly you approach the party you abandon.'—*Life of Wilberforce*. By J. C. Colquhoun.

believers in the Gospel of the Grace of God, some of the closest followers in the world of the Apostle Paul, should consider it such an essential part of their system as to call the denial of it heresy if not infidelity, is surely passing strange. Why should they be so devoted to a doctrine, which, if heartily believed and realised, would break the stoutest heart, or drive the strongest mind raving mad; which virtually robs the Law of its terrors, by making it impossible to believe that such a threat will ever be executed; which weakens the power of the Gospel, by enveloping the Love, that it is its glory to proclaim, in a dense cloud of hopeless darkness; which damps the Christian's joy and hope, by telling him that evil will never cease, but that the most frightful discord will for ever mar creation's harmony; and which drives multitudes into positive infidelity, by representing the Bible as absolutely committed to the truth of something utterly incredible? It is partly because so few of them have time and inclination for a searching investigation of what appears at first a very difficult subject, and partly because, on great questions, they will move only together. It is morally impossible for so large a number of persons to rid themselves simultaneously of such a deeply-rooted prejudice, and the force of party discipline prevents anyone breaking the ranks, unless he is prepared either to leave his party altogether or to be ostracised by it.*

Personally, I have no desire for either one or the other. As to everything that concerns the Gospel, I am still distinctively 'Evangelical;' though I never have been, and never will be, in bondage to the arbitrary bye-laws, narrow prejudices, and antiquated traditions, of any party whatever. But I see so clearly how utterly unscriptural this doctrine is, and what incalculable injury it is doing to the cause of Christ, that no personal considerations can make me hesitate for a moment to speak what I believe. For 'not the truth which a man knows, but that which he says and lives, becomes the soul's life; truth cannot bless, except when it is lived for, proclaimed, and suffered for.' I well know my own powerlessness to influence public opinion; but, when a gun is ready loaded and

---

* I am sorry to be obliged to say, that the spirit and temper displayed by some persons who have a great 'name to live,' since the delivery of these sermons, only too painfully illustrates the following observations of Mr. Spurgeon in 'Morning by Morning,' on the words 'Ephraim is a cake not turned' (Hos. vii. 8). 'A cake not turned is soon burnt on the side nearest the fire; and although no man can have too much religion, there are some who seem burnt black with bigoted zeal for that part of truth which they have received, or are charred to a cinder with a vainglorious Pharisaic ostentation of those religious performances which suit their humour. The assumed appearance of superior sanctity frequently accompanies a total absence of all vital godliness. The cake which is burned on one side is dough on the other.'

cocked, a child may pull the trigger; and that I believe to be precisely the present state of this question.* I have been astonished at the number of persons who, since the delivery of these sermons, have told me how long such thoughts have been working in their minds, and how much relieved they have been by finding expression given to them. The mine seems ready to burst; and perhaps the only thing needed is to let it be seen that this monstrous excrescence, which Satan has contrived to fasten upon the Divine Revelation, can be cut away from it, without touching its foundations, except vastly to strengthen them, and without robbing it of one particle of its glory, but rather

---

* A list of some works recently published in favour of the view presented in these pages will be found at the close. To Mr. White's book I am indebted for the first gleam of light that I ever received upon this subject; and I can heartily endorse the following remarks of Mr. Davis:—

'The same truth had been enforced by the Rev. Edward White, one among the earliest and best of the writers of this century on the subject; though his volume, as was almost inevitable at the period when he engaged in the controversy, was not wholly free from error. The *gist* of all recent arguments may be found there: and I acknowledge with deep gratitude my own obligation to it. Although I only accepted confidently, after long study, his general conclusion, I shall never forget how much light his earnest pages threw upon my faith, and the great relief that I derived from their perusal. The volume was written by Mr. White in early life, and he would probably modify much of its argumentation now; but, published with admirable moral courage, and a noble disregard of temporal interests, it has done good service in the cause of Truth.'

enabling that glory to shine forth with greater brilliancy than ever. If the following pages should be made use of by the Spirit of God to conduce ever so slightly to that end, I shall feel that I have not run in vain, neither laboured in vain. I am overwhelmed with a sense of the favour that God has bestowed upon me in awakening me out of a hideous dream. To be employed in awakening others out of it also would seem too great an honour for me to believe possible, but that He so constantly chooses the weak things of the world to confound the mighty, and things which are not to bring to nought things that are.

One word to those who put the subject aside, not wishing to have their minds 'disturbed' about it. Do they love their neighbours as themselves? If they had believed themselves to be condemned to endless suffering, would not their hearts bound at the bare possibility that they might be ultimately released from their misery, even at the expense of being blotted out of creation? But as the question relates only to others, albeit including perhaps their own fathers or mothers, husbands or wives, brothers or sisters, sons or daughters, who may have died out of Christ, they do not wish to be *disturbed* (!) with such a hope being suggested for *them*, and refuse even to examine the grounds on which it is maintained. They object to being troubled with *controversy*! What can account for this? Only the palpable fact that the doctrine has no hold whatever on their real feeling, but is simply an abstract theory, which they are compelled to admit on the supposed authority of Scripture. A particular interpretation of certain texts has been so drilled into them from childhood, that they cannot conceive any other as possible; and therefore to throw doubt on the Eternity of Evil, they regard as tantamount to throwing doubt on the truth of Scripture.

But surely they ought to see the difference between an infidel, who says, See what horrible doctrine Scripture teaches, and a believer, who says, See what horrible doctrine the traditions of men have falsely attributed to Scripture; between one who uses the popular theory as a weapon wherewith to attack the Bible, and one who, instead of vainly attempting to parry the blow, endeavours to wrest the weapon out of his hand. To the former, ordinary Christians may well be excused for turning a deaf ear. But to the latter, however weak and insignificant he may be in himself, it might be expected that they would strain their ears in listening, if only in the faint hope that he might be able to throw a gleam of light on the darkness, by suggesting at least the possibility of understanding the testimony of Scripture in some less gloomy sense. Why do they ever cease to examine and re-examine the Bible for themselves, to see if there is not some way of escape from the oppressive burden which their traditional belief lays upon them? Why are they not perpetually asking everyone they know, who is competent to give an opinion, whether the original words necessarily convey the meaning commonly attached to them? Why do they not eagerly grasp at the veriest straws, that offer the slightest hope of helping them out of this slough of despond? If it were a question that could in any degree shake the foundation of their faith, or interfere with their peace of mind, the case would be very different.* But as it is, when the result of shaking off their old tradition would be enormous gain without a particle of loss, their resenting even the suggestion of such a hope is intelligible only on the supposition that their theory has not enough effect upon their feelings to make them willing to be troubled with any thought about it. And here is just the root—one root at least—of the dislike felt by many persons to

---

* The Eternity of Evil has lately been called a '*vital* doctrine.' It seems hard to understand how it can be essential, or in any way conducive, to the *life* of a believer.

have the subject broached. They cannot bear the trouble of thinking; to weigh evidence and judge for themselves is too much for them. They have also an uneasy feeling, that if they should find themselves to have been wrong in one point they may likewise be wrong in another, and where is it to stop? So they have a horror of anything being disturbed; they want just to think and feel, and believe, and act, as they have always done. From the eternal torment of their dearest friends, down to the chanting of a psalm or the arrangement of a service, they love 'old' things, and dread anything 'new,' mistaking the 'old paths' of habit for the old paths of truth.*

Much the same answer may be given to another question, which, as a matter of feeling, I should like to

---

* The statements above have been abundantly justified by the tone of numerous letters which have since reached me. One person 'was *happy* to say' that this book had not shaken his faith in the doctrine of eternal evil; another, who was rather staggered by it at first, afterwards felt 'greatly *relieved*' to find that he could still retain his old opinions; while a third promised to read it, but 'without even *wishing* to agree with me.' In each of these cases, which are fair samples of many others, the feeling of satisfaction was not at being able to believe in endless suffering, supposing it to be revealed, but at finding, as they thought, that it *was* revealed: they positively *wished* the doctrine to be true. It disturbed them less, to think that millions of their fellow-creatures will writhe in eternal agony, than it would have done to discover and acknowledge that they themselves had been in error. So Jonah would rather that all Nineveh had perished, than that he should have appeared to be a false prophet.

dispose of at once. If the doctrine, it may be asked, is as bad as you represent, how can many of the believers in it so excel in holiness? Everyone becomes like that which he worships. How, then, can any spark of love remain within the breast of one who worships a God capable of inflicting endless suffering upon His own creatures? What kind of character must be formed in the worshipper of a God, whose goodness will never extend beyond causing eternal good to preponderate over eternal evil? The truth is, they do *not* worship such a God. They have two distinct Gods, the one to argue about, the other to love and adore. When Scripture has to be defended against the charge of teaching an incredible doctrine, their own mistaken view of its language compels them to assert that the doctrine is perfectly credible. When sinners have to be warned to flee from the wrath to come, no terrors are thought too great to set before their eyes. But their own God is a wholly different Being. When they enter into their closet and pray to their Father which is in secret, they see only the God and Father of our Lord Jesus Christ, the God whose name is Love, and whose love has been begotten in themselves by the Word. No thought of endless torment enters into their conceptions of Him they worship; or if Satan be able to obtrude it for a moment, it is instantly repelled as a hideous spectre. That they *must* receive *some* injury from entertaining it even in theory is certain. All moral truth sanctifies; and therefore any error must to a certain extent interfere with sanctification; and the various ways in which this error does so have been pointed out in the eighth and ninth of the following sermons. I am now only endeavouring to remove what might be felt as a preliminary objection, by showing how the almighty power of divine grace can diminish the evil that would naturally flow from false doctrine. Faith filters the adulterated draught which is taken by the intellect, letting the pure truth contained in it sink down into the heart, while the residuum lies floating on the brain, clouding the mind no doubt, and producing a certain degree of unsteadiness in the walk and conversation, but not poisoning the blood, as it would naturally do if it were allowed to take its course. However good these eminent saints may have been, they would have been better still if they had been free from this theoretical error. Multitudes of saints, whom I never dream of approaching in holiness, have believed both in Eternal Evil and in Transubstantiation. I cannot hope to overtake them in the Christian race; but I hope to get nearer to them than would ever have been possible if we had continued to be equally weighted. How encouraging to know that in this race it is *not* one only who receives the prize; that the superior excellence of one is no loss to another; and that without any reference to the rest, each one will receive his own reward, have his own praise of God, and reap to the full extent of that which he has sown. May we all, in our several callings, and according to our abilities and opportunities, so run that we may obtain.

S. M.

PS.—Since writing the above, I have received letters from a number of persons, who consider my throwing off this 'tradition of men' to be a departure from the faith, and who express their intention of earnestly praying that I may be brought back to the truth. As regards some of them, I fear, from the very little effect which their prayers seem to have upon their own spirit, that they can be of little avail to others. But there are many humble-minded Christians amongst my friends, who are just as sure that the doctrine of Eternal Evil is the truth of God, as the devoutest Roman Catholic can be with regard to Transubstantiation. *Their* prayers will be heard. And I never more needed them, than under the conflict, to which God has called me, in assaulting this old stronghold of Satan. To contend with enemies is nothing. To withstand friends to the face is painful in the extreme. Let them pray on, with all their might, and without ceasing. Every one of their prayers will be answered, though not in the way they expect. If offered in faith, and humility, and love, they will bless not only me, but themselves also. And I know no greater blessing with which God could reward their intended kindness to me, than by bringing them out of the dismal shadow of this strong delusion, and enabling them to rejoice in the light, which is now gladdening the hearts of multitudes of their fellow Christians.

THE STUDY OF SCRIPTURE.

'If thou criest after knowledge, and liftest up thy voice for understanding; if thou seekest her as silver, and searchest for her as for hid treasures; then shalt thou understand the fear of the Lord, and find the knowledge of God.'—Prov. ii. 3-5.

'The theological student is often a student chiefly of some human system of divinity, fortified by *references* to Scripture, introduced from time to time as there is occasion. He proceeds—often unconsciously—by setting himself to ascertain, not what is the information or instruction to be derived from a certain narrative or discourse of one of the sacred writers, but what aid can be derived from them towards establishing or refuting this or that point of dogmatic theology. Such a mode of study surely ought at least not to be exclusively pursued. At any rate, it cannot properly be called a *study of Scripture*.

'There is, in fact, a danger of its proving a great *hindrance* to the profitable study of Scripture. For so strong an association is apt to be established in the mind between certain expressions and the *technical* sense to which they have been confined in some theological system, that when the student meets with them in Scripture, he at once understands them in that sense, in passages where perhaps an unbiassed examination of the context would plainly show that such was not the author's meaning. And such a student one may often find expressing the most unfeigned wonder at the blindness of those who cannot find in Scripture such and such doctrines, which appear to him to be as clearly set forth there as words can express; which perhaps they are, on the (often gratuitous) *supposition*, that those words are everywhere to be understood exactly in the sense which he has previously derived from some human system—a system through which, as through a discoloured medium, he views Scripture. But this is not to take Scripture for one's guide, but rather to make one's self *a guide* to Scripture.'—*Essays on the Writings of the Apostle Paul.* By Archbishop Whately.

CONTENTS.

SERMON I.

THE IMAGE OF THE INVISIBLE GOD 1

SERMON II.

THE OLD AND THE NEW CREATIONS 7

SERMON III.

THE FULNESS OF CHRIST AND THE RECONCILIATION OF ALL THINGS 15

SERMON IV.

THE RECONCILIATION OF ALL THINGS NOT REQUIRING THE RESTORATION OF EACH INDIVIDUAL CREATURE, BUT EXCLUDING ETERNAL EVIL 23

SERMON V.

THE WAGES OF SIN 34

SERMON VI.

EVERLASTING DESTRUCTION 49

SERMON VII.

	PAGE
IMMORTALITY	68

SERMON VIII.

THE INJURY DONE TO THE CAUSE OF CHRISTIANITY BY THE DOCTRINE OF ETERNAL EVIL	81

SERMON IX.

ITS INJURIOUS EFFECTS UPON CHRISTIAN CHARACTER	92

SERMON X.

THE LIGHT WHICH IS THROWN UPON THE DARKER FEATURES OF PROVIDENCE AND REVELATION BY THE SCRIPTURE DOCTRINE OF THE RECONCILIATION OF ALL THINGS, AFTER THE EVERLASTING DESTRUCTION OF THE WICKED	103

APPENDIX.

FIRST INTRODUCTION OF THE POPULAR DOCTRINE	119
LIFE AND DEATH	128
IMMORTALITY	131
'IMMORTAL' AND 'INCORRUPTIBLE'	136
'ETERNAL,' 'FOR EVER AND EVER'	138
ETERNITY	141
DESTRUCTION	142
ANNIHILATION	145

CONTENTS.

	PAGE
'UNQUENCHABLE FIRE'	146
'ETERNAL PUNISHMENT'	150
CORRECTION AND RETRIBUTION	155
'THE SMOKE OF THEIR TORMENT'	156
ETERNAL EVIL	159
MORAL EFFECTS OF THE POPULAR DOCTRINE	168
THE DIVINE CHARACTER AND THE HUMAN CONSCIENCE	171
THE DESERT OF SIN	178
THE DOOM OF JUDAS	179
PLATO AND THE NEW TESTAMENT	181
ARCHBISHOP WHATELY	183
REV. ANDREW JUKES	187
MR. JAMES GRANT	197
THE POWER OF PRAYER	210
BE TRUE	213

THE GLORY OF CHRIST.

SERMON I.

Who is the image of the invisible God.—COL. i. 15.

THIS is one of those passages with reference to which, however confident we may feel as to their general meaning, we soon become conscious that they point to something far beyond the grasp of our finite minds. However true may be the glimpses we are able to obtain of what it reveals, they are but glimpses after all; and far beneath our deepest soundings there lies a fathomless abyss, of which the ever-increasing knowledge of eternity will only enable us to say with more intelligent conviction, 'Oh the depth!' We have need to enter upon the consideration of it with holy awe and deep humility, veiling our faces before the unapproachable light, taking the shoes from off our feet before we tread on such holy ground, and saying, 'Open Thou mine eyes,'—'I beseech Thee, show me Thy glory,'—so far as I may be able to bear it.

What is meant by 'the *invisible* God'? Certainly not, invisible to the bodily eye. For that would imply that God had some shape or form, though invisible to us, of which Christ's body was the 'image' or visible resemblance; and as form can be produced only by a boundary line, it necessarily involves limit. Besides, the creative act being immediately afterwards ascribed to Christ, shows that He is here spoken of in His Divine nature. It is to the inward eye of the mind, and that not of man only, but of any creature whatever, that God is in Himself invisible. His dwelling in light that no man can approach unto, refers to no physical light, but to the incapacity of any created mind to know anything of His Being, His Nature, His Attributes, or His Character, except as they are revealed in and by His only-begotten Son.

An 'image' is the most complete representation that can be made of any material object; so much so, that if the image were perfect, it could not be distinguished by sight from the original, and therefore to see it would be as good as seeing the original. This is the idea here employed to set forth one of the deepest truths that have been revealed to us with reference to the Divine Existence. But for the manifestation which He has made of Himself in Christ, the eternal God would have dwelt for ever alone and unknown: in perfect light wherein was no darkness at all, but in light unseen by any—except Himself. In Christ there is a full and complete manifestation of God. Whatever there is in Him to be known, may be known by Christ, just so far as our own powers of vision are able to see Christ. Our view may be dim or distorted, so that we see the image obscurely or untruly; or the image may be of such vast dimensions, that we are unable to take it all in: but so far as we do see it, we see God. 'He that hath seen me, hath seen the Father.'

Now just what Paul here asserts in a figure drawn from the sense of sight, St. John asserts in a figure drawn from the sense of hearing—'The Word.' Words represent thoughts. Until we speak, thoughts dwell only within our own mind. But as soon as we speak, if the language be perfect and perfectly understood, the hearer understands them as well as we understand them ourselves. But for Christ, God would have dwelt in 'eternal silence.' Thought there would have been, all-embracing thought, that could never receive the addition of one new idea; but it would have been thought that led to nothing, that terminated in itself, and remained absolutely unknown to any, except the solitary Thinker. Christ is the utterance of that one universal thought; and an utterance so clear and full, that as far as the language is understood and rightly interpreted, the thought is perfectly revealed.

Again, in the Epistle to the Hebrews, the same truth is stated under yet other figures. Christ is said to be 'the brightness of His glory, and the express image of His person.' The word rendered 'brightness' means—

shining forth. Without Christ, the glory would have existed, but could never have been manifested. Through Him it is to illumine the universe with the light and warmth of its glorifying beams. The word rendered 'express image,' is literally—character. It means, in the first place, the mark stamped upon anything by a die: and then, from that, any distinctive mark upon a person or thing, which, as we commonly speak, gives it a character. Our special use of the term, as referring to moral conduct, is an unintentional witness to our consciousness of the fact, that in responsible creatures the really distinguishing marks are moral qualities. The lines that are cut into a man most deeply, and stamp him as what he is, are not social or intellectual or physical distinctions, but the characters of holiness or sin engraved upon his soul. He may be a helpless cripple, all but an idiot, and a pauper as well, and yet rank higher in the scale of being than the veriest giant in body and mind that ever swayed the destinies of an empire. It is not, however, in this limited sense that Christ is the 'character' of the Divine Being, but universally, in everything by which He is distinguished from all other beings; He is the impression, struck off from the whole of what constitutes the Eternal God.

And now we ask, When did He begin to be 'the image of the invisible God'? Some would reply, At the Incarnation. But can the Apostle be speaking of what began at the Incarnation, when he goes on to say, 'For by Him were all things created'? And how could St. John's language be harmonised with that view? He speaks of Christ as the Word, *before* He 'became flesh,' and seems anxious to declare in the most emphatic manner that He was *always* the Word, by adding, '*The same* was in the beginning with God,' that is in the same capacity, as the Word. So also was He always the image of God,' in the essential conditions of the Divine existence. The Godhead so existed, that in the Son lay the capability of Divine manifestation, the possibility as well as the guarantee of all the revelation that should ever be made of God. The first step in the *putting forth* of that power was the first act of creation. But from eternity He was the 'image,' or the 'word.' The word was as yet unspoken, but it was formed, and ready for utterance at the right moment. The image was veiled, but it existed in all its perfection, ready to be unveiled in due time. The process of speaking the word, of unveiling the image, began, as we have said, with creation; it has been going on ever since, and, we doubt not, will go on to all eternity.

The taking of our nature upon Him was evidently a most marked and important step in the great work. His death and resurrection scarcely less so. But *everything* that has ever been done, great or small, was necessary to the perfection of the revelation. If the most trifling of Christ's dealings with any of you this day had been otherwise than it was, God would not have been so well known to the intelligent universe as He will be now. The very hairs of your head are all numbered : and well they may be ; for every one of them is a string of the instrument from which the divine harmony is sounding forth, that is to give ever richer and fuller expression to the Eternal Word. One hair too many or too few, one hair turning white too soon, or remaining black too long, would introduce discord into the music, and impair the perfection of the image. But no such thing is possible until Omniscience is deceived or Omnipotence overpowered. Strange and mysterious as it seems, when we remember that part of the material with which He has to work is the free-will of intelligent responsible creatures, yet is it most certain, nay, inseparable from our fundamental conceptions of a Supreme God, that He *must* work, and none *can* let it ; that in one way or other He must order all things after the counsel of His own will, inasmuch as ' Of Him, and through Him, and to Him are all things.' May we all be able to say from the bottom of our hearts, ' To whom be glory for ever. Amen.'

SERMON II.

Who is the image of the invisible God, the first-born of every creature. For by Him were all things created, that are in heaven and that are in earth, visible and invisible, whether they be thrones or dominions or principalities or powers; all things were created by Him and for Him; and He is before all things, and by Him all things consist. And He is the Head of the body, the Church; who is the beginning, the first-born from the dead, that in all things He might have the preeminence.—COL. I. 15–18.

WE have already spoken of Christ as 'the image of the invisible God,' in the essential nature of His Divine existence. And now we proceed to enquire in what sense He is 'the first-born of every creature.' Our first impression would naturally be that it referred to His preeminence in dignity amongst all creatures,—the term 'first-born' being often used solely with reference to rank, irrespective altogether of time. But this view is quite irreconcilable with the following words, which speak of Him as the Creator: 'For by Him were all things created.' Here, therefore, it can mean only, that He was born *prior to* all creation; referring to that mysterious relationship within the Godhead of which we know absolutely nothing, except that it bears some analogy to the relation of father and son among ourselves. A son becomes in time equal to his father in everything but relationship. The father continues father, the son continues son; that is all. In the Godhead, that knows no time, to which all the past and all the future are one ever-present moment, the Father and the Son were always equal, except in relationship. But of the essential nature of this relationship we are unable to form the slightest conception.

It is quite possible, indeed, that the expression may have been selected to include a reference to the fact, that He who, in His Divine nature, was born from all eternity, *before* creation, was also afterwards to assume the form of a creature, to take creaturehood into the Godhead, and a form of creaturehood in which birth takes place; and that in that nature he was to occupy the position of the first-born in point of preeminence, being exalted to the highest rank in all creation. But the primary reference must be to His Divine nature, or the Apostle's argument becomes hopelessly dislocated.

'For *in* [not 'by'] Him were all things created.' As the seeing power of our body resides in the eye, and the hearing power in the ear, so the creative power of Deity resided in the Son, as part of the self-manifesting power. 'That are in heaven, and that are in earth'—heaven being used to include everything beyond the region of this globe. 'Visible and invisible'—the world of matter and the world of spirit. 'Whether they be thrones or dominions or principalities or powers.'—It is very questionable whether the Apostle meant to say that the heavenly hosts are arranged in ranks, answering to the several terms here employed. From the third chapter of this epistle it appears that the Colossians pretended to be very learned in matters connected with the unseen world. They probably marshalled the armies of heaven according to some fanciful arrangement of their own. And Paul, waiving any argument on such a purely speculative matter, says—Well, whatever they are, call them what you please, they are all the creatures of His hand.

Still it must be remembered that in writing to the Ephesians he directly calls the evil spirits 'principalities and powers'; so that there can be no doubt as to the same principle of rank and order prevailing in the unseen world, that we see to prevail in all the visible creation. From an archangel to an insect there is no dead level to be found; all is gradation; the highest creature having enough to humble him, and the lowest enough to ennoble him, in his immediate connection with, and dependence upon, the Creator Himself. Equality is the dream of man's littleness and ignorance, and all his levelling propensities are merely the rebellion of his pride and self-will against God's universal law of rank, and order, and subordination.

> Order is Heaven's first law; and that confessed,
> Some are, and must be, greater than the rest.

This is just what makes the abuse of authority one of the greatest crimes—because it turns a power, which God has given for the purpose of benefiting others, into an instrument for oppressing them.

> He from whose hand all power on earth proceeds
> Ranks its abuse amongst the foulest deeds.

All things were created by Him'—Here is the creative power, that resided 'in Him,' actually put forth. 'And for Him'—as an intermediate step towards what is declared to be the great end of all things, 'the glory of God the Father.' All will conduce to the glory of the Father, by first bringing glory to the Son. 'Every tongue shall confess that Jesus Christ is Lord, to the glory of God the Father.' He is the point from which all the glory of the Godhead shines forth, and the point to which it all returns—the focus and centre of the universe.

'And He is before all things.' It is very difficult to see why the Apostle here goes back to Christ's pre-existence. Probably some phase of the Colossian errors, if we knew it, would account for the train of thought. In the concluding words, however, we shall find no difficulty—'And in Him all things consist,' or hold together. He is the universal Sustainer and Preserver, as well as the universal Creator. In Him, observe, not 'by' Him. The sustaining of creation is not effected by a succession of acts: but as a house rests on its foundation, so creation rests on the Divine power, which resides in the Son; interpenetrated throughout by His sustaining energy, it 'consists.'

The importance of this last truth will appear in a subsequent sermon. For the present we must pass it over, and proceed to the Apostle's next step in the unfolding of his argument.

Depending upon this primal glory of Christ as the Eternal Son, follows an additional glory, in connection with the new creation, which was to arise out of the ruin of one part of the old creation. 'In Him was Life,' the original life of all things. And in Him is that higher life, eternal life, which can be reached only through death.

It was in the eternal purpose of God to raise one portion of His creatures to a height of dignity and honour far above any other; to bring it into the closest possible relationship to Himself. Creaturehood was to be taken into the Godhead. In that created form all the fulness of the Godhead was to dwell for ever: 'creature and Creator were to meet at that point;' and from that point was to flow forth in ever-widening circles, and with infinite variety of application, the Divine love, which would embrace the universe. Nearest to the Throne were to stand some, in such intimate relationship to the Incarnate Son that He would not be ashamed to call them brethren; partakers of the very nature that He had Himself assumed, receiving their new life directly from union with Him, and associated with Him in the government of the universe. But to reach that height of glory, He and they alike must first pass through death. Why, we know not. We can partly understand that aspect of it in which Christ's death was necessary to make atonement for the guilt of sin, and our own death is necessary to purify us from the defilement of sin. But why a state of things requiring so terrible a process should ever have been allowed, why it should have been rendered necessary that death and resurrection must intervene before we can reach the destined glory, are questions which only the shallowest minds will imagine that they can answer, and about which the highest possible attainment is to be able to rest satisfied with the assurance, 'What I do, thou knowest not now but thou shalt know hereafter.'

But whatever be the reason, the fact is certain. And its grand interest to us lies in the fact, that *we* are the creatures destined to be raised to such a stupendous height, to sit with Christ on His throne, and shine as the stars for ever and ever. It is *our* nature that the Son has already taken into the Godhead, and out of *our* race is now being gathered that ' Church ' which under its immediate ' head ' is to occupy the foremost place in all creation, as the mystical ' body ' of Christ.

It was necessary to take this glance at the glory of

the Church, in order to appreciate what the Apostle here wishes to show,—namely, the glory of Christ as its Head.

'And He is the Head of the body, the Church.' Throughout these verses 'He' and 'Him' are emphatic; doubtless in implied opposition to some Colossian errors. And this perhaps also accounts for the abruptness with which he speaks of 'the body.' The natural way of expressing it, and that which he elsewhere adopts, is 'the Church, which is His body.' But with reference to controversies that were prevailing about the Church *as* a body, especially about its head, Paul asserts that '*He* is the Head of the body;' a position which he immediately proceeds to establish.

'Who is [inasmuch as He is] the beginning.' Christ is the beginning, the origin, of the new creation, which was to spring from death; as He was the beginning of the old creation, which sprang from nothing but what was contained within the Deity itself. And this He becomes by being 'the first-born from the dead;' not the first who was ever restored to life, but the first-*born* from the dead, the first who arose from death into that new life which His Church is to partake of. It is not, however, mere *priority* of resurrection that constitutes Him the Head of the body, but the fact that His resurrection, including of course all that led to it, from His incarnation to His death, was both the essential condition and the effectual guarantee of our resurrection. When the Head rose, the whole body rose also *in Him*; God 'quickened us together with Christ, and raised us up together, and made us sit together in heavenly places in Christ Jesus.' So that He obtained His position as 'Head of the body' by becoming its origin, by overcoming death, and opening the kingdom of heaven to all believers.

'That in all things'—the new, as well as the old, creation—'He might have the preeminence.' In His Divine nature He has preeminence over it, as having called it into being. In His Divine and human nature united He has preeminence over it, as having raised it from its fall, and placed it in a position of security and honour far above that which it originally held.

The union of those two natures, with the ultimate results of what has been accomplished by the God-man, the Christ of God, will be brought before us in the next verses. Meanwhile, let us rejoice with joy unspeakable and full of glory, at the wonderful prospect set before us; let us in spirit already cast our crowns before His feet, singing, Thou art worthy, for Thou hast redeemed us; and let us seek for grace to walk even here more worthy of the vocation wherewith we are called, more worthy of God, who has called us unto His kingdom and glory.

SERMON III.

For it pleased the Father, that in Him should all fulness dwell; and having made peace through the blood of His cross, by Him to reconcile all things unto Himself; by Him, I say, whether they be things in earth, or things in heaven.—COL. I. 19–20.

THE APOSTLE began by speaking of the Son, in His Divine nature, as 'the image of the invisible God,' the Revealer of Deity. In that capacity He was the Creator of all things, the 'beginning' of the old creation. Then came the incarnation, when the Word was made flesh, creaturehood taken into the Godhead by the union of the Divine and human natures in Christ. In that capacity, by His death and resurrection, he became the 'beginning,' or origin, of the new creation, the 'Head' of that 'body' which, being gathered out of the human race, is called the 'Church.' This second glory was added to the first, 'that in all things He might have the preeminence.' And the reason why it was necessary that He should thus have universal preeminence, was that the whole fulness of the Godhead was permanently to abide in the bodily form which He assumed, and therein to effect a complete and everlasting reconciliation between the creature and its Creator.

The word 'fulness' means either that which fills something else, or that which is filled with something else. In Eph. i. 23, the Church is called 'the fulness' of God, as the special *receptacle* of Divine fulness. Here, 'the fulness of the Godhead' is the plenitude and perfection of all that belongs to God, all that constitutes Him what He is. This in its entirety dwells in the incarnate Son. This of itself would not directly prove Christ's Deity. It would prove that He should be worshipped *as God*; 'that all men should honour the Son even as they honour the Father'—because if all the fulness of the Godhead dwells in Him bodily, He must be *equal* with God,—if not God. He must have been raised to a level with God,—and whatever reverence is due to God, must be due to Him also. And if this were admitted fully and unreservedly, the rest would be little more than a dispute about words. For it would practically come to the same thing. If you are to feel and act towards Christ *as* God, why then He *is* God *to you*. But it never is fully admitted by those who deny his Deity. And no wonder. For we instinctively feel, that God would not raise a mere creature to equality with himself; 'My glory will I not give unto another.' And here lies the importance of maintaining the absolute Deity of Christ. For if you give it up, everything else follows, the whole edifice comes down together. Now, that truth depends, not upon the whole fulness of the Godhead dwelling in Him bodily, but upon His being the Incarnate Son, the Word made flesh. His Deity rendered it possible for all the fulness of the Godhead to dwell in Him.

It is not the whole Godhead, observe, that dwells in Christ. He is not the Father, nor the Spirit; but He *is* the Son. Neither the Father nor the Spirit became man; but the Son did, and therefore Christ *is God*. And in Him, not in His humanity only, but in His entire Person as the God-Man, dwells all the *Fulness* of the *Godhead*, the whole attributes and perfections of Deity. To carry out His great self-manifesting design, God saw fit that the whole fulness of Deity should be embodied in a visible created form. He selected the human form; which the Son, consequently, took upon Himself, being made in the likeness of man, and thereby rendered it capable of containing all the Divine fulness.

This residence was to be a permanent one: the fulness was to 'dwell,' not sojourn, in Him. It was not a mere temporary expedient to meet a necessity that had arisen. This is one aspect of it, no doubt. And it is the first which presents itself to us in the Gospel. But here we rise far above that to the great design of self-manifestation, and the universal reconciliation of all things to Himself, towards which man's redemption is only a step in the process.

'And having made peace through the blood of His Cross, by Him to reconcile all things unto himself.' If there could be any doubt as to the 'all things' here being coextensive with the 'all things' that were 'created' by Christ, it would be at once removed by the same classification being employed, 'whether they be things in earth or things in heaven;' it is the whole universe. In the Epistle to the Ephesians we are told that this is to be 'gathered together,' literally headed up, 'in Christ.' While He is to be peculiarly the Head of the Church, He is also to be the Head of the Universe! And as this is here called being 'reconciled' to God, it is manifest that the universe is to be brought not merely into subjection, but into *harmonious* relation to God.

This is said to be effected by 'having made peace through the blood of His Cross.' Here is the heart of the whole system, the pivot on which everything turns, the central point between the creation and the reconciliation of all things. On which observe, first, that it was accomplished by the same eternal Son, Who ever was, in the conditions of His Divine existence, and ever will be, in the endless fulfilment of those conditions, the one sole 'image of the Invisible God,' the Manifester of Deity from first to last: and secondly—which is the most wondrous thing of all, and constitutes it, perhaps, the exceptional fact in the history of the universe— that it was accomplished, not by doing, but by suffering; not by acting, but by being acted upon; not by any exercise of power, but by an abandonment of all power, and stooping to the lowest depth of humiliation. He was 'crucified through weakness.'

And what did this do? Did it merely illustrate in His own person one of the deepest laws of the universe, that only through death can the highest life be attained? No. It did that, no doubt; but it did more. Our views of this question must at best be limited and imperfect, and it is unwise to insist upon rigid definitions. But if Scripture teaches anything, it teaches that there was some moral necessity for it, arising out of God's own essential and unchangeable character. Whether we are able to see it or not, it is a matter of revelation, that in order to put away sin, and bring in everlasting righteousness, on which depends eternal life, it was required by the righteousness of God, that the Son of His love, in human form, should be 'made sin for us,' that sin should be 'laid upon' Him, and that He should pay the death penalty which was its righteous due—that He should 'put away sin by the sacrifice of Himself.' No wonder the Apostle puts this in the very forefront of the great reconciliation, which is to be the ultimate end of Christ's work. For if the universe is to be harmoniously and securely headed up in Christ, above all things must it be necessary that sin should be done away with. Any other reconciliation that may be effected must be altogether subsidiary to the bringing into conscious harmony with God, those moral intelligent creatures who were alienated from Him by wicked works.

Now we pass over at present any consideration of the bearing of this upon the destiny of the fallen angels, which will come before us subsequently. And we proceed to inquire how it affects those intelligent creatures, who have never fallen, the holy angels, or any other sinless beings that may exist throughout the universe. They do not need the same kind of reconciliation that we do: in their case there is neither guilt nor enmity to be removed; they are already at 'peace' with God. But still we believe that Christ's redeeming work will confer infinite blessing on every one of them to all eternity. It is not from curiosity, nor even from sympathy alone, but from their own personal interest in it, that 'the angels desire to look into' the mystery of the cross. There do they learn, and there will they ever learn, their deepest lessons in the knowledge of God. One object in man's redemption was, 'that in the ages to come He might show the exceeding riches of His grace in his kindness toward us through Christ Jesus.' As the fruits of this are unfolded to all eternity, their minds will expand, and become more capable of receiving from the fulness of God; they will rise ever nearer and nearer to God—nearer to His heart, and nearer to His throne. By this, and perhaps by other means of which we can understand nothing, they will be saved from the possibility of ever falling; they will be kept eternally at one with God; the peace will never be broken, the harmony never be disturbed. This we believe to be the chief benefit conferred upon them by Christ's death. It may be, that to have restored them, if they had fallen, He must have taken their nature; but to establish them in holiness, so that they never can fall, the work He accomplished in our nature may very possibly be sufficient. In the dispensation of the fulness of time, they will be 'headed up in Christ,' and so brought into indissoluble union with God.

And now as to the rest of creation, animate or inanimate. How will it be reconciled to God? By harmony and order being restored where they have been disturbed, or preserved where they are as yet unbroken. Sin has introduced discord and confusion into the universe. To what extent we know not. But we learn from the Apostle's statement that, however far it has extended, it will at length cease wholly and for ever. When sin comes to an end all suffering and all disorder will come to an end also. From the highest creature nearest the throne, down to the minutest atom of matter, everything will be in its right position and fulfilling its proper function. What will be the actual state of things resulting from that in the material world, whether here or elsewhere, we have no means of knowing. We expect new heavens and a new earth, but what they will be like we cannot tell. As to the moral world, however, there can be no doubt. God is Love. And if all His creatures are to be reconciled to Him, then, in every breast throughout the universe, amongst all ranks and classes, with all their endless diversities, must Love reign supreme. Christ is that Love incarnate, and with that Love the Spirit of Christ will fill all things.

SERMON IV.

By Him to reconcile all things unto Himself; by Him, I say, whether they be things in earth, or things in heaven.—COL. I. 20.

THE ultimate object of Christ's redeeming work is to reunite creation to its Creator, to restore universal and eternal harmony, so that discord and disorder shall never again by possibility enter, but God be 'all in all.' How does this bear upon the future destiny of the wicked—whether men or devils?

We can hardly be surprised that the Apostle's declaration here should encourage some to hope that they will all be eventually restored. Nor can it be denied, that, as regards men, there are other passages that seem strongly to confirm the hope. But notwithstanding this, it is quite impossible to maintain such a view, if we admit the Bible, as a whole, to be a revelation from God. If it teaches anything at all, it teaches that some will *never* be saved. It declares that there are vessels of wrath fitted to destruction, just as plainly as that there are vessels of mercy prepared unto glory. Ample proof of this will come before us, as we proceed. It may be sufficient at present to remind you of our Lord's words concerning Judas, 'Good were it for that man if he had never been born.' How could He possibly have said this, if Judas, after however long a period of suffering, is to enjoy an eternity of happiness?

Is this belief then required by the Apostle's statement concerning the reconciliation of all things? Certainly not. For, although by the 'all things' created, and the 'all things' reconciled, we must in each case understand the whole universe, without any exception, yet, on examining the Apostle's language, we see that he takes the scriptural and philosophical view of creation, not as carried on in every fresh development of being, but as accomplished once for all when the germs of the several orders of beings were called into existence; 'By Him *were*'—not *are*—'all things created.' In each case, therefore, he speaks of the universe as a whole. And the reconciliation of all things is, not the restoration of every particular form of life that has ever been developed out of the original creation, but the restoration of perfect harmony to creation as a whole; so that, when it is accomplished, all shall again be 'very good.' We are told nothing of the changes that will have previously taken place in the various kinds of beings, how many creatures will have come into existence, lived their little life, and passed away for ever; but we are assured that whatever forms of existence are found throughout the universe 'in the dispensation of the fulness of times,' will be 'gathered together in one,' 'headed up in Christ,' and according to their several capabilities made eternally at one with their Creator.

We are therefore placing no limit whatever upon the universality of the Apostle's statement, when, on the most positive testimony of God's word, we are compelled to reject absolutely and unhesitatingly the possibility of universal *individual* salvation.

What, then, will become of those who are not saved? The popular view is, that they will live for ever, in unmitigated enmity against God, and consequently in unmitigated suffering; in other words, that evil of every kind, moral and physical, will continue for ever.

If anything were needed to show how diametrically opposed this is to the reconciliation of all things, it would be the desperate shift to which the advocates of that view are driven, in order to escape from the dilemma. All things in heaven and earth, they say, will be reconciled to God, but not all things in hell. Then, if hell is to be excluded from the 'all things' to be reconciled by Christ, it must be excluded also from the 'all things' created by Him—for there also the Apostle uses the same classification, 'both which are in heaven and which are in earth.' But St. John says, 'Without Him was not *anything* made that was made.' In point of fact, however, Scripture knows nothing of any hell beyond the region of this earth. By 'things in earth' is meant not merely things on the surface of this globe, but everything connected with it.

There are other inspired statements also as to the object of Christ's redeeming work, which are quite as hopelessly irreconcilable with the popular view. In Heb. ii. 14, we read—'That through death He might destroy him that had the power of death, that is, the devil;' which is explained in 1 John iii. 8—'For this purpose the Son of God was manifested, that He might destroy the works of the devil.' Could anything be more directly opposed to these statements than the supposition that one part of the universe is to be set apart for the eternal exhibition of Satan's works in their fullest possible maturity? Instead of losing his 'power of death' he will retain it in a more tremendous form than ever. Some have argued against the destruction of this earth, on the ground that it would give Satan a triumph. This may or may not be so. But most assuredly, if Satan is to be the author of *eternal sin*, and consequently of *eternal suffering*, he will have an eternal triumph, and God will suffer an eternal defeat. How would the Almighty be compensated for this, by the power of eternally torturing him? The enemy would retain his 'spoils.' Some of them would have been taken from him, but enough would be left to enable him to hurl back hate and defiance against Him who created, and tried to redeem, the victims of his wiles. This hatred would be as hard for God to bear from any of His creatures, as it would be for them to bear the heaviest infliction that He could lay upon them. For 'God is Love!' and love cannot bear to be hated.

This brings before us another consideration. The popular doctrine is totally opposed to the central truth of Scripture as to the Divine nature, namely that 'God is Love.' Here we tread on different ground. To the statements we have just been considering, the doctrine in question is *directly* opposed. The argument against it from the love of God is one of inference only. Now some persons tell us, that we are wholly incapable of drawing any such inference whatever, both because our moral judgment has been warped by the fall, and also because our mental capacities are necessarily limited. That an undoubted truth lies at the bottom of this objection, we readily admit. The existence of evil is in itself a tax upon our faith. We have to believe in God's love, notwithstanding some appearances to the contrary. And with the grand proof of His love afforded us in the gift of His Son, our faith ought to be able to bear the strain. Though it is not what we should have expected, though we cannot understand it, yet, if all evil will sooner or later come to an end, and result in eternal glory to God, and eternal blessing to the universe, we can easily believe that when that time arrives, when, with all the facts before us and minds capable of grasping them, we look back upon the shadow that was allowed just for an instant to darken the scene, every trace of which is gone, except the ever-increasing blessedness and glory that infinite wisdom and grace evolved out of it,—we shall ourselves perceive the permission of sin and suffering to have been as much the result of infinite Love, as anything else that God ever did.

But if evil is *never* to end, the whole case is altered. If a single creature is to be kept alive for ever in flames that would instantly consume him, were not Almighty power put forth to sustain him under the torture, so that he may never be put out of his misery,—then we cannot form the faintest conception of what Love means, as applied to God. Yet by telling us that He is Love, He implies that we *can* understand what is meant by it. And if so, we may be as certain as we are of our own existence, that He would never have created anything at all, if it had involved the necessity, or even risked the possibility, of one single creature writhing in eternal agony. It would have destroyed His own happiness. Infinitely rather would He have remained alone in solitary existence, than take a step that could possibly lead to anything so dreadful. But when it is said that these millions of suffering creatures will know Who it is that is thus keeping them alive in their torments, and will consequently hate Him with ever-increasing hatred, we reach the climax of impossibility. To suppose that a God of Infinite Love can be perfectly happy, while conscious of being the object of eternal hatred to multitudes of His own creatures, is the most violent moral self-contradiction that could possibly be invented.

Let us endeavour to illustrate the foregoing distinction. If you had to work out a sum in arithmetic, involving a vast number of figures, and a variety of complicated calculations, you would readily admit the possibility of making some mistake. If an arithmetician, in whom you had perfect confidence, assured you that the result of your calculations was wrong, you would feel quite sure that you *had* made a mistake, however unable you might be to discover it. But if all the arithmeticians in the world assured you that two and two make five, you would *not* believe them; nor would you feel the slightest doubt as to the accuracy of your own calculation, that they make four. You would not be at all disturbed by any charges of presumption, or any appeal to your own admitted fallibility. It might be said, If you allow that you may err in one case, but not in the other, where do you mean to draw the line?—where does your infallibility end, and your fallibility begin? At all this you would merely smile; or if you gave a serious answer, it would be to the effect, that confidence is a matter of degree, and that the degree of confidence you felt, as to two and two making four, was precisely the degree of confidence you felt as to your own existence. In either case you *may* be mistaken; but you feel fully justified in acting *as if* it were impossible. You *see* the one, and you *know* the other. Just so—if evil be of limited duration, I can easily attribute all the difficulties connected with it to my own ignorance. I cannot make the sum come right; but I have not the least doubt that that results from some mistake in my calculation, which I am unable to discover. The problem is too vast for me. But when you say, that Infinite and Almighty Goodness will allow evil to maintain a kingdom of its own to all eternity, and that Infinite Love will be eternally and supremely happy, while knowing that it is eternally hated by millions of creatures who are writhing in hopeless agony, I simply reply that you might as well try to persuade me that two and two make five, or that the three angles of a triangle are equal to four right angles.

What! even if God declared that it would be so? There is happily no need to say what I *should* do, on the impossible supposition of God declaring anything so self-contradictory; for as a matter of fact, He *has not* declared anything of the kind. On the contrary, His own Word, from beginning to end, plainly declares the very reverse. In every variety of language, with every kind of metaphor and illustration, directly and indirectly, positively and negatively, by assertion and inference, it teaches that evil *will* come to an end, that evil-doers will utterly perish, that the devil and his works will be totally destroyed, and the whole universe be brought into a state of reconciliation with God. Scripture, therefore, confirms the judgment of that moral instinct, which God has implanted within us, and which pronounces it *impossible*, that He whose name is Love *could* have allowed it to be otherwise.

And this fact enables us with perfect freedom to pursue the subject one step further.

It is believed—indeed it is essential to the consistency of the theory—that the endless sufferings of the condemned will heighten the enjoyment and enhance the blessedness of all holy creatures throughout the universe. Now here we can speak not from inference, but from intuition. Our feelings, of course, are liable to considerable alteration when we are placed in other circumstances; but again we say, that there must be *some* limit to this, or we should wholly lose our identity. And for myself I can only express the confidence I feel by repeating the formula in all seriousness, that I am just as certain as I am of my own existence, that before long I should rush to the Throne in despair, and entreat to be annihilated, in order to escape from the intolerable thought of the unceasing agonies of the condemned. And, not believing myself to be an exceptional case, I am equally confident that this would be the feeling of every creature in the universe, who possessed a spark of love within his breast. They would come again and again with the same importunate cry to the great Creator, saying, Lord, if it must be that this is never to end, if the condemned *cannot* be put out of their misery consistently with Thy glory, oh, then blot *us* we pray Thee out of existence, or send us into an eternal sleep—

anything to escape the horror of the thoughts that haunt us incessantly; we cannot, indeed, see the writhings of their agony or hear their shrieks of despair, but we know what they must be, we can never forget them for a moment, and the thought of them makes life unendurable to us.

How do the advocates of the doctrine attempt to meet this? Why, they say, that sin being committed against an Infinite Being must deserve infinite punishment, and that a feeling of satisfaction at wrong-doing, unrepented of, receiving its due reward is part of our moral nature—one of the results of our being made in the image of God. The latter part of this statement is perfectly true; the former a palpable fallacy, which has often been conclusively disposed of. For a sin to deserve infinite punishment it must be committed not merely against, but still more *by*, an infinite being. The opposite position makes a finite being capable of performing an infinite act, nay, it gives an infinite value to every moral act that any responsible being can possibly perform. For if whatever he does wrong deserves infinite punishment, then whatever he does right must deserve infinite reward. So that the appeal to metaphysics not only utterly fails, but supplies a powerful argument against the theory of endless suffering. *

* It should have been added, that the theory of infinite guilt is irreconcilable with the doctrine of Scripture, that there are degrees of guilt; that which is infinite admitting of no degrees. Yet Mr. Grant, who contends for infinite guilt, objects to the doctrine of Destruction, that it

These four positions, then, appear absolutely impregnable. First, that the doctrine in question is directly at variance with the declarations of Scripture as to the devil and his works being destroyed, and all things reconciled to God. Secondly, that it is utterly irreconcilable with any intelligent belief that God is Love. Thirdly, that it does the utmost conceivable violence to some of the deepest instincts that God has implanted in our nature. And lastly, that it involves a metaphysical impossibility.

In our next discourse we shall show, that it contradicts the plainest statements of God's word as to the final doom of those who will not come to Christ that they may be saved.

does away with degrees of punishment and therefore of guilt. Strange, that he did not see how fatal the objection is to his own doctrine, how perfectly frivolous as against that which he was opposing.

SERMON V.

The wages of sin is death; but the gift of God is eternal life, through Jesus Christ our Lord.—Rom. vi. 23.

STRANGE and startling words these must sound in the ears of the Christian world. If anyone were to preach such doctrine as this now, he would probably meet with the same reception that Paul met with at Athens. Some would ask, What will this babbler say?—other some, He seemeth to be a setter forth of strange gods—because he preached Jesus and eternal life. A few, less ignorant and therefore less bigoted, would say to him, May we know what this new doctrine, whereof thou speakest, is, for thou bringest certain strange things to our ears? And if he replied, We write none other things unto you than those ye read; our doctrine stands out on almost every page of the Bible as plain as words can speak; it is simply this, that the wages of sin is death, but the gift of God is eternal life, through Jesus Christ our Lord; they would at once say : Oh, impossible; that text cannot be in the Bible, you must have got it out of the Apocrypha; we have read the Bible all our lives, but no such idea as that ever entered our minds. We always believed that death was impossible to man; we know, of course, that his body, the lower part of his nature, goes to corruption, but as long as the higher part of his nature, the soul, lives, the *man* does not die; and even the body is dissolved only for a time, it will be raised again, and then he will live for ever, whole and entire, and can never die. Eternal life is no peculiar gift of God through Christ, it is the common possession of every man. Indefeasible immortality is his great glory, the thing in which alone he is equal to his Creator. The wages of sin is not death, but to spend eternal life in sin and misery; and the gift of God is to spend it in holiness and happiness.

Yet no; the text is not out of the Apocrypha, but out of the Epistle to the Romans. And it is only one of a multitude in which the same truth is quite as plainly, sometimes even more plainly, declared.

We will first take those passages in which life and death simply are the alternatives put before us. There is no need to quote them; a glance at the Concordance will show anyone, who is not already aware of it, how incessantly the Bible assures us, that if we live after the flesh we shall die, but if through the spirit we mortify the deeds of the body we shall live; that he who hath the Son hath life, but he who hath not the Son of God hath not life; that he who believes in Christ shall never die, while he who rejects Christ will fall under the power of 'the second death.' Life and Death, Life and Death—these are the two words with which the Bible rings from beginning to end.

Now if endless happiness and endless misery are the alternatives intended, why are they *never* stated in plain language?* Why are they so incessantly and persistently set forth under figures that are directly calculated to mislead? Why is the case so infinitely understated—on one side at least—that of endless misery? If there was any single truth that we should expect to have been stated in the fullest and most explicit terms, it would surely have been this. And yet there are only three or four expressions in the whole Bible which even appear to teach it, not one of which, on fair examination, is found to do so; while we find a doom incessantly threatened, which is quite awful enough in itself, quite enough to fill the impenitent sinner with horror and dismay, but which at its utmost severity, however 'many stripes' may be incurred in the process of destruction, is infinitely less than endless misery. That life and death may sometimes be used figuratively, of course we admit. That the

---

* It will be shown in the next sermon, that neither 'everlasting contempt' nor 'everlasting punishment' nor 'everlasting fire' necessarily involve everlasting pain. If that be the sinner's doom, it is never once declared in Scripture, unless you take one single part of a scenic representation near the end of the Apocalypse, and, while compelled to admit that every other part of it is in the highest degree figurative, insist upon that being taken literally.

future destiny of the righteous and the wicked are often described in figurative language, of course we admit also. But we maintain that the whole of that figurative language points not to endless misery but to destruction; and that if endless misery be the real doom of the lost, and death be only a figure to describe it, then both that figure, and every other similarly employed, are utterly misleading.

Let us look at it closely. It is admitted by all that the death, which is the wages of sin, and which when inflicted is called 'the second death,' means the death of the whole man—body and soul. Now we can infer what is meant by the death of the soul only from what we know of the death of the body. The second death must bear some analogy to the first death, or it would be simply a misleading term. What, then, happens to the body when it dies? It becomes utterly incapable of feeling, or acting, or performing any one of its appropriate functions. It is not that it performs them badly—that is disease—but that it does not perform them at all. When, then, death is said to be inflicted on the soul what are we to understand? Why surely that it will be reduced to the same condition. But the popular theory is that it will live for ever, performing all its functions, but performing them badly. In other words, that instead of being punished with death, it will be afflicted with a loathsome and painful disease, which can never be cured, and from which death will never release it,—that it will be always dying, but never die.

The same thing holds good with regard to the share which the raised *body* is to have in the second death. The popular theory will not allow even it to die. It is to be kept alive in agony for ever. What a teacher the Bible must be, if this is the meaning of God being 'able to destroy both body and soul in hell!'

It may be said that after the first death, consciousness remains in the surviving soul; and that therefore consciousness may remain after the second death. So it might, if the second death were only another death of the body; but as both body *and soul* are to be destroyed by it, no remaining consciousness is possible.

This one word, therefore, the key-word to the whole subject, is amply sufficient to decide the question. It would be difficult to conceive a more violent perversion of the plainest possible teaching, than that which makes death to mean eternal life in misery. And this perversion is all the more inexcusable, on account of the earnestness with which the whole Bible labours to guard us against it. Every expression that human language can supply, and every metaphor that the material world can yield, to impress upon us that the wicked will wholly cease to exist, are piled one upon another, almost continuously, from Genesis to Revelation. They are said to perish—to pass away—to fade—to wither—to be destroyed—consumed—devoured—

burnt up—ground to powder—cut down—plucked up by the roots—broken to shivers—put away like dross—besides other similar expressions. What dependence can be placed upon the teaching of Scripture, if all this means that they will live for ever, with all their powers and faculties of body and mind in full exercise, though at enmity with God, and consequently in a state of unmitigated suffering?*

---

* ' They are to be as " chaff driven away before the wind," or " burnt up;" as " stubble before the wind;" as " thorns burned in the fire;" as " trees cut down," "rooted up," and " burned in fire." They are to be as " beasts taken and destroyed;" as " a light put out ;" as " waters melting away;" as " the whirlwind passing by;" as "the cloud consumed and vanishing away;" and as a " dream" which " flees away." They are to be as '' ashes under the feet ;" as " powder" ground down; as a " vessel dashed in pieces;" as a "garment eaten by the moth," or " consumed in rottenness;" as " grass withering away ;" as " fat consumed into smoke;" and as "tow" and " tares" " burned in the fire."'—*Rev. W. Ker.*

' In exact conformity with our view will be found the illustrations of future punishment in the Old and New Testaments. These are some of the illustrations of the former. The wicked shall be dashed in pieces like a potter's vessel: they shall be like the beasts that perish: like the untimely birth of a woman: like a whirlwind that passeth away: like a waterless garden scorched by an eastern sun: like garments consumed by the moth. They shall consume like the fat of lambs in the fire: consume into smoke: melt like wax: burn like tow: consume like thorns: vanish away like exhausted waters. The illustrations of the New Testament are of the same character. The end of the wicked is there compared to fish cast away to corruption : to a house thrown down to its foundations : to the destruction of the old world by water, and that of the Sodomites by fire: to the death and destruction of natural brute beasts. They shall be like wood cast into quenchless flames: like chaff burnt up: like tares consumed: like a dry branch reduced to ashes. Every one of these images point—not to the preservation of life in any state of pain, but to the loss of life, the utter blotting out of being and existence.'—*Rev. H. Constable.*

But let us look at a few passages, and see if there is anything in them to suggest such a strange interpretation of the words.

Matt. iii. 12. 'Whose fan is in his hand, and He will throughly purge His floor, and gather His wheat into the garner; but He will burn up the chaff with unquenchable fire.' Could any figure be employed more utterly repugnant to the idea of perpetual continuance *in* whatever is here represented by 'unquenchable fire'? or could any figure more forcibly depict utter destruction *by* its irresistible power? The only difficulty is to say anything that can make it plainer or more decisive than it appears in itself. We really can do nothing but ask anyone, who still feels a doubt, to try the experiment of throwing some chaff into an intensely hot fire, and see what becomes of it. The fallacy of the common idea lies in supposing that, if fire be unquenchable, what is put into it must be indestructible. But we shall have more to say upon this in the next sermon.

Matt. x. 28. 'And fear not them which kill the body, but are not able to kill the soul: but rather fear Him which is able to destroy both soul and body in hell.' We select this from a host of passages in which the destruction of the wicked is spoken of, because both body and soul are so emphatically specified, and because the contrast drawn between the power of man and the power of God, renders the meaning of 'destroy' so perfectly clear. To 'destroy' the soul is to 'kill' it. This man cannot do. He *can* make the soul very wicked and very miserable. What he is not able to do, is to put it out of conscious existence. That power he does possess with regard to the body; not, as we explained in a former discourse, by putting out of existence its component atoms, but by causing such a disarrangement of them, or producing such an effect upon them, as leaves the body totally incapable of performing any one of its functions. The quibbling about 'annihilation' is wholly beside the mark.* No one contends for annihilation, but for destruction—which is quite another thing.

Luke ix. 24. 'For whosoever will save his life shall lose it: but whosoever will lose his life for My sake the same shall save it.' What is the 'it,' which he shall either save or lose hereafter? Evidently 'his life.' What else can it be? He may lose it hereafter in a much more awful manner than he can possibly lose it now; or he may save it hereafter for much higher

---

* The language commonly employed on this subject is instructive. Our opponents charge us with believing in 'annihilation,' and denying 'everlasting punishment;' both of which charges are absolutely groundless. We doubt whether God will ever annihilate a single particle of matter that He ever created, and we hold everlasting punishment as strongly as they do. But we understand the punishment to be 'everlasting destruction,' and what we deny is eternal evil. From both of these terms our opponents shrink with instinctive dread; the one expresses too strongly what they do not believe, the other puts too clearly before them what they do believe.

enjoyment than he can possibly have from it now. But the thing which he will either save or lose, is his *life*: the difference being, that at present he can only lose it partially, man not being ' able to kill the soul,' while then he will lose it entirely, being ' destroyed, soul and body.'

Gal. vi. 8. 'He that soweth to his flesh, shall of the flesh reap corruption; but he that soweth to the Spirit shall of the Spirit reap life everlasting.' Corruption means literally the decay of a dead body, and so comes to represent death or destruction. It is the same word in the original, that in 2 Pet. ii. 12 is applied to the slaughter of animals, and in Col. ii. 22 to the consumption of food.

2 Thess. i. 9. 'Who shall be punished with everlasting destruction from the presence of the Lord, and from the glory of His power.' The peculiar value of this text is in connection with the last verse of Matt. xxv., which we shall have to consider in our next sermon; ' These shall go away into everlasting punishment.' Here we are distinctly told what the 'everlasting punishment' is, namely, 'everlasting destruction.' It no more follows that everlasting punishment should be eternally in process of infliction than that everlasting destruction should be eternally in process of accomplishment. The wicked will no more be undergoing continuous punishment for ever, than they will be undergoing continuous destruction for ever. The

destruction will take place once for all, 'when Christ shall come to be glorified in His saints,' but its effects will be everlasting, inasmuch as there will be no recovery from it. That punishment therefore will be strictly everlasting — as lasting as the life of the righteous, for it will be the eternal deprivation of the blessedness which they would otherwise have been for ever enjoying.*

Heb. x. 26, 27. 'For if we sin wilfully after that we have received the knowledge of the truth, there remaineth no more sacrifice for sins, but a certain fearful looking for of judgment and fiery indignation, which shall devour the adversaries.' Of course the word 'devour,' like any other of those we have quoted, may be used figuratively—indeed it is used figuratively here; but we maintain that, as employed to describe the effects of a 'fiery indignation,' it can denote only utter destruction. And this is confirmed by what immediately follows; in which it is compared to the stoning of an offender against the Mosaic Laws. 'He that despised Moses' Law died without mercy under two or three witnesses. Of how much sorer punishment, suppose ye, shall he be thought worthy, who hath trodden under foot the Son of God.' Some have argued that as the dignity of Christ is *infinitely* greater than that of Moses, the punishment threatened must be *infinitely* sorer. But this is a mistake. For the sin

* But see Appendix.

was, in each case, committed against God, and the contrast is between rejecting a revelation made through Moses, but quite sufficiently attested to be from God, and rejecting a much more important revelation made through Christ. And though perhaps not very much weight may attach to the argument, yet, as far as the expression goes, it seems scarcely likely that any comparison would be instituted between endless suffering and the mere stoning of a man to death. The punishment alluded to would be *so* 'much sorer' as to make any reference to the other almost absurd. But understand it, in the light of other Scriptures, as a far more terrific destruction than anything that can befall a man in this life, and the comparison is natural and forcible.

Heb. xii. 29. 'For our God is a consuming fire.' The word rendered 'consuming' is as strong a word as the Greek language could supply. The popular theory makes God to be only a scorching fire; those who are exposed to His wrath being for ever tortured, but never consumed, by it. These words furnish the answer to an objection that may possibly be raised against the view that the soul as well as the body will be destroyed in hell. Material fire, it may be said, could not destroy that which is immaterial. Perhaps not. But the God, who is Himself a consuming fire, is not confined to the use of material instruments for effecting any destruction that may be required. That He will make large use of material fire, there appears no reason to doubt. But who imagines that He will use nothing else?

1 Peter i. 23-25. 'Being born again, not of corruptible seed, but of incorruptible, by the Word of God, which liveth and abideth for ever. For all flesh is as grass, and all the glory of man as the flower of grass. The grass withereth, and the flower thereof falleth away: but the Word of the Lord endureth for ever.' The contrast is between the regenerate and the unregenerate, those who are subjects of the new birth, and those who are merely subjects of the old birth. The regenerate partake of endless life, because they are begotten of God through the Word, the effect of which must necessarily be abiding. The unregenerate in their natural state are like grass which withers and falls away. If this referred merely to the frailty of man's present life, there would be no force in the contrast; for in that the regenerate and unregenerate are alike. The contrast is between the imperishable life of those who are born of the incorruptible enduring seed, and the transitory existence of man in his natural fallen state—'all flesh.'

2 Peter ii. 12. 'But these, as natural brute beasts, made to be taken and destroyed, speak evil of the things that they understand not; and shall utterly perish in their own corruption.' The form of the original shows that they are not compared to the brutes in their evil speaking, but in the ultimate consequence

of it.* That consequence is described in precisely the same terms as the slaughter of the animals. It is literally, 'made for capture and destruction,' and 'shall utterly perish in their own destruction.' The words 'their own' show that there will be a fitting difference in the manner of it; but it must be destruction, if there is to be the smallest propriety in comparing it to the killing of an animal.

1 John ii. 17. 'And the world passeth away, and the lust thereof: but he that doeth the will of God abideth for ever.' A careful examination of the context will show that the 'world' is here not the material world, but the world of ungodly men. And the contrast between its passing away, and the righteous abiding for ever, is in perfect harmony with the whole teaching of Scripture.

In our next discourse we shall consider the four expressions which are thought to teach an opposite doctrine: namely, that the wicked will abide for ever, no less than the righteous, only in misery instead of in happiness.

Before concluding, however, let us answer a question that must naturally occur to any reflecting mind, and the answer to which is not a little instructive. There is

---

* From a comparison of this text with Jude 10, it seems probable that St. Peter had their conduct as well as their destruction in his mind: although it is only in the latter point, that he directly likens them to the lower animals.

no difficulty in the doom of the wicked being described simply as 'death;' but how is the term 'life,' standing alone as it so often does, sufficient to describe the blessedness of the righteous? Other expressions no doubt make it abundantly clear that their bliss will not consist simply in endless existence. But how is all that included in 'eternal life'? The answer to this involves the essential principle of the whole matter. In Christ 'all things consist' or hold together; as from Him they all at first derived their existence. In Him is life, and in Him only. Nothing can permanently live that is separated from Him. It may be allowed to retain for a time an unnatural existence; it may continue in a dying state as long as He sees fit; but it 'hath not *life*,' and it must ultimately perish. The death of those who 'have not the Son' is a necessary consequence, arising out of the essential conditions of all existence. Irresponsible beings, animate or inanimate, may live by unconscious union with Christ, the nature of which perhaps we cannot understand; but moral creatures, by the very conditions of their being, can only live permanently by conscious willing union with, and subjection to, the great Head. As long as they remain without that, they are only 'dead while they live,' and if they continue so, must in due time perish.

Eternal life, therefore, necessarily implies eternal moral union with Christ, and so carries everything with it. 'Because I live, ye shall live also;' there is no need to add 'in holiness and happiness,' for it must be so. An eternally dying life is impossible. When this state of trial and probation is over, and the final judgment comes, there are but two alternatives—life or death.

This day life and death are set before you; therefore choose life; for why will ye die?

SERMON VI.

Who shall be punished with everlasting destruction from the presence of the Lord, and from the glory of His power.—
2 Thess. i. 9.

HAVING shown the clearness and fulness with which Scripture foretells that the doom of impenitent sinners will be utter destruction, we now proceed to examine those particular passages which are thought to teach that their doom will be—not everlasting destruction, but—eternal life in hopeless misery. Multitudes of texts are brought forward against universalism, which have no bearing whatever upon the present argument. There are only four expressions in the whole Bible, which even appear to teach endless suffering, as distinguished from everlasting destruction.*

As to the first there is no difficulty. 'Many of them

---

* A text commonly adduced, in Isa. xxxiii. 14, 'Who among us shall dwell with the devouring fire? who among us shall dwell with everlasting burnings,' has no reference to future punishment, but to the perpetual invasions of Judæa by their enemies. The people in their distress say, 'Who can live in such a state of things as this? Who can bear these constant desolations?' As the Egyptians said to Pharaoh, 'Knowest thou not yet that Egypt is destroyed?'

The parable of the Rich Man and Lazarus refers to the intermediate state. The Rich Man was in 'Hades,' not in 'Gehenna.' Both words are translated 'hell' in our Bible.

that sleep in the dust of the earth shall awake, some to everlasting life, and some to shame and everlasting contempt' (Dan. xii. 2). It does not at all follow, because they will be *objects* of everlasting contempt, that therefore they will remain *conscious* of it for ever. In Is. lxvi. 24, the same word, here rendered 'contempt,' and there 'abhorring,' is applied to the '*carcases* of the men that have transgressed against Me;' and *they* could not of course be conscious of it. This passage, therefore, is in perfect harmony with the general teaching of Scripture: the wicked will awake to a sense of shame, and to become the objects of everlasting contempt. Whether the remembrance of *individuals* will be preserved for ever may perhaps be questioned; but it will never be forgotten, as one of the most marvellous illustrations of the power of evil over those whom it possesses, that multitudes of intelligent creatures, having life and death set before them, chose death rather than give up the pleasures of sin for a season.

We may therefore proceed to the next passage, namely, Matt. xxv. 46. 'And these shall go away into everlasting punishment: but the righteous into life eternal.' This is more relied on than any; so much so, that it supplies the conventional term for the doctrine of endless suffering. You are never asked whether you believe in 'everlasting destruction,' or any similar term, but whether you believe in 'everlasting punishment.' Now it is surely of itself a noteworthy circumstance, when the advocates of a doctrine invariably select, as the name for it, an expression that occurs only once in the whole Bible, although the subject to which it refers is so constantly mentioned in every form and variety of language. But let us see whether our Lord's saying does necessarily teach what is supposed. The question turns on the meaning of the two words rendered 'everlasting' and 'punishment.'

As to the former, there is no doubt whatever; both its etymology and its use are decisive. It is taken from a word which means an age or period of time, and it consequently means lasting through the period referred to. What that period may be in any particular case, we can only learn, either from the context, or from our previous knowledge of the facts; the word itself tells us nothing. For instance, the Mosaic ordinances were over and over again declared to be 'everlasting;' that is, they were to last through the whole period of that dispensation; and the 'hills' are called 'everlasting,' because they will last throughout the present state of natural things on the surface of our globe—that is, until 'the heavens shall pass away with a great noise, and the elements shall melt with fervent heat,' and 'the earth also with the works that are therein shall be burned up.' So, again, the fire that consumed Sodom and Gomorrah is called in Jude 7 'eternal fire,' because the *effect* of it *still* remains. Indeed, without these plain proofs of the sense in which the word is used in Scripture, it seems strange that our own familiar use of that whole class of expressions—everlasting, eternal, endless, unceasing, continual, perpetual, always, never, for ever—with an implied limit, should not have saved us from attaching the idea of absolute endlessness to them when found in the Bible. The common answer to this is, that in so speaking we use exaggerated language, which it is impossible to attribute to God's Word. If so, then a Jew is quite justified in adhering to the Mosaic ritual, for that was most positively declared to be everlasting. But it is altogether a mistake. Such language is no exaggeration at all; it expresses the simple truth, that the thing referred to lasts continuously throughout the whole period, which is implied by the nature of the case. Perhaps no language in the world possesses a word which necessarily implies absolute endlessness—certainly not the Greek. A stronger word than that commonly used in the New Testament for everlasting, is applied by Jude to the 'chains,' in which the fallen angels 'are reserved under darkness;' and yet the duration of those 'everlasting chains' is expressly limited 'unto the judgment of the great day.'

Let us see, then, how this bears upon the subject before us. When the word 'eternal' (or 'everlasting,' which is only another translation of the same word) is applied in Scripture to the existence of God, or to the future glory of the Church, we understand it as meaning absolutely endless, *because* we know, from other statements, that neither the one nor the other will ever come to an end.* When it is applied to the future punishment of the wicked, we know that—as far as regards the *consciousness* of punishment—it *cannot* mean absolutely endless, be-

---

* This meets the objection, that if we put a limit to the misery of the condemned, we must also put a limit to the happiness of the saved: in other words, that if the wicked perish, so must the righteous,—if the wicked have not immortality, neither can the righteous have it,—if there is no eternal life out of Christ, neither can there be any *in* Christ. 'Eternal' means lasting throughout the period referred to; and that period may be limited in one case and unlimited in another. But see Appendix on 'Everlasting Punishment.'

We may also ask, how the way of holiness could be called '*the* way everlasting,' in *contrast* to every 'wicked way' (Ps. cxxxix. 24); if the two ways were both everlasting, the one being the way of everlasting holiness and happiness, the other the way of everlasting sin and misery.

'The certainty that the blessedness of the righteous will be truly everlasting does not depend on the use of the adjective αἰώνιος in connection with the life promised to them. If we had no evidence beyond the use of that word, we should not, so far as the proof turns upon language, have a certainty that immortal life is the inheritance of the saved. But we are not left to the imperfect assurance of an adjective of ambiguous meaning. The heavenly heritage is declared to be "incorruptible, undefiled, and unfading," and "the crown of glory, one that fadeth not away;" "the corruptible is to put on incorruption, and the mortal to put on immortality." The future life of Christ's faithful servants is set forth as flowing from Him, and being like unto His life: "Because He lives, they shall live also;" "He is their life, and their life is hid with Him in God;" "they shall be made like unto Him;" "whether they wake or sleep, they are to live together with Him;" "they are to be for ever (πάντοτε) with the Lord;" and, "their vile bodies are to be changed, and fashioned like unto His glorious body."'— *Appeal to Scripture.* Rev. *J. Barton, M.A.*

cause Scripture positively declares that evil will come to an end, and the irreclaimably wicked be utterly destroyed. 'Everlasting punishment' therefore, as used by Our Lord in this parable, if it be understood of *felt* punishment, can only mean, *at the utmost,* punishment which will continue through the remainder of their existence; whilst the 'eternal life' promised to the righteous we know to mean endless indissoluble union with God in Christ.

Still it may be said, that although such a view may be logically tenable, yet the impression naturally produced by the contrast is, that the duration in each case is the same. This impression, so far as it concerns the duration of happiness and misery, is produced by coming to the passage with that belief in our minds. The Romanist, who has been taught from infancy to believe that the words 'This is my body' mean, 'This is the substance of my body,' is confirmed in his impression every time that he hears those words. He wonders how you can be so blind and perverse as to reject such plain teaching. In answer to all your arguments from Scripture and reason, he recurs again and again to his one text, 'This is my body;' just as the advocates of Eternal Evil recur again and again to, 'These shall go away into everlasting punishment.' Look at a straight stick under water, and it will appear crooked. You may know that it is not crooked, and be able to prove it to a demonstration; but as long as you look at it through the distorting medium it will appear so. In the same way, while you look at this passage through the doctrine of Eternal Evil, it will appear out of line with the general teaching of Scripture. And however completely you may be silenced in argument, it will still continue to *look* crooked. But let your mind be thoroughly possessed with the revealed truth, that the wicked are to perish for ever, and then, if you look at the passage with a right understanding of the terms employed, it will wear no such distorted appearance;* the stick will not only be *proved* to be straight, but taken out of the water and *seen* to be so.

Notwithstanding all this, I quite believe that our Lord did mean to ascribe the same duration to the punishment of the wicked, *in one of its two elements*, that he ascribes to the life of the righteous. In what will that punishment consist? In *suffering* and in *loss*. Many or few stripes will be inflicted, according to each one's deserts; while in every case they will end in the final loss of life, as the necessary consequence of not being united to Christ, in whom alone can anything permanently 'consist.' Now this latter element in the punishment necessarily involves the termination of the

---

* This is described by the *Christian Advocate* as 'settling the matter beforehand.' No; it is only acting upon the principle laid down in one of our own Articles, that one passage of Scripture is not to be interpreted so as to contradict another.

former, but itself has no termination. To all eternity will they pay the penalty of having rejected Christ, in the loss of that eternal life which they would otherwise have possessed. Like the cities of Sodom and Gomorrah, they will be 'suffering the vengeance of eternal fire,' in the 'everlasting destruction' which their persistence in evil has brought upon them.

Understand the 'punishment' here to include both these elements, and then, so far from there being the slightest difficulty in the statement, it becomes a simple comprehensive expression of the whole truth. As regards the element of suffering, the punishment is everlasting in the sense of continuing through the remainder of their existence. As regards the element of loss, it is as everlasting as the gain of the righteous. To insist upon the suffering being absolutely endless, is to force an arbitrary interpretation upon the words, which brings them into violent antagonism with the whole teaching of Scripture.*

If it be thought strange that our Lord should use language which He knew would be so grievously perverted, it is quite enough to adduce once more the

---

* If anyone thinks that the word rendered 'punishment' cannot properly apply to a penalty, consisting of loss or deprivation, he has only to refer to Thucydides (book ii. ch. 87), where he will read κολασθήσεται τῇ πρεπούσῃ ζημίᾳ, he shall be punished with the proper ζημία, which Liddell and Scott's Lexicon explains to mean 'loss, damage, opposite to κέρδος (gain), a penalty—in money, a fine.'

But see Appendix.

words, 'This is my body.' What gross superstitions He foresaw springing up and corrupting nearly the whole Church for ages, and what wholesale massacres of His faithful people for refusing to admit the monstrous lie! A word of explanation would have rendered all this impossible. But it was not given. And millions of Christians have lived and died as perfectly certain that 'This is my body' teaches transubstantiation, as that 'everlasting punishment' means eternal life in misery.

The next argument we have to consider is drawn from our Lord's words, recorded in Mark ix. 47, 48: 'And if thine eye offend thee, pluck it out: it is better for thee to enter into the kingdom of God with one eye, than having two eyes to be cast into hell fire: where their worm dieth not, and the fire is not quenched.'

The question is, For what purpose are they cast into hell fire—to be destroyed, or to be tortured for ever? Now, without again referring to our Lord's express declaration, that God is able to destroy both soul and body in hell; or to His warning, recorded in the preceding chapter (Mark viii. 35), that whosoever is not willing to sacrifice his life, if required, by fidelity to Him, will ultimately 'lose *it*'; we might be content to ask whether the contrast is not evidently intended (though more pointedly brought out in Matt. v. 29 'that one of thy members should *perish*'), between the loss of a single member now and the loss of the whole body hereafter. But let us examine the figures more closely.

We will take the 'fire' first, as the simpler. What is the meaning of 'unquenchable fire'? Does it mean fire that will never cease to burn? Certainly not. If a fire broke out in London, which could not be quenched, it would burn on *until* it had burnt down the whole town, and *then* it would go out of itself for want of any more fuel to consume.* So Our Lord means that, when the wicked are cast into hell, there will be no hope for them; they will neither be able to escape from the fire nor to extinguish it. It will burn on till it has utterly consumed them. 'He will burn up the chaff with unquenchable fire.' † And even if it were certain, that a visible memorial of evil will be preserved, in

---

* In verses 43 and 45, the phrase is rendered 'that never shall be quenched'; but it ought to be 'unquenchable.' The idea is precisely the same as in the Baptist's 'unquenchable fire.'

† I have been favoured with the following criticism by a member of my congregation:—

'I believe you have not mentioned in any of your sermons that the Greek authors used ἄσβεστος (unquenchable) in the sense of violent or excessive, without any reference to its duration, or the possibility of its being quenched or stopped. Homer speaks of ἄσβεστος γέλως, Il. i. 599, and after saying that in the attempt of the Trojans to burn the Grecian fleet, φλὸξ ἀσβέστη (an unquenchable flame) spread itself over one of the ships (xvi. 123), he saw nothing absurd or contradictory in adding in the same book (xvi. 293) of Patroclus that he extinguished the blazing fire, and that the ship was left half burned— κατὰ δ' ἔσβεσεν αἰθόμενον πῦρ.'

some material fire kept burning for ever, there would be no reason to conclude that what is cast into it is indestructible; even if we had not been so plainly told, that the wicked will be destroyed, consumed, devoured, burnt up, by it.

In the 'undying worm' we have the same fact presented under a different aspect. It is nothing to say that the two *figures* thus combined are mutually inconsistent (inasmuch as the fire would destroy the worm); it is enough if the things they *represent* are consistent. The fire represents death in its most terrific, the worm in its most repulsive, aspect—its painfulness and its loathsomeness. The worm not dying means precisely the same as the fire not being quenched. And if we came to such expressions without preconceived ideas, we should never imagine that either of them were endless. Just as, when we are told that the fire is unquenchable, we should understand, that it would burn on, until it had consumed everything within its reach; so, when we are told that a worm feeding on a carcase 'dieth not,' we should understand that the worm would go on devouring the carcase until there was nothing of it left. What becomes of the worm after that, we should never stay for a moment to consider, because it does not come within the range of the figure. Who could imagine that the carcase would be miraculously renewed, so that though the worm was for ever preying upon it, it would never be devoured? So far from the worm not dying, affording any proof that the body will continue for ever in existence, it is manifestly intended to show that it will not. The ravages of the worm must bring the carcase to an end, unless additional corrupt matter is perpetually supplied to compensate for the loss.

Instead, therefore, of finding anything here even to suggest the idea of endless suffering, we must do extreme violence to both the figures, in order to force it upon them. Besides the improbable notion of an eternal fire and an eternal worm, we have to imagine a living human body so constructed that fire will go on for ever scorching but never consuming it, and also a dead body which will for ever supply food to a worm that unceasingly preys upon it—which will, in fact, possess more astounding vitality than any living body that was ever known.

We have taken for granted, you will observe, in the preceding argument, that it is a dead body upon which the worm is supposed to be preying. This is surely self-evident; for from what other fact in nature could the figure be drawn? Any doubt, however, is set at rest by turning to the passage in the Old Testament to which Our Lord manifestly refers. In Isa. lxvi. 24 we read: 'And they shall go forth, and look upon the carcases of the men that have transgressed against Me: for their worm shall not die, neither shall their fire be quenched; and they shall be an abhorring unto all flesh.' Surely this passage should have preserved us from attaching the idea of eternal suffering to the same expressions, when applied by Our Lord to the final doom of all impenitent sinners. Here they *cannot* mean eternal suffering, or any suffering at all; for the Prophet speaks only of the dead bodies of persons previously slain—which are exhibited to view, disgraced and degraded, 'an abhorring unto all flesh.' But as our Lord evidently means to represent the wicked as cast *alive* into hell-fire, the figure must there be held to include the sufferings which they will endure in the process of destruction, as well as their subsequently becoming objects of 'everlasting contempt.'

Before passing on, perhaps we ought to mention an argument that has been drawn from the words which immediately follow: 'For every one shall be salted with fire; and every sacrifice shall be salted with salt.' It is said that salt represents preservation from corruption, and that therefore the preservation of the wicked from being destroyed by the fire, is what Our Lord here asserts. But the words are—'salted *with* fire,'—not salted so as to be proof *against* it. Besides, salt preserves *from* corruption, not *in* corruption; so that this interpretation would directly contradict what had just been represented by the worm. The universalist might draw a plausible argument from the word, to the effect that the fire was remedial; but no ingenuity can make it teach eternal suffering. I believe it does refer to the purifying effect of fire; but to the purification of the universe by the destruction of the wicked, not to their own purification. Every sacrifice was mingled with salt; which represented, no doubt, freedom from corruption. As the whole universe is to be reconciled to God, and presented to Him an acceptable sacrifice, by Christ, every taint of corruption must be eradicated from it. And Christ here warns us, that unless we *will* submit to the purifying fire of self-sacrifice during our period of probation, cutting off the right hand or plucking out the right eye that would cause us to offend, we *must* submit to be cast into the fire of hell, which will effectually put an end to our corruption, by utterly destroying us body and soul.

We now come to the last argument which is adduced to support the doctrine of Eternal Evil—drawn from some of the closing scenes in the Apocalypse. The particular passages quoted are, ch. xiv. 9–11, xix. 3–20, and xx. 10; of which we may say, generally, that they describe the devil and certain victims of his wiles as tormented for ever and ever in a lake of fire.

Now it is very natural that anyone, who already believes in eternal torment, should understand these passages as referring to it. But one, whose mind was thoroughly imbued with the whole tenor of inspired teaching upon this subject, and who consequently knew that evil was *not* to last for ever, would no more suppose them to teach that either men or devils will literally suffer endless torment, than he would suppose, from other parts of the same scenic representation, that when Christ appears to inflict punishment upon them, He will ride on a white horse, and be clothed with a vesture dipped in blood; that out of His mouth will go a sharp sword; that an angel will stand in the sun, and call to all the fowls that fly in the midst of heaven to come and gather themselves together to the supper of the great God. Is it not palpable that the whole scene is figurative to the highest degree, and that we must interpret the figures by the light which the general teaching of Scripture throws upon them? Now, we can give a very much stronger reason for denying that the smoke of their torment ascending up for ever and ever is to be understood literally, than for denying that Christ will ride on a white horse. For of the latter we can only say that it seems extremely improbable; while of the former we can say that it is absolutely impossible, because it would contradict the plainest and most positive declarations of God's word, that the wicked are to be utterly destroyed and evil come to an end.

Even without this appeal, however, taking the representations just as they stand, we find the strongest ground for denying any literal interpretation of them. In the first place, this perpetual torment is said to be endured 'in the presence of the Lamb'; whereas St. Paul says that the wicked will be 'punished with everlasting destruction *from* the presence of the Lord.' Again, chap. xiv. 9-11 and ch. xix. 3-20 refer to judgments inflicted before the millennium, while it is not until the end of the millennium that the general judgment takes place, and the wicked receive their final doom. This is made still more obvious by what follows the statement of the beast and the false prophet being cast alive into the lake of fire, in ch. xix. 21: 'And the remnant were slain with the sword of Him that sat upon the horse.' If the being cast into a lake of fire represents the commencement of endless suffering, what does the being slain with a sword represent, when put in contrast with it? Again, we may observe, that the beast and the false prophet are not persons but systems. And more decisively still, that death and hell (Hades, the place of departed spirits) are cast into the lake of fire; which cannot mean the inhabitants of Hades, for it has been previously emptied of its inhabitants in order that they might stand before the great white throne.*

---

* In addition to what is mentioned above, let it be observed, that after the last judgment St. John 'saw a new heaven and a new earth, for the first heaven and the first earth were passed away;' and therefore, it would seem, the lake of fire also, which was on the first earth. That it is *referred to* afterwards, affords no proof of its continued existence on the new earth, where 'there shall be no more death, neither sorrow nor crying, neither shall there be any more pain:' for in ch. xxii. 12, reference is made to the Lord's coming, which cannot be an event of eternal continuance. Then where is it? For of any 'Hell' separate from this earth Scripture gives not a hint. Can anyone sup-

If it be asked what the lake of fire does represent, we would reply—the partial overcoming of evil and destruction of evildoers at the beginning of the millennium, with their complete overthrow at the close of it. Fire is the most irresistible agent of destruction that we know; and it is used here to give us the most vivid idea that could be presented to our minds of the complete destruction of what is represented by the persons and things cast into it. The devil probably represents all the evil connected with the unseen world; the beast and the false prophet the most conspicuous typical developments of human wickedness; death and hades the physical evils introduced by sin. All will come to an end; every trace of sin and its results will be swept away for ever.

How far literal fire will be made use of, and whether any visible monument will be preserved of the mighty overthrow, are questions to which it is equally difficult and needless to give any decided answer. But with regard to the word 'torment' being used here, we can have little doubt that it refers to the sufferings which will accompany the final death of the wicked; it will not be a simple act of annihilation, but a process of

pose that these glowing descriptions of earth's future blessedness merely refer to the surface of our planet, while underneath its crust, 'death,' and 'sorrow,' and 'crying,' and pain,' are to reign and rage eternally with greater fury than ever? Whatever be the interpretation of it, there can be no doubt that in the prophetic *picture*, the 'ages' have passed away, and 'the smoke of their torment' has ceased to ascend.

F

destruction. What will be the nature or duration of the torment we are not informed, and need not attempt to guess. All we know is that it will produce no change in their character. 'He that is unjust, let him be unjust still: and he which is filthy, let him be filthy still: and he that is righteous, let him be righteous still: and he that is holy, let him be holy still' (ch. xxii. 11). After the final judgment, the wicked will continue wicked, and must therefore perish; the righteous can never fall again, and must therefore live for ever.

I know not how it may appear to you, but to me it appears as clear as daylight, that neither this passage nor any of the others, nor all of them together, prove the doctrine of Eternal Evil one whit more than 'This is My body' proves the doctrine of Transubstantiation. If, however, any of you should still think that the difficulty of reconciling these passages with the general teaching of Scripture has not been wholly removed, let me beg you to consider whether it is at all greater than the difficulty of reconciling some other passages with the Deity of Christ, or the Atonement, or Justification by Faith, or indeed almost any doctrine in the whole Bible. We never admit the smallest doubt of Our Lord's deity, merely because we are unable to interpret one or two texts, without such an amount of what a Unitarian would call special pleading, as, if heard alone, would probably confirm, rather than shake, his conviction of its untenableness. Neither ought we to admit the smallest doubt of the 'everlasting destruction' of the wicked, merely because it requires some degree of thought and patient examination to get a right understanding of the very few texts that may seem opposed to it. And in our belief that we have not misunderstood either those particular passages, or the general teaching of Scripture, I shall be greatly mistaken if we are not confirmed, when we come to look at the whole subject from a practical point of view, and consider the mischief which has been done by the popular theory, as well as the light which is thrown on some of the darker features of revelation by a right understanding of the truth on this important matter.

But first we shall endeavour to show how the error arose, and also how inconsistent it is with the revelations of Scripture concerning man's Creation, Fall, and Redemption.

SERMON VII.

In the day that thou eatest thereof thou shalt surely die.
GEN. II. 17.

No sooner was Christianity established in the world, than Satan set himself to corrupt it. His greatest success was the infusion into it of Judaism and of heathen philosophy; resulting in sacerdotalism and in the doctrine of Eternal Evil. In each case, as usual, the error was engrafted on a truth; in the former on the priesthood of Christ and of all Christians, in the latter on the Resurrection of the dead and everlasting life in Christ. The purpose of the former was to hide God from our view; that of the latter to present Him in such an aspect as would inspire us with horror.

As regards that, with which alone we have now to do, the root of the whole mischief lay in the Platonic philosophy with regard to the immortality of the soul. To this day is that supposed inherent immortality man's proudest boast. It seems so glorious to think that he *must* live for ever. Glorious indeed, for it clothes him with one of God's own essential attributes. He cannot climb up to equality with God in His omnipotence, omniscience, or omnipresence; the one point in which alone his vain imagination can hope to place him on a level with his Creator, is his presumed indefeasible immortality,—that whatever else may happen, he must and will live for ever. We may see at a glance how easily this idea, so agreeable to man's pride, would be engrafted upon the Christian's belief in a state of consciousness after death, a subsequent resurrection, and eternal life through Christ. And then, how natural and consecutive appear the links in the chain. All live, in a limited sense, after death,—all will stand, absolutely alive, before the judgment seat,—the saved will continue to live for ever in perfect holiness and happiness,—the lost will—what?—had Satan ever an easier task than to suggest—live for ever in sin and misery? What else is possible? Their restoration is hopelessly barred by the plain declarations of Scripture; their souls are presumed to be indestructible; and for what purpose can their bodies be raised, unless to be habitations for those immortal souls? The inference is irresistible—body and soul must both be tormented for ever. How easily may an apparently innocent error find entrance! How disastrous may be its results! To a heathen it was little matter whether he believed in the immortality of the soul, or not. Christianity was poisoned by the infusion.

But how was this to be reconciled with the constant testimony of Scripture, that the wicked will *not* live for ever, but be destroyed and utterly perish? Why did not a host of texts open their eyes and show them their mistake? In reply we may ask, again, Why does a straight stick put into water look crooked? And why will no arguments make it look straight? Simply because it is seen through a distorting medium. So may men search the Scriptures for ever, with a pre-established belief in their own indestructibility, and they will be only more and more confirmed in their belief of eternal evil. The longer they look at the stick, the more certain they will become that it is crooked. This accounts for the otherwise perplexing fact, that some of the most determined advocates of this doctrine are men who have studied the Bible all their lives, and in many points have the deepest understanding of it. And it also accounts for the rapidity and thoroughness with which many persons change their views, as soon as their eyes are opened to see the fundamental fallacy that underlies them. The moment the stick is taken out of the water, it appears perfectly straight.

Let us, then, see whether there is any ground for this postulate, of natural immortality, either in reason or in Scripture.*

---

* 'I permit the Pope to make articles of faith for himself and his faithful,—such as, that the soul is the substantial form of the human body, that the soul is immortal, with all those monstrous opinions to be found in the Roman decretals.'—*Martin Luther.*

'To the Christian, indeed, all this doubt would be instantly removed

The ground on which reason is appealed to in its favour, is the supposed indestructibility of matter; the inference being that, if the lower part of our nature cannot be annihilated, it is very unlikely that the higher part can. But this argument involves two palpable fallacies: first, that because matter is indestructible by man, it must also be indestructible by God, and secondly, that any compound thing can be *destroyed* only by being *annihilated*. With regard to the former, it is hard to believe that the Creator could not put out of existence whatever he had called into existence. With regard to the latter, it simply confounds the destruction of a material object with the destruction of its component parts. It is not necessary that *they* should be destroyed in order to destroy *it*. A vessel is destroyed when it is broken to pieces; it ceases to exist *as such*. Now, as we know nothing of the composition of the human soul, we can form no idea as to the kind of process that would be required for its destruction,— but to say that it *cannot* be destroyed is simply absurd.

Indeed, so far from reason suggesting the smallest

---

if he found that the immortality of the soul was revealed in the word of God. In fact, no such doctrine is revealed to us. The Christian's hope, as founded in the promises contained in the Gospel, is the resurrection of the body.'—*Archbishop Whately*.

'That the soul is naturally immortal is contradicted by Scripture, which makes our immortality a gift dependent on the Giver.'—*Richard Watson*.

'The doctrine of the immortality of the soul, and the name, are alike unknown to the entire Bible.'—*Olshausen*.

argument in favour of its indestructibility, all the analogies from the material world are directly against it. Not a single material organisation can be found that is indestructible: why should any spiritual organisation be so? Would not reason itself lead us to conclude that it must be at least as easy for God to destroy a soul as for man to destroy a body?

But what saith the Scripture? Does it represent man as created indestructible?

First, we are told that 'God created man in His own image.' But how did that make him necessarily immortal, any more than omnipotent or omniscient? An image of a person or thing does not necessarily last as long as the original. In what the likeness did consist, we are plainly told, namely, in his moral nature: 'Renewed in knowledge after the image of Him that created him,' 'Which after God is created in righteousness and true holiness.'

Then we are reminded, that ' God breathed into his nostrils the breath of life, and man became a living soul.' But a 'living soul' simply means an animated being, and is applied to the lower animals as well as to man.* The expression 'God breathed' is purely figurative, and affords no countenance whatever to the heathen notion of man's soul being an emanation of Deity; indeed, the very circumstance here referred to is actually brought forward to illustrate the frailty of

* Gen. i. 30, margin.

man's life; 'Cease ye from man, *whose breath is in his nostrils*, for wherein is he to be accounted of?'

Then it is said that the threat, 'In the day that thou eatest thereof, thou shalt surely die,' virtually implied, that as long as he remained obedient he could not die. It certainly did no such thing. Though obedience would save him from any such abrupt cutting short of his days as disobedience would incur, it by no means followed necessarily that he could never die from the natural decay of his vital powers. There is a plain intimation afterwards, however, that he would have been preserved from any such decay, had he remained obedient. 'And now, lest he put forth his hand and take of the tree of life, and eat, and live for ever.' The Tree of Life either represented, or actually was, the provision made by God for preserving man from death; which implies, that otherwise he would have been liable to death, even if he had remained obedient. For observe, it was not by supplying him with food that the Tree of Life would have kept him alive. God had given him every green herb for food. And yet, with a full supply of food, and under the most favourable circumstances possible, within and without, it was necessary for him to eat of that tree, in order that he might live for ever. Is not the inference irresistible, that he was created with a nature, which would sooner or later have worn out, but for the special provision that was made to counteract this natural tendency?

There is certainly no appearance as yet of indefeasible immortality. All we can gather is, that man was made *capable* of living for ever, provided certain conditions were complied with.

Further light will be thrown upon this, as we proceed to enquire, what was the punishment threatened to Adam by the words, 'In the day that thou eatest thereof, thou shalt surely die.'

Some have understood it to mean moral death, or the separation of his heart from God. But surely this took place *before* he ate the forbidden fruit. It was the *cause* of his doing so; whereas death was evidently threatened as the *consequence* of it.

Others suppose it to mean, that he would at once become mortal, and therefore necessarily die in course of time. But this is not at all sufficient to meet the language, and is also at variance with what is said of the Tree of Life.

The question is, what must Adam himself have understood by it? With such a tremendous issue at stake as the fate of a whole race, surely the consequences of disobedience must have been set before him to their fullest extent and in unmistakable language. The penalty which God meant to inflict could not surely be something *infinitely greater* than that of which Adam was warned.*

---

* 'Adam was not threatened with never-ending torments! Quite true.' So says the *Bible Treasury*. And Dean Close argues, that, as

Now what could he possibly have understood by the threat, except that he would *die*, and cease to exist *as a man?* How could he ever have imagined that when God said he should die, it was really meant that he should live for ever in sin and misery? or that such would be the necessary consequence of his act in any way whatever? If, after sinning, he had found himself and his posterity exposed to a doom so *infinitely* greater than that which he was warned of, might he not have replied against God, that had he been aware of its consequences, nothing would have induced him to commit the act? No; he believed that God meant what he said. There is not a word in the inspired narrative which affords any warrant for the belief, that Adam had the least idea of any separate conscious existence out of the body. And if he had, how could the threat of *death* give him the slightest warning of the unutterable woe that is supposed by the popular doctrine to be the penalty of sin?*

---

the happiness of the redeemed will exceed anything that hath entered into the heart of man to conceive, so will the 'torments of the damned.' But surely it is a totally different thing, for a promised reward to exceed what the promise itself could convey, and for a threatened punishment to exceed what the person, who was warned of it, could possibly conceive to have been intended.

* From the words 'Adam was not deceived' (1 Tim. ii. 14), many thoughtful persons have concluded that Adam, seeing the ruin in which his wife was involved, deliberately chose to share her fate. If he supposed that fate to be eternal life in misery, it is absolutely inconceivable that he could have been actuated by any such motive: for what comfort could it have been to either of them to witness the other's

But why was the threatened penalty not inflicted on the day that Adam sinned? Because provision had been made in the everlasting covenant of grace, for bestowing upon man as a free gift that eternal life which was at first offered him as the reward of obedience. That covenant was 'ordered in all things and sure' before man was created; and it was to be sealed with the blood of the Lamb, who in the mind and purpose of God was 'slain before the foundation of the world.' But for Christ, Adam would have died on the day he sinned, and the whole human race of course have perished with him. Thus Christ is 'the Saviour of all men,' and 'gave his flesh for the life of the world.'

That it was through Christ his life was spared, was at once made known to Adam, with what degree of clearness it may be difficult to say, by the promise, and by the ordinance of Sacrifice. On the former it is unnecessary here to dwell; but the latter has too important a bearing upon our present subject to be overlooked.

The idea represented in sacrifice was—the penalty of sin being laid upon another. What then was inflicted on the animal offered in sacrifice? Death. It was killed—it ceased to exist. It was not kept in prolonged torture, but slain outright. Now, fully admitting that

---

everlasting agonies? But it is quite possible that he might choose to *die* with her, rather than to live without her.

In what other way, we may also ask, is it possible to understand the willingness of Moses to be blotted out of the book of life, and of Paul to be accursed from Christ, for the sake of others?

some difference may be expected between a type and its antitype, there surely must be *some* likeness between them. And there certainly is none whatever between the death of an animal and a man's eternal life in misery.

This is placed beyond a doubt, when we consider the true sacrifice for sin. Our iniquities were laid upon Christ. He paid the penalty of sin. He delivered us from the curse of the Law, by being made a curse for us. And what was the penalty he paid? What did he suffer for us? Eternal life in misery? No, he 'tasted *death* for every man.' The advocates of eternal suffering try to escape from this by saying, that the dignity of the Sufferer rendered His temporary sufferings a sufficient equivalent for the eternal sufferings of those whom He redeemed. To which it has been sometimes replied, that on such a view, the slightest possible pain endured by Him would have been sufficient to redeem the world. A more satisfactory answer is, that Christ is positively declared to have endured *the* penalty due to man's sin; and what He did endure was mental and bodily suffering, *ending in death*. The mental anguish which he endured in the garden and on the cross, however much greater in degree, was doubtless the same in kind, as that which would have come upon Adam, if he had known that the death penalty was about to be inflicted upon him. It would only have been necessary that he should have been given some due appreciation of what he had lost, to break his heart and terminate his existence; just as the hiding of His Father's face broke the heart of Jesus and ended His sufferings for ever.*

We are not left to these inferences, however, irresistible as they are, on the question of man's natural immortality. St. Paul makes as decisive a statement as could be uttered in human language: 'Who will render to every man according to his works; to them who by patient continuance in well-doing seek for glory and honour and immortality, eternal life.' (Rom. ii. 6, 7.) If all men possessed immortality, naturally and indefeasibly, how could it be classed with glory and

---

* It may be argued, that as the soul of Jesus did not cease to exist after death, so neither would the soul of Adam have ceased to exist if the death penalty had been inflicted on him. This is an intricate point, on which I would speak with great diffidence. It seems very doubtful, how far we may infer what *would* have happened in Adam's case, if there had been no redemption, from what does happen to men now in consequence of that redemption, or what did happen to Christ when his atoning work was finished, and he had drained the last dregs of the cup of wrath. But this we may confidently say, and it is quite enough for our present purpose, that whatever would have happened to the soul of Adam after death if he had been left to bear the penalty of sin, it could not possibly have been doomed to a condition of eternal anguish, or else the penalty of which he was warned, would have been but an inappreciable fraction of the penalty which he actually incurred.

I cannot forbear suggesting the enquiry, whether the sustaining of our blessed Lord's human spirit during the hiding of His Father's countenance, so that it should not be utterly crushed, may not have been the answer to those prayers and supplications, which He offered with strong crying and tears unto Him that was able to save him *from death*, and in which we are told He *was heard*, in consequence of His reverent submission to His Father's will.

honour as one of the things which were to be sought by patient continuance in well-doing? Or how, we may further ask, could it have been 'brought to light by the Gospel?' According to the popular theory, neither the Gospel, nor well-doing, has anything to do with it: man was created immortal, and immortal he must ever remain, do what he will.*

Before concluding, it may be well to answer a question which is often asked, namely, why is it still 'appointed unto man once to die,' when Christ has 'tasted death for every man'? The answer is, that the death which we have now to undergo, is not the penalty of sin at all, but merely a result of the condition in which God has seen fit to place man since his fall; the result, in fact, of his being cut off from the Tree of Life, whatever that may mean. His being deprived of that was not the penalty incurred by sin. Immediate death was the punishment with which he

---

* The Apostle's desire to 'attain unto the resurrection of the dead' is no parallel. His aim was to share, not in the general resurrection, but in the first resurrection, which is exclusively of 'them that are Christ's.'

I have not quoted 1 Tim. vi. 16, 'Who only hath immortality,' because it might be said, that there is nothing in that to debar the Creator from communicating His own immortality to any of His creatures. Still, to my own mind it appears perfectly certain, that the Apostle would not have used such an expression, if he had believed in man's inherent indefeasible immortality.

Neither have I quoted 1 Cor. xv. 53, 'This mortal must put on immortality,' because it might be said to refer only to the body. But if it does, then it is a mere repetition of what has been stated in the preceding words, 'This corruptible must put on incorruption.'

was threatened, and, that being remitted through Christ, God might deal with him just as He pleased. He might have been replaced in his former position, with access to the Tree of Life, so long as he was obedient. In other words, he might have been given another opportunity of earning eternal life by his own obedience. But the covenant of grace had provided something better for him than that. A higher life than he could ever have attained to by his own obedience was to be bestowed upon him as a free gift. That higher life could only be reached through death. So he was cut off from the Tree of Life, and placed in a position where death became inevitable in the course of nature. Death therefore, though one of the *consequences* of sin, and therefore, according to St. Paul's argument, a standing witness of it, was by no means a *necessary* consequence, after it had been remitted as a *penalty*.* And though it should remind the believer of the death from which he has been redeemed, inasmuch as it entered into the world by sin, yet in itself it is to him only a necessary step in the development of that eternal life which is the gift of God through Jesus Christ; while to one who has finally rejected Christ, it is only a step toward the total death which is the wages of sin, and which will be inflicted on him in the judgment, when he will be destroyed body and soul in hell.

* Gen. v. 24 ; 2 Kings ii. 11 ; Heb. xi. 5.

SERMON VIII.

Thou shalt not put a stumblingblock before the blind.
Lev. xix. 14.

Being blind, he is not unlikely to stumble, whether we do or not; but that is no excuse for our putting a stumblingblock in his way. And this is what has been done to the spiritually blind by the doctrine of Eternal Evil. We have already shown that it is not only destitute of any solid foundation in Scripture, but directly opposed to its plainest teaching; and we now proceed to point out some of the injurious results which flow from its adoption.

First and foremost, it begets more positive infidelity than perhaps all other causes put together. Men are told that the doctrine of Endless Suffering rests on precisely the same authority as the Gospel; that the one is as plainly taught in God's Word as the other; and that if they deny one they have no ground for believing the other. The few texts that sound very much like it have been drilled into them from childhood; so that, when they begin to reflect, and find the doctrine absolutely incredible, it never occurs to them that these passages may possibly admit of another interpretation, and they therefore reject the whole Bible together. We are far from saying that they are guiltless in so doing; but the measure of their guilt can be estimated by God alone. We may see a marked difference between one case and another, from the half-reluctant abandonment of traditional belief to the contemptuous sneer or malignant scowl with which it is denied and defied. But God alone can know how far they have wilfully shut their eyes against the light and been only too glad of an excuse for getting rid of the Bible, because it testified of them that their deeds were evil. In no case can the Church be held guiltless for the persistency with which she has kept this millstone tied about the neck of inspiration, making it a fundamental part of the Gospel, harping on those few texts that sound like it to a carefully attuned ear, and using them as a lever to upturn the whole teaching of Scripture on the subject to which they refer. Neither can anyone, whose eyes have been graciously opened to see the delusion, be absolved from a grave dereliction of duty, unless he does his utmost to rid Christianity of such an incubus, and remove such a stumbling-block out of the way of the blind. Let those who can, 'lift up their voice like a trumpet,' and let those who cannot, at least add a hearty Amen.

But this is not all. To adopt positive infidelity requires more determination of character than most persons possess. For one who is driven into that position by the popular teaching, perhaps twenty are lulled by it into a fatal slumber. Of all the delusions that prevail upon this subject, none can exceed that which supposes the doctrine of endless suffering to be a powerful instrument for awakening sinners to a sense of their danger. The deterring effect of punishment depends far more upon its certainty than upon its severity. Now, the excessive severity of the punishment thus threatened, not only robs it of all certainty whatever, but makes almost every one feel sure that, in his own case at least, it will never be inflicted. When he is told that the only alternative before him is, at the moment of death, to enter at once into a state of endless happiness or endless woe, he feels so perfectly sure that he neither does, nor ever can, deserve the latter, that his future entrance into bliss becomes to him a matter of course. He may be quite aware that he is not fit for it yet, nor even on the road to it: but in some way or other it must come all right at last. And he is confirmed in this by observing, that in spite of the general professed belief in the saying, 'strait is the gate, and narrow is the way that leadeth unto life, and few there be that find it,' almost every separate individual, after his decease, is supposed by his friends to have entered into bliss. Few persons, in their last hours, refuse to receive a minister of religion; nearly all profess repentance and faith; and when the only alternative known to the survivors is, that they are in endless bliss or in endless torment, how can it be otherwise than that every one, except in the extremest cases, should be supposed to have entered into life? And how can this fail to make the survivors themselves expect that their own latter end will be the same? Thus the law is virtually robbed of its terrors, and the thunders of Sinai reduced to 'sound and fury signifying nothing.'

A still worse evil perhaps is the tendency of this theory to diminish the saving power of the Gospel. That power is love. 'We love Him, because He first loved us;' and 'hereby we perceive His love, because He laid down His life for us.' Therefore, whatever clouds the revelation of God's love that is made to us in the Gospel, must lessen its power to save and sanctify us. And what can possibly throw a darker shadow over it, than to combine with its glorious message such a hideous doctrine as this? That the Gospel, even with this tremendous hindrance in its way, should actually have saved such a multitude of souls, only shows what a marvellous weapon it is, and how the Spirit of God can enable it to overcome almost any amount of poison, that the craft of Satan, or the infirmity of man, may mingle with it.

That the same objection applies to the Scripture doctrine of everlasting destruction, we entirely deny. As no creature has any right to live at all, it would be perfectly consistent with infinite love for the

Creator to terminate its life whenever He pleased; even apart from the consideration of the condemned having wilfully rejected the eternal life offered them in Christ. And as to the specific punishment previously inflicted upon them for their own particular sins, that is perfectly in accordance with one of the deepest moral instincts that God has implanted within our breast, namely, that there *ought* to be retribution for wrong doing unrepented of. So long as we are sure that the retribution will not exceed what the wrong doing actually deserves, it need not in the least degree lessen our confidence in God's righteous love. What amount of punishment anyone's sins do deserve, we cannot tell. All we know with absolute certainty is, that by no possibility can they deserve *infinite* punishment. So long as there is a limit to the number of stripes, we can confidently leave God to pronounce how many or how few they should be. Scripture distinctly assigns a limit to them, by assuring us, in every variety of language, that they will end, sooner or later, in the utter destruction of the lost soul. And therefore Scripture throws no cloud at all over the proof which the Gospel affords of God's amazing love, in having given His only-begotten Son, that whosoever believeth on Him should not perish, but have everlasting life.

Another evil resulting from this theory is, that it aggravates the enmity of the world against those who are chosen out of it. Such enmity, in a more or less developed form, is unavoidable, from the very nature of the case; but that is no excuse for our needlessly provoking it. On the contrary, we should do all in our power to conciliate them that are without, 'giving no offence in anything.' A believing wife is enjoined to behave towards her unbelieving husband in such a way that he may be 'won' thereby. Now could anything be conceived more calculated to exasperate worldly people, nay to excite a feeling of righteous indignation in their minds, than the knowledge that we consider them so unutterably bad, as to deserve endless torment? No words can describe the abhorrence with which we ought to regard them, if we really believe this. It is nothing to say that we hope they may repent. That may so far mitigate the horror with which we think of the prospect before them, as to prevent our heart breaking, or our brain giving way — though it seems a mystery how we can eat or sleep, knowing that any moment their doom may become inevitable. But that does not in the least affect our estimate of their present character. Our theory compels us to regard them at present as all but infinitely wicked. For though we may admit degrees in the severity of the punishment, yet the endlessness of it reduces the difference to insignificance. Neither can we escape from this by reference to the fuller development of the evil principles within them, when the restraints of this present life are removed, and the Spirit wholly ceases to strive with them. For it must be by their conduct during this state of probation that they have incurred the penalty of being hopelessly consigned to such a condition: so that it comes practically to the same thing. Now, however bad they may be, so bad that they cannot even themselves dream of being on the narrow path to life, yet their deepest instincts assure them that they cannot possibly have incurred *such* guilt as to deserve infinite punishment. They therefore resent, consciously or unconsciously, the unmeasured imputation which our theory casts upon them. And the only thing which makes them tolerate us at all, is the knowledge that it is a mere theory, and that our feelings towards them are totally different; in which confidence they are of course greatly strengthened by knowing that we regard ourselves to have been in the same condition, until we became new creatures in Christ Jesus.

For example. Suppose a model husband, who is a thorough worldling, has a model wife, who is a decided Christian. He knows her theory to be, that if he were to die now, he would enter into a state of hopeless eternal misery; and as God cannot possibly inflict upon anyone severer punishment than he deserves, as He has declared that whatsoever a man soweth that shall he also reap, she must believe his guilt to be enormous beyond all power of conception. She hopes that he will yet repent of it, and be saved; but she knows that she may awake any morning, and find that his everlasting agonies, of mind at least, have actually commenced, and all hope of their ever being mitigated or brought to an end utterly gone. Further, so certain is she that this tremendous doom, on whomsoever it may fall, is not one whit more than he deserves, that the continuance of it, in ever-increasing intensity, is part of the permanent ultimate prospect, the hope of which should cheer her under all the trials of this mortal life, and make her rejoice with joy unspeakable and full of glory. She cannot, it is true, as yet derive any conscious satisfaction from thinking that the smoke of their torment will ascend for ever and ever; but she believes that she will do so, when she gets into a right state of mind; inasmuch as whatever conduces to the glory of God must conduce to the happiness of all whose minds are in harmony with His. And what at first sight seems to make the matter worse, is that she is so wonderfully happy under this state of things. Not only can she enter with apparent zest and enjoyment into a variety of innocent pleasures, perhaps appreciate humour, have no objection to a little quiet merry-making, and rather like a moderate amount of society; but even in her religious exercises, which ought to overwhelm her with gloom or plunge her into despair, she endeavours to assume as joyful a tone as possible. The most wonderful thing is to see her at the piano, and hear her sing charming hymns of joy and hope about the glorious prospect of eternal holiness and happiness that is set before us—with her husband in the room, whose eternal agonies are perhaps to form part of the dark background on which the glories of Heaven will stand out so brightly. Hark!

> There is a land of pure delight,
> Where saints immortal reign,
> Infinite day excludes the night,

(to *him* it will be, infinite night excludes the day)—

> And pleasures banish pain—*

that is, from *them*, the pain being all concentrated elsewhere.

How do these two manage to live so comfortably together? The answer is suggested by what we have just been saying. He knows that this theory has no place in her heart and soul, but merely lies on the surface of her brain. And if she would reflect a moment, she would see it herself. Her *feeling* is, not how bad he is, but how good he is. She never tires of praising him as a pattern of every virtue under heaven. And what does often make her sad, is the melancholy thought that *such a man* should be living only for the perishing things of this passing life, and sacrificing his prospect of glory and honour and immortality by

---

* A lady, who heard this sermon preached, afterwards told the author, that a friend, in arguing with her some years ago against the doctrine of eternal suffering, had quoted that particular verse, just as it is used above, with reference to the case of her own husband.

refusing to lay hold on the eternal life offered him in Christ. All that she sees in him to love and admire makes her realise more deeply his capability of something higher and better, and she sometimes cannot help weeping to think how he will himself be filled with shame, and what an object of everlasting contempt he will become to the universe, for having sacrificed the substance to the shadow, and sold his glorious inheritance for a contemptible mess of pottage; for having fallen into a net that was spread before his very eyes; for having sown to the flesh from which he knew that he could only reap corruption; and chosen to gratify for a moment the lust of the flesh and the lust of the eye and the pride of life,—whether in the form of sensual indulgence, intellectual gratification, or earthly distinction,—rather than to wear an imperishable crown, to possess a kingdom that cannot be moved, to sit with Christ on His throne, and to share in the government of the universe. All this is put before him in Scripture again and again. Human language is exhausted, and all human things ransacked for metaphors, to fire his ambition, and make him resolve, at any cost or any effort, to obtain such a prize, to lay hold on eternal life. But his answer is, No, it is too much trouble; let me eat and drink, and have others to eat and drink with me, and to-morrow I am willing to die. This, no doubt, makes her often weep and always pray. It is not the greater or less number of stripes he may receive that troubles her so much; it is the thought that he is throwing himself away, that by and by he will be cut down like the grass and wither as the green herb, and that one who might have been an heir of immortality will soon be amongst the things of the past—at length perhaps forgotten by all except the Infinite mind that can never forget anything. This is quite sufficient trial for her. But heavy as the burden may sometimes be, it is simply *nothing* to the unutterable anguish that would crush her to the earth, if she really felt in her inmost soul, that he actually deserved, and might any moment be plunged into eternal torment.

No, it is a hideous dream. And those whom God has been gracious enough to awaken out of it should show their gratitude by using every effort to awaken others, so that they may bask in the light and warmth of the Sun of righteousness, and know what it is to be able to believe, that God is love; feeling it no exaggeration to say—

> Could we with ink the ocean fill,
>   Were the whole sky of parchment made,
> Were every blade of grass a quill,
>   And every man a scribe by trade;
>   To tell the love
>   Of God above
> Would drain the ocean dry,
>   Nor would the scroll
>   Contain the whole,
> Though stretched from sky to sky.

SERMON IX.

Take up the stumblingblock out of the way of My people.
Isa. lvii. 14.

BEING God's people, they will not 'stumble that they should fall;' but they may receive grievous injury, notwithstanding, from striking their foot against a stumblingblock. And such injury has the Church undoubtedly received from the doctrine of Eternal Evil.

We have already pointed out some of its injurious effects upon the world. Now let us see how it affects those who have been called out of the world, and have received the gift of eternal life, through faith in Christ Jesus.

Perhaps its worst effect is that it must necessarily, to whatever extent it is realised, cloud their view of God's love. They cannot get rid of an uneasy feeling, though hardly perhaps aware of it, which prevents them looking up to Him with entire confidence and perfect love. The knowledge that God is a 'consuming fire' to sin, and therefore to impenitent sinners, greatly helps us to love Him, and to confide in Him; for it assures us, that sooner or later there will be an end of evil, and that the whole universe will become 'very good.' But if there is never to be an end of it, if God is not to be a consuming fire, but only a torturing fire, in which His enemies will be kept alive for ever, then a perpetual effort must be made to keep the whole subject out of our minds, if we are to feel any confidence whatever in our Father's love. This was spoken of incidentally in a previous sermon; so that we may pass on to another consideration, which is not quite so palpable, but which exercises a more powerful influence than is commonly supposed.

The popular doctrine reduces to a minimum the grace of Christ in dying for us. People strangely talk as if the depth of misery from which we have been rescued, was a measure of Christ's self-sacrificing love in coming to our rescue. Surely it leans all on the other side. The same amount of sacrifice, that I might think very great for anyone to make, in order to save me from a small punishment, may appear trifling, if made in order to save me from a very heavy one. A Christian once told me how much distressed he was by his inability to overcome the feeling, that it would have been rather hard, if we had been left under condemnation, and nothing been done to save us from it. No wonder! The marvel is that such thoughts do not press so continually upon the minds of all men, as to make them search and see what it is that lies at the bottom of them, or at least constitutes their sting. If we are all born in such a condition, as without help would render it practically inevitable that we should spend an eternity in misery, it is *not* easy to think very much of the grace, that was willing to make even the sacrifice that has been made, to deliver us from such a doom. As another believer once said to me, ' Who would not have done it ? '

But embrace the teaching of Scripture, and the whole aspect of the case is altered.

For from what does Christ save us?

In the first place, from non-existence. But for Christ, Adam would have died the day he sinned, and we of course should never have existed. Would that have been at all hard upon us? What right have we to exist at all? None whatever. And we are indebted for our existence to the provision made in the everlasting covenant of grace, which was to be sealed with the blood of Jesus Christ. Is not that free grace?

In the next place we are saved from that death which is the wages of sin, and which would be inflicted upon us at once on account of our own sin, but for the intercession of Christ. We are saved from the penalty of Adam's sin, in that we came into existence; we are at present saved from the penalty of our own sin, in that we continue to exist a moment after committing it; death being the natural wages of sin. And in these two ways Christ is absolutely 'the Saviour of *all* men' alike—He 'gave His flesh for the life of the world;' and in Him 'God reconciled the world unto Himself, not imputing their trespasses unto them.' The life of the world was forfeited in Adam, and freely given back in Christ. Everyone who lives long enough to know God's will, has forfeited his own life by not submitting to it. The infliction of that penalty is suspended, and far more than the remission of it freely offered to those who are willing to accept it through Christ. If they refuse it, they commit a worse sin than Adam's, and incur a heavier doom, a more fearful death. For them 'there remaineth no more sacrifice for sin, but a certain fearful looking for of judgment and of fiery indignation, which shall devour (not keep alive in torture, but *devour*) the adversaries.' What is there 'hard' in this? Nothing whatever. We have only to clear away that terrible fiction of eternal suffering, and then we can see in its true light the wondrous 'grace of our Lord Jesus Christ, who, though He was rich, yet for our sakes became poor, that we through His poverty might be rich;' and to some extent can appreciate that love, which God commends to us, 'in that when we were yet sinners, Christ died for us.'

Another loss which the Christian sustains through the belief of this unscriptural doctrine, arises from the difficulty it interposes in the way of his cultivating that highest of all Christian graces—'joyfulness.' Again and again is he urged to 'rejoice evermore,' again and again is he told that 'joy and peace in believing' are among the fruits of the spirit. Now the main element of joy is hope. Peace comes from a sense of present reconciliation; but real joy can be produced only by the prospect of what is to come. We '*rejoice* in *hope* of the glory of God.' But how is it possible to rejoice in a prospect that includes the endless suffering of millions of our fellow-creatures? It would be simply impossible, but for that happy, though not blameless, inconsistency between our opinions and our feelings, that we have so often had occasion to notice. What is it you are so earnestly longing for? Is it for your own individual happiness only? Far from it; you are not so selfish. You are longing for the groans of creation to cease, for sin and suffering to be at an end. Some terrible act of wickedness shocks you, some heart-breaking tale of woe makes you weep in sympathy, and you say, Ah, well, it will soon be over; this is not to go on for ever, it is 'but for a moment,' and then all will be peace and holiness and joy; 'Creation itself shall be delivered from the bondage of corruption into the glorious liberty of the children of God.' What are you talking about? Do you ever think what you are saying? Sin and suffering at an end! Why it will be multiplied a hundredfold. No enmity against God that is now felt by the most hardened sinner in the world, can compare with the intense hatred of Him that must be felt by those who are writhing under His hand in hopeless agony; whom He will neither allow to die, nor cease to torment. Nor can all the groans that have ever been wrung from creation approach the unutterable anguish of an eternal hell. What is it, that all the sin and suffering will be transferred to another globe, or buried within the centre of this? It will exist, and exist for ever. And this is part of the glorious future that you are hoping for, and praying for, and the thought of which is to make you 'rejoice with joy unspeakable and full of glory'! Happily you are able generally to keep it out of your mind, and think only of the bright side; but your efforts can be only partially successful; and I believe that this terrible phantom does more than all other causes put together, to damp Christian joy, and render it well nigh impossible heartily to rejoice. The present is often far too dark to rejoice in, and you are almost afraid to think of the future, for there starts up an apparition of something darker still. The result is a degree of gloominess, and cheerlessness, a want of buoyancy and elasticity, that constitutes a hindrance to yourself and a stumblingblock to others. It impedes your running in the race, paralyses your arm in the battle, and mars the attractive grace, with which you should seek to 'adorn the doctrine of God your Saviour.'

Again, this doctrine tends to produce an injurious effect upon the mind, by almost abolishing any moral superiority of one man over another, and making the Apostolic doctrine that there is 'no difference' as regards all having 'come short of the glory of God,' to mean that all are equally bad. You admit, no doubt, in words, and certainly feel, that there is a very great difference amongst them. But your theory reduces it almost to nothing. For if all deserve endless suffering, the difference between the intensity of the suffering in one case or another, is hardly appreciable to us: the fact of its being hopeless and endless is so overwhelming to the mind, that everything else sinks into insignificance. You are therefore obliged to do violence to your moral instincts by making an effort on principle to think as badly as possible of all men; for if the smallest sin deserves endless suffering, it must be practically impossible to think too badly of any sinner. But on the other hand, if the wages of sin is death, if sin—that is, separation from God—renders it impossible for any moral creature permanently to live, if life is drawn from God, and can be sustained only by union with God, so that without God any creature must necessarily perish, then, in the amount of punishment that may be inflicted in the process of his death, in the greater or less severity of his dying agonies, there is abundant room for all the difference that our moral instincts require between the most opposite extremes of human character, that are to be found amongst those who are out of Christ.

Lastly, we may observe, that this doctrine injures the moral sense of those who accept it, by the inevitable discord which it creates between their opinions and their feelings. It would be a still worse evil, if they really felt as they profess to believe; and we have at every step to give them credit for not doing so. But still they cannot do such violence as this theory requires, to the harmony that ought to subsist between the mind and the heart, without throwing a shade of unreality over the whole of their inner being— and, we must add, casting doubt upon the sincerity of all their religious convictions, in the eyes of the world around them. Why do they not go mad at the sight of such multitudes rushing into endless woe? Or, if faith have such enormous power as to save them from that, why do they not put on sackcloth and ashes, cover their faces, and wail with a bitter lamentation? Why do they not rush frantically about the streets, stop everyone they meet, and, with horror and dismay depicted upon their countenances, warn them of the unutterable woe that lies before them?* Why do they ever let a smile play upon their features? How can

* Mr. Grant thinks that the question must have arisen in the minds of my hearers, 'Why did not he himself feel and act thus, when he believed it?' I doubt whether there was a single hearer so destitute of intelligence as to think anything of the kind. The answer of course would have been—For the same reason that others do not; that is, as I was endeavouring to show, because the doctrine has no real hold upon any one's soul. I was proving this from the inconsistency invariably seen between the natural, and the actual, effect of such a belief upon the conduct. If I had been an exception to this, it would of course have so far weakened my argument.

they eat and drink and sleep amidst such a scene of horror? They know that a human being dies every second; they believe that only a small fraction of them are saved; and yet they go on, laughing and singing, buying and selling, building and planting, marrying and giving in marriage, just as if it was all a myth. They rejoice at the birth of a probable inheritor of this tremendous doom; and make merry at a wedding, which may probably add thousands to the wretched inhabitants of that eternal prison-house.

Are you about to marry? Stop and think! You may have children, grandchildren, great-grandchildren; your descendants may go on multiplying, generation after generation. You know that but few are saved, and, whatever confidence you have about your own children, it must grow less and less about every successive generation; so that the ultimate result of the step you are about to take, will probably be the addition of a few to the number of the blessed, of many to the number of the lost—the intensity and the duration of the happiness or misery of each being the same. Dare you take the step? What! face an eternity, spent in the knowledge that thousands of your own descendants are mingling with their frantic curses against God for creating them scarcely less bitter curses against you, for having been the willing instrument of bringing them into existence—for the horrible selfishness of having, merely to gratify yourself, taken a step that you knew *might* at least lead to such a result!* And if you *are* prepared to encounter even this, do you expect to find any minister of religion, that believes in an eternal hell, who will dare to join you in wedlock? 'No!' he would say: 'Find some one who believes that evil is limited, but good un-limited; that life may continue for ever, but that death *cannot*; that heaven is a place to live in, and hell a place to die in; and *he* may bless your marriage. For if it sends a thousand to hell, and only one to heaven, the gain would then be so incalculably greater than the loss, that there would be scarcely an appreciable drawback to the satisfaction with which the proceeding might be regarded; the unlimited happiness of one of course infinitely outweighing the limited misery of any possible number. But don't ask *me* to do it; my tongue would cleave to the roof of my mouth, and an horrible dread would overwhelm me.'†

Surely our Great Enemy well knew what he was about, when he succeeded in inducing the Church to accept this monstrous perversion of God's Word. She was led astray unwittingly; and millions of saints are now adoring the grace that pardoned, and to such a

---

* The Author has since become acquainted with the case of a person who was for some time actually deterred from marriage by the above consideration.

† It must surely be obvious to anyone of moderate intelligence, that the above is merely intended to depict the doctrine in its true colours, by showing what might naturally be expected from those who heartily believe it.

great extent neutralised the effect of, such a disastrous error. But Satan was not deceived. Again has he tried, only too successfully, his old lie, in a different meaning, but from the same wilful enmity against God—'Thou shalt not surely *die.*' His main object was the same in both cases—namely, to persuade man that sin would bring no penalty at all. At first, he did it by a direct assurance of impunity, and then afterwards by putting before him, as the only alternatives, eternal happiness, or something that no one, in his own case at least, would ever believe possible. And really, if we could admit the possibility of eternal evil, if we could believe that anything might provoke God to inflict infinite punishment upon a finite creature, if we could ever imagine Him unwilling to let an enemy escape out of His hands, even by annihilating him,—it would be in the case of that dark spirit of evil, who has wilfully led multitudes of His dearest children to believe their Heavenly Father *capable* of what this doctrine attributes to Him.

But no! Scripture assures us that the devil and his works are to be destroyed together, that the long conflict between good and evil is to end in the consuming fire of hell, that evil will be a thing of the past, and all things be reconciled to God through Jesus Christ, so that He Himself may be all in all.

Amen! Even so, Lord Jesus, come quickly!

SERMON X.

The Lord hath made all things for Himself: yea, even the wicked for the day of evil.—Prov. xvi. 4.

The subject of our present discourse, though not at all essential to the argument which we have been endeavouring to pursue, is far too important to be overlooked. Few minds have not been perplexed and distressed by difficulties connected with the existence and the destruction of evil. Those difficulties cannot be wholly overcome. God evidently intends them to remain difficulties to the last. He might, if He had seen fit, have made everything in His Word so perfectly clear that no one could possibly have entertained a moment's doubt. But He has not done so. He sees it needful, for our present state of discipline and probation, that we should have to struggle with difficulties of belief just as we have to struggle with temptations to sin. In His Providence and in His Word, He has left just as much difficulty as it is good for our faith to bear. Whatever we add to that by misinterpreting them is injurious to us by putting too great a strain upon our faith. The exercise of rowing is beneficial to the body, just because of the difficulty which the water interposes to the progress of the boat. Remove the difficulty, and all the benefit of the exercise is lost. But it by no means follows that it is good for a man to row till he bursts a bloodvessel, or is lifted fainting out of the boat. Now, I verily believe that it is just this doctrine of the eternity of evil, which renders the difficulties connected with the existence of evil—not insuperable, for that they must remain under any circumstances— but so crushing as to damage our spiritual constitution by overstraining our faith. Exclude this, and there is nothing that faith ought not to be able to bear; but this cannot be laid upon it without injury to one part or another of our moral being. Sometimes faith itself breaks down; sometimes it is able to hold up, but with an effort that warps the judgment, hardens the heart, and blunts the moral sense.

Now let us take the facts before us, in conjunction with the teaching of Scripture, and see precisely what the difficulties are.

Scripture tells us, that evil was permitted to enter for the glory of God. 'The Lord hath made all things for Himself: yea, even the wicked for the day of evil.' It tells us that this will be accomplished by some being raised out of it to a higher life than they could otherwise have reached, while it is allowed to do its work upon the rest and destroy them; there being 'vessels of wrath fitted for destruction,' as well as 'vessels of mercy which He had afore prepared unto glory.'

Now where lies the difficulty in this?

Not in the idea that God should create beings for a temporary purpose. A flower blooms for a few days, and is then gone for ever. An insect dies, and few persons imagine it will ever reappear. Why should the principle stop there? Why should not creatures of a higher order live for a time, and then vanish away? It is only our pride that makes us think it at all improbable.

Nor in what is called the 'partiality' of creating one being for one purpose, and another being for another purpose. Has a horse a right to complain that God has been partial, in placing him in such a vastly inferior position to a man?—or a reptile to complain that he is still lower than a horse? If no one questions the justice of such enormous differences being made *in the creation of them*, why should there not be as great differences in His treatment of them after they are created? If God may create one a horse, and the other a man, why may He not create one man for life, and another man for death?* Partiality is making a difference in our treatment of two persons who have equal claims upon us. The Creator, therefore,

---

* It has been thought that this argument is invalidated by the fact of all men being created with a capacity for immortality, and eternal life being offered to them all in Christ. I cannot see how that affects the question, so long as Divine sovereignty is actually admitted. But the reader must judge for himself; and he will probably decide according to the prevailing bias of his own mind.

cannot possibly be guilty of it; because no creature has any claim upon Him whatever, having not the smallest right to exist at all. For one creature to complain that some other creature has been called to a higher destiny than his own, is simply absurd, and shows that he has no adequate sense of his dependent position.

The only difficulty is, that any creature should be placed, during his existence, in such a condition that he would rather not have existed at all. Differences are nothing. Whether others are better or worse off, does not touch the question. The sole difficulty lies in the fact of any sentient creatures being brought into an existence, whether long or short, in which evil predominates. And it is one, which, as it appears to me, applies almost equally to responsible, and to irresponsible creatures. For, although the assurance of a future state of retribution for us is an immense satisfaction to our moral instincts, it hardly touches the question before us in its ultimate form, which is this: —How can it consist with Infinite Love to place any responsible creatures in a position where it is certainly known that they will bring irremediable suffering upon themselves? Granting that it is their own fault, why were they given the opportunity of committing the fault?—that is, why were they created? I confess that this consideration relieves me from all temptation to accept any of the improbable theories that have been suggested about the brute creation—whether the supposition of a previous existence to account for their sufferings, or of a future existence to compensate for them. I see no greater difficulty in the creation of beings, who would have to suffer for no fault of their own, than in the creation of beings who would have to suffer *by* or *for* their own fault. It makes a wonderful difference, of course, to a responsible creature, during his state of probation, to know that a way of escape is set before him, and that it is his own doing if he perishes. But taking a comprehensive view of the question, it seems equally to concern the sufferings of animals and those of men or devils.

How then can the difficulty be met? Only by admitting that evil is *necessary*, in order to bring out a greater good than would otherwise have been *possible*. And the admission is demanded both by reason and by revelation. To deny it, is both to deprive of all meaning our Lord's agonising cry, '*If it be possible,* let this cup pass from Me,' and also to make God love Evil for its own sake. For if the good could have been reached equally well without it, evil must have been permitted for its own sake—in other words, it must be in itself a positive good. But this seems to limit either the Wisdom or the Power of God. And to this objection it is difficult to give a complete answer. The declarations of Scripture, that 'it is impossible for God to lie,' and that 'He cannot deny Himself,' clearly point out the direction in which we are to look for it. They assure us of what reason itself might have suggested, that there are necessities and impossibilities in God's own essential nature. But when we try to peer into those depths, we soon discover the weakness of our eyesight. Some may be able to see a little farther than others. But sooner or later all have to give it up, and acknowledge the incapacity of the finite to fathom the Infinite.

This, however, observe, is a purely intellectual difficulty, which taxes our humility rather than our faith. It arises from the necessary limitations of our own minds. When once we have subdued our pride sufficiently to admit this without reserve, all the rest becomes comparatively clear. Every *moral* difficulty is removed. All the darkness lies behind us, and it is our own fault if we will keep looking back, and letting its shadow rest upon us. Before us all is bright, if only we look far enough; for, however long evil is to last, it will be 'but for a moment' in eternity. However many creatures are to be destroyed by it, and pass out of existence, they will be but an inappreciable fraction of those who are to be blessed by what accrues from the overcoming of it. 'In the ages to come,' will the ever-widening circle of created intelligence be learning deep lessons of truth from the never-to-be-forgotten story of evil. There will be no need to keep any creatures eternally under its power, in order to show them what it is. The destruction that it brought on all who persisted in it, and the living witnesses of the redemption from it that was wrought out by the Son of God, will be enough to show 'the exceeding sinfulness of sin,' and 'the exceeding riches of His grace in His kindness towards us by Christ Jesus.'

On this view, even we ourselves are capable of seeing, that to produce an infinite good by any finite evil, is an act of pure love; and that to have shrunk from doing so would not have been love, but weakness. The moment, however, that you make the evil to be infinite, the whole aspect of the case is altered, and you become hopelessly enveloped in darkness that may be felt. And the popular theory does make the evil infinite, at least in duration. In two out of the three points of comparison, the evil will equal the good—namely, in duration and intensity. Hell will be as wicked and miserable, as heaven is holy and happy. And the one will be as lasting as the other. Heaven will exceed it only in the *number* of its inhabitants. How can we believe that, merely for this balance of gain, God would ever have put forth His creative power?

You will have observed, that in the preceding argument, we have taken for granted the sovereignty of God in determining which of His creatures are to live, and which to die. And this is so self-evident, even to our own reason, and so positively asserted in Scripture, that I believe no one, who is capable of reflection, or who admits the truth of Scripture, would ever think of questioning it for a moment, but for this monstrous bugbear, which perpetually comes up, frightening us out of our senses, and throwing us off our balance. Few persons are aware how strongly it is declared in God's Word; because they have instinctively shrunk from paying any attention to those passages. Many Christians are able to find great comfort in the texts, which speak of God's sovereignty in saving some; but they generally pass by with a thrill of horror, or at least a painful feeling of uneasiness, those which speak quite as plainly of His sovereignty in leaving the rest to perish. They tell you that they believe in election, but not in reprobation.

Let us, however, look the matter full in the face—because the texts are there, whether we like them or not. To attempt to get rid of the difficulty by ignoring them, is merely to act like the ostrich, who, when pursued, thrusts its head into the hole of a rock, and imagines that it can no more be seen than it can see. If you believe the Bible, hear what it says:—

Prov. xvi. 4.—'The Lord hath made all things for Himself: yea, even the wicked for the day of evil.'

1 Sam. ii. 25.—'Notwithstanding they hearkened not unto the voice of their father, because the Lord would slay them.' Not—The Lord would slay them because they hearkened not to their father.

John x. 26.—'But ye believe not, because ye are not

of my sheep.' Not—Ye are not of my sheep because ye believe not.

Rom. ix. 6–24.—On which we need only remark at present, that the absolute *national* election and rejection of Isaac and Ishmael, of Jacob and Esau, are adduced to illustrate the absolute sovereignty with which God determines the ultimate destiny of all His creatures.*

1 Pet. ii. 7, 8.—' Unto you therefore which believe He is precious: but unto them which be disobedient, the stone which the builders disallowed, the same is made the head of the corner, and a stone of stumbling, and a rock of offence, even to them which stumble at the word, being disobedient: *whereunto also they were appointed.*'

Now what is it that shocks people so much in these texts, and makes them stigmatise anyone as a 'Calvinist,' who professes to believe them in their plain obvious sense? Simply the idea, that the doom of the wicked is endless misery. Who can wonder at the blasphemies of the infidel against God's Word, when he is told by its own advocates that it teaches this? And who can wonder at the quibblings, the evasions, the straw-splittings, with which Christians try to soften the truth down, or explain it away, so that

---

* The words ' Esau have I hated' imply no more than that Jacob was absolutely preferred to him. The same Hebraism is found in our Lord's saying, ' If any man will come after Me, and *hate* not his father,' &c.

it may not *sound* quite so dreadful? But once see that the end is *death*, preceded by a retributive judgment, in which they will reap precisely what they have sown, neither more nor less; and then we maintain that there is nothing which should make us hesitate to admit the plain teaching of Scripture, that 'He will have mercy on whom He will have mercy, and whom He will He hardeneth.'

Indeed, as we have already intimated, even our reason should teach us that it must be so. In the first place, how can we imagine that the Creator would call beings into existence to thwart His own purposes, baffle His designs, and permanently oppose His will? How can we attribute anything so suicidal to infinite wisdom and infinite power? One moment's realising apprehension of what is involved in the relative position of creature and Creator, would make us feel its utter impossibility. In the next place, how could God keep the universe in order, if even the minutest part of it were beyond his control? How could He govern anything, unless He governed everything? Is it not as necessary for Him to decide whether you shall live or die, as it was for Him to decide whether you should be a man or a horse?

Is this Fatalism? No--it is precisely the opposite extreme. Fatalism makes God to have the control of *nothing*; Predestination makes Him to have the control of *everything*. There is a common subterfuge, which tries to evade the difficulty by steering a middle course, and making God to have the control of everything, *except* what depends upon the freewill of responsible creatures; that is to say, it makes Him the God of the mineral, vegetable, and purely animal kingdoms, but leaves Him no power to deal effectually with any higher orders of creatures, except by force. This view, however, is quite as unscriptural as it is irrational. For Scripture not only implies God's control of the wills of responsible creatures, by telling us of some being appointed to death, and others appointed to life, but also directly asserts it, by ascribing the acceptance of eternal life to Divine influence upon the will. 'As many as were ordained to eternal life believed' (Acts xiii. 48). 'Who, when he was come, helped them much which had believed through grace' (Acts xviii. 27). 'No man can come to Me, except the Father which hath sent Me draw him' (John vi. 44). 'All that the Father giveth Me shall come to Me' (John vi. 37). 'Whose heart the Lord opened, that she attended unto the things which were spoken of Paul' (Acts xvi. 14).

Now, if you ask, 'How can these things be?—how can any creature be responsible for his own actions, if that which directs them, and gives them all their moral character, namely, his will, is under the control of another?'—we acknowledge at once, that it is utterly impossible either to explain or to understand it. And

Paul himself distinctly admits this in the passage we have just quoted. He supposes the difficulty to be propounded in the plainest way. 'Thou wilt say then unto me, Why doth He yet find fault? For who hath resisted His will?' That is, how can we be blamed for what we do, if our wills are under the control of His will? And what is his reply?—'Nay but, O man, who art thou that repliest against God? Hath not the potter power over the clay, of the same lump to make one vessel unto honour, and another unto dishonour?' That is, he just reasserts the fact, without attempting to explain it at all. He gives it up as incapable of explanation; and only warns the objector, that he had better leave the difficulty alone, and beware of acting as if he was not responsible, when God tells him that he is. Oh for the honesty and courage and confidence of a man, who is not afraid to state a difficulty plainly and fully, which at the same time he acknowledges himself unable to remove! Paul knew the truth of what he was preaching, and therefore he proclaimed it—whether men would hear, or whether they would forbear.

Observe however again, that this difficulty is purely intellectual. It is most important to notice, in examining this whole range of subjects, how the moral difficulties give way, and only those of an intellectual nature remain; in other words, how the whole strain is left upon our humility, and scarcely any upon our sense of right and wrong. On that deep moral instinct,

Abraham ventures to plead with God against a certain course of action which He appeared about to take— 'Shall not the Judge of all the earth do *right*?' To that same moral instinct Jehovah Himself appeals— 'Judge, I pray you, betwixt me and my vineyard,' and again—'Are not my ways equal, are not your ways unequal?' Our Lord also asks the Jews—'Why even of your selves judge ye not what is *right*?' And Paul assures us that 'God is not *unrighteous*, to forget our work and labour of love.' Where is any such reference made to our power of solving metaphysical difficulties? No: the more we attempt to grapple with them, the more are we made to feel our own littleness, and, when they touch upon the actions of Deity, to exclaim, 'Oh the depth both of the wisdom and knowledge of God! how unsearchable are His judgments, and His ways past finding out!'

The only question of practical importance to us is, how we are to deal with those passages of Scripture which refer to the two sides of this truth respectively? They have been treated in three ways. The first is what we may call the ostrich method—of looking only at one side, and ignoring the other altogether. The second is, to make the statements fit in together, by explaining them both away; to blend the two colours into a neutral ambiguous tint, that means nothing, and fades away the moment you look steadily at it. The third, and only honest way, is to deal with them as you do with opposite sides of a globe. We know they are both there, we can bring either of them into view in a moment, but we cannot see them both at once. Whichever side is turned towards us, the other is, for the time, concealed. We may, or may not, remember it is there, but we cannot see it. What! not if the globe be made to turn round with great velocity? Yes: and hereafter we may be able to see all round this metaphysical globe: but at present we must be content to see one side at a time. Whichever side is put before you in any passage of Scripture, believe that it truly represents something in the mind of God; look steadily at it, get a clear view of the truth so presented, and let it take its full effect upon you. When God tells you that He has 'made all things for Himself, yea, even the wicked for the day of evil,' tremble lest you should be found amongst them! When He tells you that if you are so, it will be your own fault, because 'you *will* not come to Christ that you may have life,' acknowledge it, and beware of replying against God! When He tells you that He 'willeth not the death of a sinner, but that all should come to repentance,' believe Him absolutely, and you will experience an immediate sense of relief; a gleam of hope will shine into your soul. When He pleads with you, saying, 'Why will ye die?'— when He beseeches you to be reconciled to Him, believe in His sincerity, and yield to His entreaties. When He says, 'Whosoever will, let him take of the water of life freely,' embrace the offer, and drink your fill. When He tells you that Christ 'is made unto you wisdom and righteousness, and sanctification and redemption,' believe Him, and rejoice at your completeness in Christ. And when, after all this, He tells you that it was 'through grace' you 'believed,' that He 'loved you with an everlasting love, and therefore with lovingkindness has been drawing you'—that 'He predestined you to be conformed to the image of His Son,' and therefore has 'called,' and 'justified,' and will hereafter 'glorify' you —accept it all without reserve, and say, 'Who maketh me to differ? What have I that I have not received? By the grace of God I am what I am. What shall I render unto God for all His benefits conferred upon me?' And if Satan tempt you to fear lest you should not be able to endure unto the end, but should turn back unto perdition, then believe the assurance, that 'He who has begun a good work in you will perform it unto the day of Jesus Christ.' Say, 'I know whom I have believed, and am persuaded that He is able to keep that which I have committed unto Him;—

> 'The work which His goodness began,
>   The arm of His strength will complete:
> His promise is Yea and Amen,
>   And never was forfeited yet.
> Things future, nor things that are now,
>   Not all things below or above,
> Can make Him His purpose forego,
>   Or sever my soul from His love.

'My name from the palms of His hands
  Eternity will not erase,
Impress'd on His heart it remains,
  In marks of indelible grace.
Yes, I to the end shall endure,
  As sure as the earnest is given
More happy, but not more secure,
  The glorified spirits in Heaven.'

APPENDIX.

FIRST INTRODUCTION OF THE POPULAR DOCTRINE INTO THE CHRISTIAN CHURCH.

An able article has appeared in the *Rainbow* for April 1869, by the Rev. H. Constable, from which we make the following extracts:—

'The end of the ungodly, according to Scripture, is their destruction or death. As this death is the punishment of sin, and as there is no recovery from it, it is called everlasting punishment and destruction. This was also the doctrine of the apostolical age of the Church, as we find it declared in those "Epistles of the Apostolical Fathers" which have been preserved to our time. The best and soundest of the Fathers of the age immediately succeeding were also of this opinion. Justin and Irenæus, men who suffered martyrdom for their Master, and Theophilus of Antioch, all maintained the old scriptural doctrine. If the opinion of the Church had never departed from it, we would probably have never heard of the view of Origen.

'At an early period, however, doctrine on this point began to be corrupted, and the corruption grew with a rapid growth. Of all the systems of philosophy in vogue at the time, the most sublime was that of Plato. Of a part of human nature, the soul, it took a very lofty and captivating view. It abandoned the body for ever to its dust, but it ascribed to the soul a life which should have no end.

'The reader of Scripture knows how earnestly and frequently Paul warned the Church against philosophy.[*] He is the only one of the apostles who has specially done so, as he was probably the only one of them who had any acquaintance with philosophical systems. In his warnings he does not make any exception; he does not condemn the Stoic or Epicurean Schools, and exempt that of Plato; he prohibits

---

[*] Col. ii. 8; 1 Cor. i. 22.

with all the weight of his authority the introduction of any philosophical system or dogma into the Church. He warned that it would spoil and corrupt, not elevate or strengthen truth. It might be that every system of philosophy had its portion of truth, but he knew that every system was also poisoned with error. Accordingly, while he has quoted more than once from the poets, he has never quoted from the philosophers of heathenism.

'Many of the early fathers forgot this warning of the apostle, and it is amongst these, precisely, that we find the origin of error upon the great doctrine of future punishment. Educated in Platonism, they thought that they might, with great advantage to the cause of Christianity, bring at least a portion of their old learning into its service. Some brought less, some more, according as they were more or less thoroughly acquainted with Christianity. But on one point they were substantially agreed. All of them, with Tertullian, adopted the sentiment of Plato— "Every soul is immortal."* On this point Plato took rank, not among prophets and apostles, but above all prophets and apostles. A doctrine which neither Old Testament nor New taught directly or indirectly, nay, which was contrary to a great part of the teaching of both, these fathers brought in with them into the Church, and this gave to the old Sage of the Academy a greater authority and a wider influence by far than he would ever have had otherwise. It was in effect Plato teaching in the Church, under the supposed authority of Christ and His apostles, doctrine subversive of and contrary to the doctrine which they had one and all maintained. This dogma of Plato was made the rigid rule for the interpretation of Scripture. Christ, and Paul, and John, all were forced to Platonise. The deduction of reason was palmed off on men's minds as the teaching of revelation. We have read the writings of the early fathers with carefulness, at least on this question. It is impossible, of course, to affix a date to a nameless forger, but we think it quite possible, if not probable, that the first known holder of the theory of eternal life for the reprobate was the author of the writings known under the title of "Clementina," and falsely attributed to Clemens Romanus. It is indeed difficult, if not impossible, to ascertain the exact sentiments of this writer. If his work is not itself interpolated, he appears to hold directly opposite opinions in different parts of it. In one place he speaks of the soul as if it would at length be extinguished in the fire of hell; in another as if, from its essential immortality, its sufferings could have no end.† To our mind, he seems to

---

* Tertullian, De Ris. 327: iii. Paris, 1675.

† Clementina; Hom. Ter. vi.; Hom. Undec. xi.; ed. Antwerpiæ, 1698.

ORIGIN OF THE POPULAR DOCTRINE. 121

have lived at a period and a place where opinion was changing from the Apostolical to the Augustinian point of view, and that it is thus we are to account for his inconsistency. It is enough for our present purpose to note that he has fully adopted the lofty language of Plato on the nature of the human soul, and thus laid the sure foundation for that change of doctrine which he did not, perhaps, himself fully adopt. With him the soul is of "the same substance with God," and is hence "immortal" and "incorruptible."* And all this he has placed in the mouth of an apostle who, in his genuine sayings, has taken precisely the opposite view of human nature.† This nameless forger is, so far as is known, the first maintainer of the doctrine of eternal life in hell.

'We now come to a man who has at least the recommendation of having a name. We know his antecedents, and can give some fair opinion of what his judgment is worth. He is Athenagoras, who lived from about A.D. 127 to A.D. 190. He was born at Athens; was educated there in the philosophy of Plato; became a Christian, and settled at Alexandria, where his great object seems to have been to show that Christianity and Platonism were one and the same in substance. Beyond a question, he held to its full extent the doctrine of eternal life for the reprobate, as it was afterwards elaborated by Augustine. He based it on an argument of reason, for, it is as clear as daylight, this theory of the soul's immortality is pre-eminently a Rationalistic deduction. He laid it down that God's grand object in making man was *that man should live.*‡ He does not say a word about God's having man's happiness, or his own glory, in view in creation; but that *simple existence* was his end. Hence, he argues, as God's end cannot possibly be defeated, man *must* live for ever, be he good or evil, miserable or happy. This is indeed *Rationalism*, except that it is Rationalism of a very poor order. One text of Scripture Athenagoras never dreams of advancing for his opinion; but then he has his master's sonorous phraseology for our nature. With him, as with Plato, the soul is "immortal," it *must* continue to exist; it was made immortal at its creation, and cannot be subjected to death; no change can affect its invulnerable being; for it is, and was, and always will be "incorruptible."§ Athenagoras, being a Christian as well as a Platonist, took the liberty to add to his master's theory. Plato dropped the body altogether at death, and was only glad to do so as being with him only

---

* Hom. Decimasenta, xvi.; Hom. Undec. xl.
† 1 Peter i. 24; 2 Peter ii. 12.
‡ St. Justini Opera: Paris, 1615. Athenagoræ, 53, c.; 57, b.
§ p. 31, a.; 53, d.; 57, d.; 64, c.

a clog, a prison, a curse to the soul. Here Athenagoras struck out a new line for himself, which diverged, we must say, fully as much from Scripture as from Plato, and was no improvement to either system. The body, according to our Alexandrian philosopher, was originally created immortal, but became mortal by Adam's sin. At the resurrection, however, it will, in the case of the wicked as much as of the righteous, resume its original immortality. The glorious chapter of St. Paul, in which he describes the resurrection of the just, and the change which passes on their corrupt, dishonoured, weak, and natural bodies, to fit them for an eternal life, is applied by Athenagoras to the resurrection of the unjust as much.* Monstrous as this idea is to us— abstaining as our modern Augustinians do from this application of Paul's great chapter—such an application is a necessity to them, and Athenagoras was reasonable here. The mortal body must put on immortality if it is to endure an eternity of pain.

'But while Athenagoras, the Platonist, is at Alexandria maintaining the novel doctrine of eternal life in hell, he has a worthy fellow-labourer in Mesopotamia, in the person of Tatian, the Marcionite heretic. It is curious and instructive to trace, when we can, the progress of error. Tatian had been, in his earlier days, a scholar of Justin Martyr, and after the death of the latter professed great reverence for his old master's opinions, and affected to consider them identical with his own.† Justin, a great admirer of Plato, had, to a great extent, adopted the phraseology of Plato concerning the soul, and called it immortal and incorruptible. We know, however, that his meaning was, that it was immortal *as compared with the body*, and did not suffer death when the latter did, but continued to exist in a separate state. We know this from a very remarkable passage in his writings, in which he describes with much minuteness the death of the soul when God withdraws from it the life he had given to it.‡ Tatian, well aware of this prominent doctrine of Justin, introduced a view of the soul of wicked men which, so far as we know, was quite peculiar to himself. He supposed that when the body of the wicked died the soul also died with it, being forsaken by the higher spirit; that, at the resurrection, it is raised to life again along with the body, and then receives an immortality which makes it capable of enduring endless pain.§

'In Athenagoras, Tatian, and the forger of the "Clementina," we have the earliest known advocates of the theory of eternal life in hell. From their writings we gather the marvellous power which the introduction of the Platonic dogma of the soul's immortality had upon the doctrine of the Church. But this theory required a more powerful

* 54, a.; 50, a.; 65, c. † 158, a. ‡ 224, b. c. § 152, b. c.

advocate than any of the above writers, and it found it somewhat later in the person of Tertullian. A perfect master of the Latin tongue, a powerful reasoner where not led away by his peculiar errors, of a vehement nature and a vivid imagination, he was well suited to impress an idea on an age disposed to accept it; and, spite of his heresies, spite of his strange hallucinations, he left the lasting impression of his mind upon the Church of succeeding times. Accordingly, the theory of eternal torments culminated, in the second century, in this fierce African theologian. He did not hold it more plainly than Athenagoras and Tatian, but he impressed it with a power to which they were utter strangers, and he freed it from some of their statements which would expose it to animadversion. In his utter ignorance of the Hebrew language, he attempted to find some scriptural support for the base of his theory— the immortality of the soul—in the description given in Gen. ii. 7, of the creation of man.* But he does not rely on this alone, or even chiefly; he appeals boldly to the natural argument, and when he feels pressed here, he throws himself on the revelations of a sister, to whom divine visions of the soul were vouchsafed.† Thus fortified he uses, to their utmost possible latitude of meaning, most of Plato's terms for the soul. It is, even in the case of the wicked, not subject to death, but must ever continue immortal: it is ever indissoluble, indivisible, an eternal substance, having the very same immortality which belongs to Deity.‡ But it is in the descriptions of the endless agony of the lost that Tertullian surpassed his predecessors, and threw them into the shade. He does not draw any veil over his scene of punishment. Without saying that he took a positive delight in the contemplation of it, he depicts its fancied circumstances with a minuteness and a force that has scarcely been surpassed by the imagination of Dante, or the agonising details of a Jesuit or a Revivalist preacher. Nor can we say that he was wrong, if his theory were but true. No amount of terror, horror, disgust, that could possibly be awakened here in the human mind could be too great, if only by it a single soul could be persuaded to fly in time from this wrath to come. The delicacy that tells us there is such a hell, but that good manners or regard for feeling should lead us to conceal its naked and terrible aspect, is a false delicacy, which risks eternity rather than give pain for a moment. Tertullian certainly was not guilty of this false delicacy. He believed in eternal torments, and he drew faithful pictures of them. With him hell was a scene where endless slaughtering (*æterna occisio*) was being enacted, where

---

* Tertulliani Opera: Paris, 1675; p. 270, b.
† 269, c. d.   ‡ 269, 346, 281.

the pain of dying was to be ever felt, but never the relief which death could bring.* And God was the author and inflictor of this!

* * * * * *

'The theory of Origen was man's revolt against this doctrine of man. This fearful picture of God could not be laid in its bare horrors before the mind without drawing forth a protest. It came in the form of *Universal Restoration.* Tertullian had consigned reprobate men and devils to endless suffering in hell; Origen converts hell into a purgatory, and sends men and devils forth from it purified and humbled to the feet of the great Father and to the joys which are at His right hand for evermore. It is the old story of human thought—from one extreme to its opposite. The truth always lies between the two.

'Origen had seized hold of a scriptural truth—the final extinction of evil, which was just as much a part of our Father's revelation as Tertullian's eternity of punishment. Each had his share of truth, and if the question lay between these two human systems it could never be set at rest. If Tertullian could appeal to Scripture for the overthrow of the wicked, whether angels or men, as being of an endless nature, Origen could point from the same source of truth to a blissful coming time when all that had breath should praise the Lord.†

'What was there which prevented Origen from going back to the old scriptural doctrine of death as the end of sinners, which places the two scriptural truths just mentioned in harmony and not in opposition? It was the very same human dogma of the immortality of the soul which had led Athenagoras and Tertullian to their endless life in hell. This dogma of Plato, this creation of human reason, this tradition of men, made the revolt from Tertullian to be only the exchange of one human system for another, instead of being a return from man's heresy to God's truth.

* * * * * *

'But Origen, while he only became acquainted with the Hebrew language in his old age, was a Greek scholar from his youth. He had the advantage, which Augustine had not, of being thoroughly acquainted with the language in which the gospel was inscribed. He knew the meaning of its terms, and among the terms which described the future punishment of sinners, who in this life rejected Christ, were all the terms of the Greek language which describe the utter destruction of organisation, the utter loss of life, and being, and existence. What was to be done with these?

---

* p. 364, d. † Psalm cl. 6.

ORIGIN OF THE POPULAR DOCTRINE.

'Were they to be explained away? This is what the holders of Augustine's theory have done. They put an insufficient, an unnatural, or a positively false meaning on the terms of the New Testament. With them death means life, and life means happiness, and destruction means preservation, and so on. Having put these convenient meanings on the phraseology of Scripture, they can look placidly upon a thousand passages, which contradict what they teach from platform, and pulpit, and press, and instil into children's minds almost with their mother's milk. Origen could not, or would not, do this. He gives, as any Greek scholar not possessed with the spirit of Augustine would do, their proper force to the terms of the New Testament—the same meaning which Plato, or Euripides, or Demosthenes, or Cicero, would attach to them.

'We will give an example of this. Every one is familiar with the solemn warning of our Lord, "Fear not them which *kill* the body, but are not able to kill the soul: but rather fear Him who is able to *destroy* both soul and body in hell." We remark in the English version the change from "kill," in the first clause, to "destroy," in the second, a change exactly answering to the Greek original, which uses ἀποκτείνω in the first clause, and ἀπόλλυμι in the second. The maintainers of Augustine's theory attempt to take advantage of a change which is in reality only a heavier blow to their system. They explain "destroy" as a term of inferior force to "kill." Listen to Bengel, from whom better things might be expected. He tells us that the word "destroy," and not "kill," is used when the soul is spoken of, because "the soul is immortal;" "cannot die."* Now anyone who came unprejudiced to this passage of our Lord would acknowledge that every law of right reason would lead us to conclude that the force of the term in the second clause must at the least *equal* that in the first, else the warning is diminished in its intensity. The real reason why our Lord varied His phrase was because "destroy" in the Greek was a *term of far greater power* than "kill." Let us hear the Greek scholar Origen on the true force of this word destroy. He is commenting on 1 Cor. iii. 9, in connection with Jeremiah i. 10:—"See what is said to the people of God: 'Ye are God's husbandry, ye are God's building;' therefore the words of God over nations and kingdoms are, 'to root out, and to throw down, and *to destroy*' (ἀπόλλυμι). If it be rooted out, and that which is rooted out be not *destroyed*; if it be thrown down, while the stones of the overthrow are not *destroyed*; *that which is thrown down still*

---

* Bengel on Matt. x. 28.

exists. It is therefore the result of God's goodness, after the rooting out, to destroy what is rooted out; after the throwing down, to *destroy* what is thrown down." Such is the mighty power which Origen, a Greek scholar, gives to this word "destroy." With him it means blotting out of existence.

'But it will be asked if such be the true force of the words applied in Scripture to future punishment, how did Origen defend his theory of universal restoration, with these meeting him in the face? Very easily. Origen never found any difficulty in Scripture. If it was for him, well and good. If it was against him, he made it without any ceremony speak as he wished.

'Every reader of Scripture knows that its solemn warnings are addressed *to the sinner in person:* "*O wicked man, thou shalt surely die.*" Death, destruction, perdition, loss of life—all the multiplied phrases and illustrations of the Bible are there directed against the *persons* of the wicked. Origen's simple mode of neutralising their force is by directing them *against their sin.* And so his point is gained. Their force cannot be too strong for him, so he does not attempt to diminish it. The Augustinian, directing them correctly against the sinner, robs them of their meaning: Origen, directing them against the sin, leaves them their proper sense. It is difficult to say against which side the charge of perverting Scripture lies heaviest.

* * * * *

'But Origen had one grand truth in his system—the glorious scriptural truth of the extinction of all evil. There is a time to come, to which prophecy points onwards, when the evil which has, doubtless for wise and wondrous and *merciful* purposes, been permitted to obscure the bright face of heaven to our poor contracted view, shall have passed away. The idea of the Augustinian theorists, that evil for a time is essentially one and the same thing with evil for eternity, is as opposed to Scripture and to God's mind as it is ridiculous in the eye of common sense. With God—"*heaviness may endure for a night,*" but it shall not endure for ever; if it did, what would be thought of God or of His Word? No; with God the heaviness which endures for a night is borne for the *eternal* "*joy which cometh in the morning.*" It is *not* the same thing that evil should be allowed for some few thousand years, a speck indistinguishable between the two eternities of the past and the future—evil, too, never unmixed with good—and that evil, black, foul, and unmitigated, should, throughout all eternity, exist in the centre of God's world of righteousness. With this truth—the final extinction of evil—in his possession, and the dogma of the essential immortality of the soul admitted, the theory of Origen is fully able to stand its ground against the rival view of Augustine.

'But it is, after all, a human system, and as such is to be condemned. God's Word contradicts it in a thousand places. It holds out *no hope* to those who stand condemned in the judgment. This world and its peoples will again be all righteous, all rejoicing; but the reprobate will have passed away out of being—their names blotted from the book of life. Whatever be our opinion of Origen personally—of his learning, his brilliancy, even of the truth of much of his teaching—his teaching here places him amongst those prophets condemned in Ezekiel for "strengthening the hands of the wicked, that he should not return from his wicked way, *by promising him life.*"* In that future age which has no end, the reprobate have no abiding name or place. Their image has vanished out of the city. Life for them, whether a thing to be desired or shunned, whether with Origen in heaven, or with Augustine in hell, is the Devil's lie, repeated now from a thousand high places, as it was once whispered in Eve's credulous ear in the garden.'

* * * * * *

'For the benefit of the readers of the *Rainbow* we subjoin a table, which will enable them at a glance to see the relative antiquity in the primitive Church, of the three great theories of future punishment, which are at this day maintained in the Church of Christ. In the accuracy of this table we fully believe; for its substantial truth we are prepared to contend; and we now challenge any gainsayer to controvert it. The dates given for the death of each father are, of course, only vouched for as the most probable approximations to truth. Exactitude is now unattainable.

Eternal Death.	Died A.D.	Eternal Life in pain.	Died A.D.	Universal Restoration.	Died A.D.
Barnabas	90				
Clemens Romanus	100				
Hermas	104				
Ignatius. Martyr	107				
Polycarp. Martyr	147				
Justin. Martyr	164	The Forger of the Clementina			
Theophilus of Antioch	183	Athenagoras	190		
Irenæus. Martyr	202	Tatian	200		
		Tertullian	235		
				Origen	253

---

* Ezek. xiii. 22.

'From the above table we see how comparatively late the theory of Augustine appears in the remains of patristic writing, while that of Origen is later still. That blank space between them and primitive truth is destructive to both.'

LIFE AND DEATH.

In John xii. 25, two very different words are both translated 'life.' The one is '*psuche*,' which, when applied to man, sometimes denotes his soul, as distinguished from his body or his spirit; sometimes the immaterial as distinguished from the material part of his nature; and sometimes his natural life—an ambiguity which no doubt results from our very imperfect acquaintance with the mystery of our own being. The other is '*zoe*,' which denotes the principle or condition of *life* in any form, and therefore admits of infinite varieties and degrees, from the life of a flower to the life of God. This latter is the word used to define both the present spiritual life of the regenerate, and that future life which is to be its 'end' or result.

Now our opponents maintain that the reward of the righteous will consist in the everlasting enjoyment of the highest possible *zoe*, and the punishment of the wicked in the everlasting deprivation of it, which they contend may as truly be called death as may the present death in trespasses and sins. We have elsewhere shown how inadequate this view is to meet the general teaching of Holy Scripture, especially how it confounds the death which is the wages of sin with the death of which it is the wages, making the punishment of the lost to be the deprivation of what they never possessed. But our Lord's words in John xii. 25 might have been spoken expressly to guard against such a mistake; for it is not *zoe* only that the unbeliever will lose, but his own *psuche*, his actual existence—

the very thing which, according to the popular theory, it is impossible for anyone to lose; while the believer is to ' keep ' —or, as it is given in Matt. x. 39, ' find,' and in Luke ix. 24, ' save '—not merely *zoe*, but his own *psuche*. With this agree the words of Ezekiel (xviii. 27), ' He shall save *his soul alive.*' The popular doctrine teaches that every man will save his soul alive—the righteous ' unto life everlasting,' the wicked unto death everlasting. But that is not what Christ said, nor what Ezekiel said.

We are triumphantly asked whether the everlasting life of the righteous is ' mere existence.' Certainly not. But these and other passages of Scripture abundantly prove that eternal existence is not a thing taken for granted, but *included* in the *zoe* which is to be the ' end ' of 'holiness;' and that the death inflicted upon the wicked will be deprivation, not merely of the higher part of that *zoe*, but the whole of it—they will ' lose ' not only their happiness, but ' themselves.'

Now page after page has been written, of more or less subtle reasoning, in order to escape from the plain testimony of Scripture, and to substitute for its alternative of life or death the alternative of endless happiness or endless misery. It would be quite possible to go through it, sentence by sentence, and unravel the whole web. But it would occupy a considerable space, and the effect upon many persons would only be to make them think it was too abstruse and difficult a subject for them to understand. I prefer another plan. I will ask them, first, to determine in their own minds whether the Bible was intended to make known at least its great leading truths in a manner intelligible to plain persons of common sense reading it with due care, or whether it is addressed to philosophers and men of science alone. If they are satisfied of the former, then let them open a Concordance, and, after reading the multitude of texts which speak of life or death as the ultimate destiny of all men, let them consider whether there can be the smallest doubt—not as to what could possibly be made of all this, but—as to the impression which it is meant to convey. In all ages, in all climes, amongst all classes, there have been no more universally intelligible ideas than those of life and death. All cannot define them; but all can understand them quite enough for any practical purpose, and all understand them alike. The common sense of mankind, if allowed to act freely, would condemn the supposition that the key-words of the whole question—words that form the staple and substance of Scriptural teaching upon it—can be employed in any but their natural and familiar meaning.

Whether these terms are applied to the present respective conditions of the regenerate and unregenerate, because of their bearing some analogy to those of life and death, or because the one necessarily leads to the other, or both, may perhaps be questioned.* But even if the former view alone be maintained, the argument remains unshaken; for the death which is the *wages* of sin cannot be the same thing as the death *of* sin. Man is found at last in a hopeless state of *moral* death, and therefore God inflicts upon him *physical* death. Man has destroyed himself, and therefore God will destroy him. The common view makes the punishment of death to be the same thing as the death of which it is the punishment, with the addition only of some further suffering, which has nothing to do with death at all.

Death is deprivation of life. There are various kinds of life, and therefore various kinds of death. But there is no

---

* I believe the true explanation is to be found in the fact, that in man's fallen condition the highest part of his nature, the spirit, is *virtually* dead. Until quickened into life by regeneration, it lies dormant, and may at last become absolutely irrecoverable. (See Delitzsch's *Biblical Psychology*, or Heard's *Tripartite Nature of Man*.)

second meaning to the word death; it means deprivation of life, and nothing else. The question therefore is, What kind of life will be left to the wicked, of which they can be penally deprived by God at the day of judgment? They are already 'dead in trespasses in sins,' and 'alienated from the life of God.' In that sense they 'have no life in them,' and therefore have none to be deprived of. What is there left but conscious existence? In what other way but by the termination of that can they undergo a 'second death,' or be 'destroyed soul and body in hell?'

The case has been very clearly stated by Mr. E. F. Litton, in his able work entitled *Life or Death*:—

'If a happy life was promised, it might justly be inferred that there existed also a wretched one; but by setting forth "eternal life" simply as the promise, the inference is, that there shall be no life for those who come short of the promise. It is as though the announcement of "eternal life" was in itself sufficient; as if "eternal life" in any other condition than that of supreme happiness, where that eternal life shall be passed in fellowship with God, could not be contemplated. If this were not so, the "eternal life" which was held forth to the redeemed as the prize of their high calling would have been qualified by expressions denoting that the condition of *their* life should be one of supreme felicity. It is a fact worthy of deep consideration that "eternal life" or immortality is constantly set forth as sufficient to express what God has prepared for His people.

*   *   *   *   *   *

'It is the gift of life on the one hand, and the loss of life on the other, rather than the circumstances in which existence in the future state must be passed, that is continually advanced in the pages of the everlasting Gospel, which teaches mankind to look forward to the period when mortality shall be swallowed up of life.'

IMMORTALITY.

THE sense in which man was created immortal, namely, as '*capable* of living for ever,' on certain conditions, has been already explained. Supposing such capacity to have been part of the image of God in which he was made, why might he not lose *that*, as well as the holiness which undoubtedly formed part of it? One writer says, 'We cannot lay too much stress on the fact that man was made in the image of God.' We certainly can, if we suppose that the image could never be destroyed. The truth was admirably stated by Theophilus Bishop of Antioch in the second century—

'But some one may say, Was not man created mortal? By no means. Immortal? Nor say we this. But my opinion is, that he was neither mortal nor immortal by nature; for if he had been from the beginning immortal, He had made him a God. Again, on the other hand, if He had made him mortal, God would have seemed to be the author of his death. Therefore He made him neither mortal nor immortal, as I said before, but CAPABLE of both, that he might *advance* to immortality, and, by keeping divine commandments, receive immortality *as a reward*, and become divine. But if, by disobedience to God, he should turn to the works of the flesh, he would become unto himself the author of his own death.'

Irenæus also, the disciple of Polycarp, who was a contemporary of St. John, writes—

'*Life is not from ourselves, nor from our nature, but it is given or bestowed according to the grace of God;* and, therefore, he who preserves this *gift of life*, and returns thanks to Him who bestows it, *he shall receive "length of days for ever and ever."* But he who rejects it and proves unthankful to his Maker for creating him, and will not know Him who bestows it, *he deprives himself of the gift of duration to all eternity.* And, therefore, the Lord speaks thus of such unthankful persons,—" If you have not been faithful in that which is least, who will commit much to you?" intimating thereby unto us, that they who are unthankful to Him with respect to this short transitory life, which is His gift, the effect of His bounty, *shall be most justly deprived of length of days in the world to come.*'

The well-known words in Eccl. iii. 21 are often quoted to prove the immortality of the human soul. But the context shows that if they proved anything they would prove exactly the reverse. Solomon has just said, 'That which befalleth the sons of men befalleth beasts; even one thing befalleth them; as the one dieth, so dieth the other; yea, they have all one breath; so that a man hath no pre-eminence above a beast; for all is vanity. All go unto one place; all are of the dust, and all turn to dust again.' Oh, yes, some philosopher will say, That may be quite true of their bodies, but man has an immortal spirit within him which the beast has not. Who can prove that, replies Solomon, from anything that we see or know of ourselves? 'Who knoweth the spirit of a man that (you say) goeth upwards, and the spirit of a beast that (you say) goeth downward to the earth?'

The peculiar style of the book of Ecclesiastes creates considerable difficulty in deciding how certain passages are to be taken. But as to the general tone and tenor of Holy Scripture on this question there can be no doubt whatever. It uniformly aims at abasing man's pride, by reminding him that he is a creature of a day; that he is crushed before the moth; that he is cut down like the grass, and withers even as the green herb. 'Orthodoxy,' on the contrary, puffs him up with a sense of his own importance, by talking to him of his immortal spirit, his never-dying soul, and so forth. 'All flesh is as grass, and all the glory of man as the flower of grass,' says Scripture. No, replies 'orthodoxy'; his *flesh* may be as grass, limiting the word to the lower part of his being, his material organisation, though even that can only perish for a time, to rise again indestructible, and live for ever; but what constitutes his highest 'glory,' his spiritual nature, is essentially imperishable, and as far removed as possible from being like 'the flower of grass.' To the question of Eliphaz (Job iv. 17), 'Shall mortal man be more just than God?' 'orthodoxy' would have answered, Man is not mortal; his body no doubt dies for a time, but it is the highest glory of the *man* to be as immortal as God Himself, and, therefore, to introduce his *mortality* into the question renders the comparison nugatory.

I am well aware that the following remarks will be adduced, as if they stood quite alone, to sustain the charge of 'rationalism,' which is so freely used to supply the place of argument; but I cannot refrain from adding, in the language of one of my principal opponents, 'Let us hear what Reason has to say' on this subject.

At what point of his development does man become essentially immortal? When does the human thing, which is at first admittedly perishable, change into something imperishable? Who are immortal? All who are born? All who are born alive? or who? A child born dead is allowed neither Christian baptism nor Christian burial. How can this be accounted for, except on the supposition that the Church does not regard it as an immortal being? Are we, then, to believe that if a child dies just before its birth it perishes, but that if it dies just after its birth it must necessarily live for ever? This may be held by those who think that only the body is begotten, and that at the moment of birth, or at some previous period, a newly-created indestructible spirit is united to it. But then what becomes of original sin? On that theory it is only man's material organism that is born in sin; the higher parts of his being come into existence in a state of perfect purity, as everything must be that God creates. And what becomes of the unity of the race, or the brotherhood of man?*

According to the teaching of Scripture, the *man* is developed from his parent stock by the natural process of generation. And the question therefore arises, At what period does any, or every, separate formation from this parent stock become immortal? It is admitted that *none* of them are so from the first; when does the stupendous change from perishable to

---

* I am aware of the answers that may be made to some of the above questions; and readily admit that the implied arguments grounded on them are by no means conclusive upon the question at issue. But they suggest considerations which are not altogether without weight in the matter.

imperishable, mortal to immortal, destructible to indestructible, take place? Scripture replies, It begins in regeneration, and is completed in resurrection. When the human spirit, being quickened by the Divine Spirit, is brought to know God and Jesus Christ whom He hath sent, it 'passes from death unto life;' it 'has everlasting life,' and 'shall never see death;' it is 'made partaker of the divine nature,' and can 'never perish;' 'its life is hid with Christ in God,' and while Christ lives the possessor of that life must live also. 'The body indeed,' even in the regenerate, 'is dead because of sin, but the spirit is life because of righteousness.'* And even the body has such a principle of immortality communicated to it that it cannot remain permanently under the power of death; 'for if the Spirit of Him that raised up Jesus from the dead dwell in you, He that raised up Christ from the dead shall also quicken your mortal bodies by [on account of] His Spirit which dwelleth in you.' The wicked are raised to life again; but only to a natural mortal life, which will again come to an end. Those who are in Christ alone 'come forth unto the resurrection of LIFE;' in their case alone does this mortal put on immortality, and this corruptible put on incorruption. Most truly, therefore, do we profess, in the Nicene Creed, to 'believe in the Holy Ghost, the Lord, and *Giver of Life*;' and most appropriate are the words used in administering the Lord's Supper—'preserve thy *body* and soul unto everlasting life.'

'If man were by natural constitution possessed of immortality o eternal life, then would we expect to find the Scriptures insisting only on a modification of that life—a change of its dispositions and new

---

* If it be urged that this excludes from immortality all who die in infancy, we reply—No more than it excludes them from regeneration. The normal process is described by the words, 'Of His own will begat He us by the word of truth.' What is the nature of the process, where the mind is not sufficiently matured to receive the word of truth, we have no means of ascertaining.

direction of its powers, as necessary to his seeing the kingdom of God. Whereas, if it be true that immortal life is altogether distinct from natural life—a *new* life and from another source, then, on the other hand, we would expect to hear of a new generation, and to find it written that " except a man be BORN AGAIN he cannot see the kingdom of God." In other words, we would expect to find not merely conversion, or repentance, but REGENERATION insisted on in the Scriptures as necessary to our partaking of everlasting life. Now, what is the fact? That the Scriptures, teaching that immortality is only through Christ, and is in fact the life of God—of Him "who only hath immortality"—participated in by the redeemed, teach also the doctrine of regeneration by the Spirit of God, *an actual communication of the Spirit* as the commencement of a new life, as that life in itself; whereas the popular creed teaching that man has eternal life by nature, has been constrained to explain regeneration in such way as reconciles it with this persuasion,—to make it identical with conversion, and a change of heart or affection, which is, in fact, to deny that there is any such thing as regeneration, strictly speaking; and to interpret it as a metaphor, "a bold figure of speech," as it has actually been called!' (*Christ our Life.*)

'IMMORTAL' AND 'INCORRUPTIBLE.'

THE words properly translated 'immortal,' and 'immortality,' occur only in 1 Cor. xv. 53, 54, and 1 Tim. vi. 16. In all other passages 'incorruptible' or 'incorruptibility' would be the strict rendering of the original. On the strength of this, the chosen champion of the *Bible Treasury* replies to my quotation of Rom. ii. 7 with his characteristic courtesy, 'It is false; it speaks of incorruptibility, which Scripture distinguishes from immortality.' I am disposed to think that they are distinguished in 1 Cor. xv. 53, 54; and that the one refers to the endless life of the regenerate spirit, the other to the endless life of the resurrection body. But how entirely the above criticism fails to touch the argument drawn from Rom. ii. 7 may be seen in a moment by referring to Rom. i. 23, and 1 Tim. i. 17; in both of which places the same word, 'incorruptible,' is applied to God Himself. How can it be 'distinguished from immortality' there? Besides, supposing that the authorized translation of Rom. ii. 7 were 'false,' and that St. Paul referred only to the 'incorruptibility' of the body, how would that affect the question? According to the popular view, the bodies as well as the souls of the wicked will live for ever; in all cases alike this corruptible will put on incorruption, as well as this mortal put on immortality; so that the one has no more to be sought by patient continuance in well doing than the other.

I cannot forbear expressing my regret that the editor of a religious magazine should have admitted into its columns such a paper as that referred to above. Besides repeatedly applying the word 'infidelity' to a doctrine advocated by one, who believes in the plenary inspiration of Scripture, and also professes to ground that particular opinion on its uniform consistent teaching, the writer indulges, at every fourth or fifth sentence, in such expressions as 'It is false—simply false—clap-trap—idle inattention to Scripture—careless and false—too bad—extreme carelessness—false—dishonest—gross blunder—quite false—another blunder—trifling with Scripture.' We are all fallible, and too easily betrayed into errors of tone and spirit, as well as into errors of doctrine; but when an editor receives a paper that so grievously offends against the laws of Christian courtesy, with so very little in the way of sound reasoning to compensate for the defect, the least he can be expected to do is to remit it to the writer for expurgation. The knowledge that rhetoric will weigh far more than logic with the majority of his readers, is no excuse for taking advantage of such rhetoric as forms the staple of that short paper.

'ETERNAL' or 'EVERLASTING,' 'FOR EVER,' 'FOR EVER AND EVER.'

In endeavouring to meet the argument derived from the etymology and use of these words, two courses have been adopted.

The less informed or less candid reasoners have referred to those passages alone in which they are applied to God Himself, and have simply ignored those in which they are applied to Jewish ordinances, to the 'hills,' to Christian 'consolation,' and other things of limited duration. According to their mode of argument, it might be demonstrably proved that the life of God is not endless. For as we *know* that some of the things pronounced to be eternal have already terminated, it would follow that the word can refer only to a limited period; and therefore, as it is applied to God, His existence must have a limit.

Others, however, and amongst them the editor of the *Christian Advocate*, have attempted to grapple with the facts. And their argument is substantially this: that whenever the word is used in a limited sense, the limit is shown from the very nature of the case. Precisely so; that is just my position,—namely, that you can only know from the nature of each particular case whether the period referred to is limited or unlimited. Mr. Garbett says, that 'in every one of these cases, without exception, it is qualified by a phrase of limitation, such as, " to thee and to thy seed," " to Aaron and his sons;" where the qualifying phrases define the duration of the age to be the duration of the Jewish economy.' And just so, the whole context of Matt. xxv. 46 defines the duration of the age there spoken of to be the duration of the millennial kingdom. In neither case is the 'qualifying phrase' attached to the *word*; it is the *subject* which proves the word to indicate a limited period.

One writer argues, that when these terms are used 'in a restricted sense,' they 'refer to *a time state*, and must therefore have a meaning limited by the continuance of this worldly system, and of time.' It is shown in the note on Matt. xxv. 46, that both the 'eternal punishment' and the 'eternal life' there spoken of, do refer to a 'time state,' namely, the duration of the Millennial kingdom. But how will this view suit the common interpretation of Rev. xiv. 11? 'And the smoke of their torment ascendeth up for ever and ever, and they have no rest *day nor night* who worship the beast and his image.' Do not 'day' and 'night' indicate a 'time state'?

Dr. George Sidney Smith, of Trinity College, Dublin, an excellent scholar, and a firm believer in the popular doctrine, says: 'There is no mystery or ambiguity about the word *aionios*. Like many other words in the Lexicon, it has several meanings; but this creates no difficulty; the context is always sufficient to decide; the relation and genesis of its different meanings are well ascertained; and as a general definition, it may be safely held that it commonly means *a continuous duration as long as the subject is capable of*.' It would have been much safer to have said 'a continuous duration' *throughout the period referred to*. Of the Jewish priests it was declared that 'their anointing shall *surely* be an *everlasting* priesthood.' Ex. xl. 15. It can hardly be said to have lasted as long as it was 'capable' of lasting. It lasted until God saw fit to put an end to it, and then it was abolished. Yet how sternly an orthodox Rabbi might have rebuked the 'infidelity' of any presumptuous Jew who had ventured to assert that that priesthood was ever to be 'changed.' Heb. vii. 12. Could anything be plainer or stronger than the words 'shall *surely* be an *everlasting* priesthood'? What a perverting of Scripture he would call it 'to say that everlasting does not mean lasting for ever'!

Other texts, to which Dr. Smith's definition might more strictly apply, show even more forcibly the very limited sense of such language as our opponents press so strongly into their service.

'His master shall bore his ear through with an awl, and he shall serve him *for ever.*' Ex. xxi. 6.

'The righteous shall dwell in the land *for ever.*' Ps. xxxvii. 29.

'So shall I keep thy law continually *for ever and ever.*' Ps. cxix. 44.

'I will eat no flesh *while the world standeth.*' 1 Cor. viii. 13. This is literally *to the age*, the same expression that is generally translated *for ever*, and which it is so strongly contended must necessarily mean to all eternity.

There are three passages in which St. Paul speaks of the Gospel as a long concealed mystery. In Eph. iii. 9, and in Col. i. 26, it is said to have been hid ' from the ages;' in Rom. xvi. 25, ' through age-long times.' Our translators have rendered the three expressions—' from the beginning of the world,' ' from ages,' and ' since the world began.' But if ' *to* the ages,' which they render ' for ever,' mean to all eternity, surely ' *from* the ages' must mean from all eternity—which it manifestly does not. To express *that* idea St. Paul uses the expression ' *before* the ages.' 1 Cor. ii. 7. The 'age-long times' in Rom. xvi. 25 are not *eternal* times, according to the interpretation which is forced upon the word in Matt. xxv. 46, but the *dispensational* times, the times of the ages.

ETERNITY.

Though we can only arrive at an approximate idea of eternity, it is quite possible to get near enough to it for any practical purpose. To count a trillion, at the rate of a hundred a minute, would take more than eighteen thousand million years, a tolerably long period in itself. A trillion years would of course be just a century for every minute of that period. But a trillion is expressed by a line of only nineteen figures. Suppose the line extended to some fixed star, from which the light, travelling towards us at the rate of 150,000 miles a second, is said to have taken millions of years in reaching us. How long would *that* number of years last? Well then, every sin being supposed to be of infinite guilt and consequently deserving of infinite punishment, it would be a very small calculation, to begin by supposing that a given person—say a child of ten years old dying unconverted, or a hoary reprobate, for the distinction will soon be lost as we advance—has to endure such a period of intense mental and bodily suffering for every sin of thought, word, or deed that he has ever committed. And when all those periods have been passed through, he has to begin again, and undergo for each of his sins a period of suffering equal to the *sum total* of all those previous periods. And when those have been passed through, he has to begin again; and so on for ever, with the full consciousness that he is no nearer the end of his torment than he was at first. So that if Almighty power be continually exerted to enable his body to bear its agonies as well as when in its first vigour, his mental anguish must necessarily be for ever indefinitely increasing, because the vast periods already traversed enable him ever more and more fully to realize the immeasurable eternity that still lies before him.

DESTRUCTION.

Mr. Grant and others have laboured to show that the words 'destruction' and 'destroy' are often used by inspired writers in a figurative or secondary meaning. But the question is, whether they can be so understood with reference to the final doom of the impenitent. And on this our Lord's words, recorded in Matt. x. 28, are, surely, decisive—'Fear not them which kill the body, but are not able to kill the soul; but rather fear Him, which is able to destroy both soul and body in hell.'

The importance of this text lies in the meaning of the word 'destroy,' being so precisely fixed by the contrast. God can do to both body and soul what man can do only to the body—'*kill*' them. Nothing could seem to be more clear. I was at a loss to imagine how this argument would be met. The only possible way of even pretending to meet it which occurred to me was to urge that our Lord purposely varied the expression, so as to avoid conveying the idea of death as the chief element in future punishment. The answer to which would of course be, that the object in varying the word is manifestly to increase, and not lessen, the force of the word first used; in other words, to show how awful and complete will be the death inflicted upon those who try their strength against the Almighty. My opponents seem to have felt this, as none of them, to my knowledge, have attempted that way of escape. What other way, then, is left? I should have said, none. But nothing is impossible in controversy. 'The verse in question,' writes Mr. Grant, ' does not afford the most slender reason for the belief that God will in one single instance destroy the body and soul of any one of His creatures. It simply says that He *can* do it, that is, if so disposed.' And an anonymous writer in the *Bible Treasury*, whom the editor describes as 'a valued servant of God,' actually considers it a proof of my 'carelessness' that I have quoted the words as asserting that God 'will destroy,' &c.; whereas, he says, 'it is a question of power to be feared.' The same reply has been given by others.

Now, surely, on that supposition, it is 'a question of power *not* to be feared.' Why should we be urged to *fear* God, *because* He *could* do something which we are quite sure that He never *will* do? And why does our Lord add, 'in hell,' *the place of punishment?* God is just as '*able*' to destroy whatever He has created, out of hell as in it. Yet to believe that God will ever exercise that power is, according to Mr. Grant, 'the most unwarranted notion that ever was entertained, so far as my reading extends, by any person possessing even an approach to average judgment.' What will not men be driven to say, when it becomes 'necessary to their position?'

When the able and excellent editor of the *Christian Advocate* expressed his intention of examining this book in detail, I wrote to beg that he would grapple with the text in question. I expressed my conviction that Mr. Grant's explanation would not satisfy him, and my curiosity to know what would. His next article appeared without the slightest reference to it. Again I wrote, expressing my disappointment that he had not attempted to meet it in some way or other, but adding that his tacit surrender of it confirmed my belief in its absolute conclusiveness. A third and last article followed, but still without an attempt to touch that decisive utterance. The same result has invariably followed whenever an opponent has been tightly nailed to that text—it generally closes the correspondence. In fact, as a very able clergyman, who still feels some difficulty on the general subject, candidly acknowledged to me, it is 'logically unanswerable.'

PS.—The above was written immediately after the appearance of Mr. Garbett's third article. I have since received a letter from him, in which he endeavours to meet the argument by reference to Luke xii. 4. But that passage does not in the slightest degree affect the question, inasmuch as the question remains, *For what purpose* will anyone be 'cast into hell,' —to be kept alive there for ever in misery, or to be destroyed? To which question Matt. x. 28 gives a decisive answer. The idea expressed in Luke xii. 4, 'and after that have no more that they can do,' is of course equally implied in Matt. x., and makes no difference whatever. One correspondent, indeed, has argued that if God were to destroy the sinner entirely, *He* would have 'no more that He could do.' But even that singular idea leaves the argument quite untouched. For what our Lord says is that God's power to punish does not cease, as man's does, with the death *of the body* ('after He hath killed'), but that He is also able, in the judgment, to destroy both soul and body for ever.

It should be added, that the word rendered 'destroy' in verse 28 is the same that is used in verse 39, and translated 'lose.' It there refers to a violent death, submitted to for Christ's sake; which, not being final, is little to be dreaded in comparison with the irremediable loss of life that will be incurred by those who save their lives here at the price of unfaithfulness to Christ.

The word, in some of its forms, occurs a hundred and twenty-eight times in the New Testament, and is generally rendered either 'destroy' or in the passive 'perish.' In every instance it means precisely what is conveyed by those English terms, except when used figuratively, and then *destruction* lies at the foundation of the figure.

ANNIHILATION.

As an instance of the confusion of ideas that prevails, with reference to annihilation and destruction, may be mentioned the argument drawn from the words 'perish' and 'changed' being both applied to the predicted passing away of the heavens in Heb. i. 11, 12. 'Is change annihilation?' asks the editor of the *Rock*. No; but it is destruction, if carried far enough. When 'a potter's vessel' is 'broken to shivers,' it is not annihilated, but it is destroyed, and that simply by the process of *changing* the position and mutual relationship of its component parts. Its corporate existence is gone. It does not become a bad vessel: it ceases to be a vessel at all.

Again, an able and eminent Christian minister writes, 'Fire *destroys* nothing.' What he means is, that it *annihilates* nothing. It is the most destructive agent known.

Another writer says:—'Philosophers tell us there is no such thing as the annihilation of a particle of matter, and we have no reason to believe in the annihilation of spirits.' Scripture never teaches the 'annihilation' of the wicked, in the strictly scientific sense in which 'philosophers' deny its ever taking place, namely, the reducing of anything to *nothing*. It teaches their 'destruction,' that is, their ceasing to exist as living conscious beings; and so far from philosophy or science saying anything against this, all that it does say is directly in favour of it—at least, in favour of its possibility; for it tells us that there is no such thing as an indestructible material organism, and therefore 'we have no reason to believe' in any indestructible spiritual organism. As even man can destroy the body, it is not so very hard to believe that God can also destroy the soul, especially as Christ has positively told us that He can and will do so. Surely, He can destroy whatever He has created, even though it was created *capable of* immortality—

'He can create, and He destroy.'

The *Christian Advocate* can hardly 'resist the temptation to notice with some touch of raillery and ridicule the idea of a destruction of the soul. . . . Who can conceive,' &c. No, we cannot *conceive*, 'the kind of process that would be required for its destruction;' but to argue that therefore God is *not* 'able to destroy' it at all is what our opponents would call Rationalism.

THE 'UNQUENCHABLE FIRE' AND THE UNDYING WORM.

'AUGUSTINE, in his laboured defence of the doctrine of eternal life in hell, ransacks the realms of fact and fiction for substances and life which can resist, and are uninjured by, the power of fire. This African father tells us of worms existing in hot springs, of salamanders living in the flames, of burning mountains which are not consumed, of diamonds resisting the heat of the furnace.* The ingenious idea of another African father, Tertullian, is that fire as used by man and as employed by God are of quite opposite natures, for *that* while the former wastes in consuming, the latter repairs the waste which it produces.† A truer philosophy corrects this curious defence of African theology. In all God's known world, it tells us, *whatever life is hurt* in fire becomes extinct if continued in it: *whatever substance is injured* by fire is destroyed if it remains in it. And every one of the illustrations of Scripture refer to substances most readily consumed—to wood, and tow, and thorns, and fat of lambs.

*   *   *   *   *   *

'We are here naturally led to consider what it is that is really meant

---

* De Civ. xxi.   † Apol. xlviii.

by the terms "eternal fire," "unquenchable fire," so often applied to the fire of hell. We are not now considering the nature of the fire itself, whether it be identical with or analogous only to fire such as here consumes. What we are considering is whether, be this fire what it may, it continues throughout eternity to burn as it burns when the reprobates are first placed therein. The passage from Jude leads us to conclude that it only continues to burn *while it has anything to consume*. The fire of Sodom is called an "eternal fire," but it only burned while aught remained of the guilty cities to be consumed. It could not be extinguished until then. Jordan poured upon it could not put out its flames; Abraham's prayers could not abate its force; mercy had put forward its last plea in the bosom of God. But when all had been reduced to ashes, the fire went out, and the smoke ceased to rise, leaving behind an utter destruction which no lapse of time was to repair. It is thus we are to view the "unquenchable fire" of hell.

'We are to consider that the term is one in common use. It is not confined to hell, or peculiar to theology. It is constantly applied to fire burning here on earth, which is unquenchable inasmuch as all human efforts cannot quench it, but which, when it has done its work of destruction, smoulders away and dies out. The classical scholar will remember the famous passage of Homer where the Trojans hurl "unquenchable fire" upon the Grecian ships, though but one of them was burnt, and that one only half consumed.* In the very same way it is constantly used in Scripture. When God in one place declares that His wrath against Jerusalem "shall not be quenched," and, in another, that He will "kindle a fire in the gates thereof, and it shall not be quenched," † He means that His wrath was to continue till Jerusalem was destroyed, and the fire was to burn till its palaces were consumed. Then wrath ceased because it had spent its force, and the fire went out because it had eaten up all on which it could prey. So we are to understand that "unquenchable fire" which is the terrible fate of the lost. *Their fire is not quenched.* It preys upon them with relentless force. No cries on the part of the damned arrest it; no prayers ascend from the redeemed for the sin which they know to be unto eternal death; no further feelings of grace and pity in God's bosom interfere to check its course. It burns on, consuming, preying, reducing, until it has burnt and consumed all. When it has spent its force, it dies out for want of food, leaving behind it the endless sign of the destruction which it has

---

* *Il.* xvi. 123, 294. † Jer. vii. 20; xvii. 27.

brought on fallen archangel, and angel, and man. *This is the second death. But we can bear to look upon it because it is death.* We are not looking upon a picture which would overturn reason and banish peace from all who beheld it. Life has left the realms of the lost. The reprobates felt, but do not continue to feel, the consuming flames. These prey upon the dead, and it is dust and ashes which cover the floor of the furnace of hell.'—*Rev. H. Constable.*

'Add to this, that the well-known historian Eusebius, who wrote in the latter part of the third century and the beginning of the fourth, presents us with evidence equally to our purpose. In recording the martyrdom of four Christians he writes: "Cronion and Julian were scourged, and afterwards consumed with unquenchable fire." And, in another passage: "Epimachus and Alexander, who had continued for a time in prison, enduring innumerable sufferings from the scrapers and scourges, were also destroyed with unquenchable fire." What can show more conclusively the customary meaning of this language? The martyrs were consumed: therefore the fire was unquenchable.'*—*Rev. T. Davis.*

'It is apparent that this language borrows its expressions from the awful judgments denounced on Edom or Idumea, and may therefore be properly illustrated by a comparison with the prophecy in Isaiah. " For it is the day of the Lord's vengeance, and the year of recompenses for the controversy of Zion. And the streams thereof [Idumea] shall be turned into pitch, and the dust thereof into brimstone, and the land thereof shall become burning pitch. *It shall not be quenched night nor day; the smoke thereof shall go up for ever:* from generation to generation it shall lie waste; none shall pass through it for ever and ever" (Isa. xxxiv. 8–10).

'Now, here is language quite as strong, indeed stronger, than that which occurs in the book of Revelation, and yet *it is applied to the land of Idumea, where the fire has long been quenched, and the smoke has ceased to ascend up, except in the figurative sense of a perpetual memorial.* This language, let it be observed, according to the illustration now given, is *not* incompatible with a limited duration. The language in the book of Revelation, like that of the Hebrew prophets, is highly poetical and emblematical, and can never be justly pressed into an argument for the eternal duration of torment, as the future recompense of the wicked.

'From the above comparison of passages of the New with the Old

---

* *Eccl. Hist.* b. 6, c. 41.

Testament, it is, I think, beyond debate that the phrases "unquenchable fire," &c., are hyperbolical expressions, which, if they are interpreted as they should be, according to the meaning they have in the Old Testament, whence they are quoted, will be found to describe not a condition of *endless torment*, but very grievous suffering, to be followed by a final *annihilation*.* The fire is fitly termed "*unquenchable*," because it will utterly destroy by a resistless, inextinguishable energy.

'Another phrase demands special consideration, because it is always cited with confidence by the advocates of the popular theory. This phrase occurs in Mark, and is thrice repeated †—"*Where their worm dieth not.*" This is an expressive image quoted from the prophet Isaiah; and an examination of the original passage will, I think, convince any candid inquirer that, instead of upholding the dogma of *eternal torment*, it is at *irreconcilable variance with it*. This expression is sometimes explained metaphorically, of the conscience which excites an eternal remorse in the bosoms of the wicked. But this is evidently not its meaning. The passage is as follows:—"And they shall go forth and look upon the carcases of the men that have transgressed against me; for *their worm shall not die*, neither shall their fire be quenched; and they shall be an abhorring unto all flesh." ‡ What the prophet states is simply this—that so numerous shall be these loathsome and putrefying *carcases*, that, hyperbolically speaking, *the worms will never make an end of feeding on them, nor the fire of consuming them*. A glance at the passage will at once convince that the meaning is *not* that the "worm" of *living* persons shall not die, but the "worm" of their "*carcases*;" so that what is here intended is the *putrefaction of dead bodies*, and *not* the exquisite eternal torment of the *living*. Like the "unquenchable fire," which will not be extinguished until it has completed its work, the undying worm will do its part in the complete demolition of the wicked. This expression, instead of implying, *excludes* the idea of *conscious and everlastingly protracted pain.*

'Much light may be cast upon the nature and duration of future punishment by a consideration of the term which, with *one* exception, to which I will presently refer, is always used in the original Scriptures to signify the *place* of future punishment. This term is *Gehenna*, or *Gehennem*, and is derived from two Hebrew words—*Ge*, a valley, and *Hinnom*, the name of a person at one time its possessor. The valley of Hinnom, situate near Jerusalem, had been the scene of those abominable sacrifices which the Jews had perpetrated when they burned

---

* Rather, *destruction*.   † Mark ix. 44, 46, 48.
‡ Isa. lxvi. 24.

alive their children to Baal and Moloch. There the disgusting remains of these horrid sacrifices were left to be consumed by fire and worms; and from this place the name was derived which denotes, both in the Hebrew and Greek tongues, the place of future punishment. If *analogy* had anything to do with this appropriation of the term Gehenna, it is difficult to see how *a loathsome valley of decomposing and smouldering human remains, which were being gradually consumed*, should fitly depict a state of conscious, unending misery as the punishment of the wicked. If the valley of Hinnom was a type of the Gehenna of the damned, the *unconsciousness* and *gradual consumption* of its *dead carcases* cannot portray the *consciousness* and *eternity* of *living persons*. Analogy suggests rather that suffering to be followed by the corruption of death is the portion of the guilty in the future righteous retribution.'—*Life and Death*. By the Rev. J. Panton Ham.

It should also be observed that even if the word 'unquenchable' did prove that the fire must literally burn for ever, the common argument, derived from the necessity of its being for ever supplied with fuel, would fail of its intended purpose. For the burning mass does not *consist of* the condemned. The fire is burning before they are cast into it, and may therefore, conceivably, burn on after they are consumed. The refuse, thrown into the fires of Tophet, outside the walls of Jerusalem, from which our Lord borrows His figure, was not the fuel that kept them burning. They were kept burning by suitable fuel, in order that the refuse thrown into them might be immediately consumed. The 'consuming fire' is God's wrath against sin. In one sense, it will burn for ever, His nature being unchangeable. But when He has reconciled all things to Himself by Christ, there will be nothing left for it to consume.

'ETERNAL PUNISHMENT.'

THE interpretation given in Sermon VI. of Matt. xxv. 46 is defective, from not taking the parable and its context sufficiently into account. Like the two preceding parables, it describes, but under another aspect, the separation that will be made, at our Lord's coming, between believers and unbelievers in the visible Church.* All three set forth the importance of being ready to meet the Lord when He comes. The first shows the necessity of possessing the Spirit of God in our hearts. The second shows the necessity of devoting ourselves to Christ's service. The third shows what is the essence of that holiness without which no man shall see the Lord, namely, love. The terms, in which the consequences of being accepted or rejected are described, rise in strength and dignity according to the different aspects under which our Lord presents Himself in the three parables. The Bridegroom merely refuses to acknowledge the careless virgins and to open the door for them, while those who are ready go in with Him to the marriage supper. The Master promises His faithful servants places of still higher trust, with immediate participation in His own rejoicing, while He orders the unfaithful servant to be bound hand and foot and cast into the darkness without, where he will bitterly lament his folly. The King raises His loyal subjects to a throne, while He drives away those who have been rebels at heart into 'everlasting fire.' But in each case the rewards and the punishments are but different aspects of the same things, namely, admission to or

* I am quite aware of the difficulties attaching to this view; but those attaching to every other interpretation that has been offered seem to me very much greater. If, however, it should be held that this last parable describes a judgment upon 'nations,' rather than individuals, it becomes still farther removed from lending any countenance to the doctrine of endless suffering.

It is, surely, somewhat remarkable that such an awful doctrine as that of eternal evil should be made so largely to depend upon two words picked out of a very much disputed parable; almost the only perfectly certain thing about it being that it does not describe the final judgment, but something which takes place at the coming of Christ to establish His kingdom upon the earth.

exclusion from the Millennial kingdom. The first parable suggests only the inauguration of it by the marriage feast; the second adds the element of continued and increased usefulness and honour; which the third raises to the height of reigning with Christ.

This gives precision to the meaning of the word *aionion* (age-long) as used in the last of the three parables. The 'æonial life,' *into* which the righteous then enter, is not the life, the indefeasible immortality, which they already possessed through the risen life of Christ having been communicated to them in regeneration; it is explained before to be 'the kingdom prepared for them from the foundation of the world,' or, as Christ elsewhere expresses it, the being 'counted worthy to obtain *that age* and the (*that*) resurrection from the dead.' No resurrection, it is true, is spoken of in these parables. They deal directly only with the living; but we know from other Scriptures that the dead will be judged on the same principles, and those who have died in the Lord *at the same time.* The living shall not anticipate 'them that are asleep.' All Christ's saints, living or dead, shall obtain *the life* of *that age* and inherit the kingdom. While, on the other hand, those who named the name of Christ, but were 'sensual, having not the Spirit,' who had 'faith without works,' and 'loved not the Lord Jesus Christ in sincerity,' will be disowned by Christ at His coming, refused admission to the marriage feast, cast into outer darkness, and suffer the age-long punishment of being associated with the devil and his angels, until the day of final judgment.

This is the 'everlasting destruction' spoken of in 2 Thess. i. 10; wherein also the subjects of it are those alone who are found in opposition to Christ at His coming; those who have died in such a state 'live not again till the thousand years are finished.'

Both expressions—'everlasting punishment' and 'everlasting destruction'—might well be applied to the utter destruction, soul and body, of the finally impenitent at the day of judgment. If 'redemption,' which has been already 'obtained' and will soon be completely accomplished, may be called 'eternal redemption,' because its *effects* will be eternal, and if the fire which consumed Sodom and Gomorrah, and has long since been extinguished, may be called 'eternal fire,' because its *effects* have continued through all succeeding ages, why may not the 'punishment' which consists of 'destruction' be called 'eternal,' because its *effects* will be final and irremediable? Eternal redemption is not necessarily eternal redeeming, eternal fire is not necessarily eternal burning, nor is eternal punishment necessarily eternal punishing, or eternal destruction eternal destroying. If it be asked, How can destruction or punishment be eternal, when there will be none left to destroy or punish? we reply by asking, How can redemption be eternal, when there will be none left to redeem? And when ridicule is thrown on the 'unspeakable folly' of saying that persons can suffer punishment after they have ceased to exist, we reply that, in the sense of *feeling pain*, the word 'suffering' could not of course be applied to anyone after his destruction; but that for so applying it in another sense, we have the authority of St. Jude, who speaks of Sodom and Gomorrah as still '*suffering* the vengeance of eternal fire' long after they have ceased to exist. And he justifies this, by reminding us that, in the perpetual memorial of their having been eternally destroyed by fire, 'they are set forth for an example.'

But in the passages where alone these two expressions occur they do not refer to the final judgment at all, but to the immediate destruction of Christ's enemies from off the earth when He comes in the clouds of heaven with power and great glory; that is, to the 'gathering out of His kingdom all things that offend and them that do iniquity.' The destruction is called 'age-long,' because it will result in the 'age-long punishment' of exclusion from the kingdom and confinement in outer darkness with the devil and his angels. What will befall them at the end of that period, whether the first 'destruction' is irremediable, or whether, as some maintain, it may bring any of them to repentance, is altogether another question. It is impossible to deny that some weight attaches to the argument drawn from the word κόλασις (rendered 'punishment'), which primarily means *correction*, as distinguished from τιμωρία, which means *retribution*. But there is much to be said on the other side; and I forbear to enter into the question, as it is quite unnecessary to my present purpose. It is possible to believe that *some* may obtain forgiveness in the world to come who have not obtained it in this world, without believing that *all* will do so. But even if it could be proved, which I entirely disbelieve, that salvation will again be offered to those who, with sufficient light and knowledge, reject it now, it would still remain a revealed truth that the *finally* impenitent will not be kept alive for ever in sin and misery, but be at last blotted out of creation by being destroyed, soul and body, in hell.

It may be objected that, in this view of the parable, the wicked are represented as enduring the punishment of 'fire' without being destroyed by it; and the same remark has been made on the fact of the beast and the false prophet, who are cast into the lake of fire at the beginning of the Millennium, being mentioned as if still alive at the end of it. But there is no inconsistency in this. Fire is the symbol of God's wrath against sin. And it by no means follows, because that 'consuming fire' must ultimately destroy every evil doer, that it can inflict no *less* punishment during any preceding period.

CORRECTION AND RETRIBUTION.

It is important to remember that the final punishment of the irreclaimably wicked will not be for their own sake. The superficial remarks, therefore, that are frequently made about destruction having no terrors for those who are without spiritual desires, simply fall to the ground. As long as punishment is corrective, that is, inflicted for the good of the persons punished, it is essential that they should feel its bitterness. But when it is purely retributive, that is, inflicted with no hope of benefiting the guilty, but solely to vindicate the majesty of the law, it is not of the smallest consequence whether they care about it or not, so long as it is something which the innocent would dread. Now, whatever may be thought of any preliminary punishment that the wicked may have to undergo, it is quite certain that the last stroke, which blots them out of existence, must be for the sake of others. Their destruction will be necessary, first, that the universe may be reconciled to God; and, secondly, to make them an eternal 'example' of the destructive nature of sin; to show to all intelligent creatures throughout eternity that evil *cannot* continue; that in Christ alone all things consist, and that, therefore, they *cannot* live apart from Him. How could it add clearness or force to this reason for God to put forth an exceptional energy of His almighty power, in order to maintain a multitude of His creatures in an unnatural and wretched state of existence for ever? Would it be impossible otherwise to make creatures who are yet to come *believe* that evil ever had wrought such destruction as we are told it shall yet work? Would *no* record, *no* memorial suffice to convince them that the wages of sin is death, unless they had perpetually before their eyes the spectacle of impenitent sinners who were *never* to die, but for ever to be spending an eternally dying life?

Are God's resources so limited that He would be driven to this, surely the very last expedient that He would have recourse to for any purpose whatever? His own word alone could make us believe it. And happily that word most positively assures us that no such thing shall ever happen. 'If there be one fact in the word of God clearer than another it is His settled purpose to destroy sin and sorrow out of His universe and to make all things new. The "destruction" of every creature who is not united to Christ, "who *only* hath immortality," is the revealed law of action. It is settled that a time is coming when God will be all in all. No being destitute of the Divine nature will exist in the universe of God when He shall have completed His most glorious purpose.'*

'THE SMOKE OF THEIR TORMENT.'

NONE of the replies that I have seen to my argument on this head attempt to touch the only question that has to be considered, namely, What does that highly figurative scene represent? However clear the *picture* may be in itself, the question remains, What is the *truth* which the Spirit of God means to depict by it? Nothing can be clearer than the meaning of the words 'angel' and 'stand' and 'sun' in another part of the same scene; but a right understanding of the *words* is only the first step towards ascertaining what is meant to be prefigured by an angel standing in the sun. And to fix the meaning of 'torment' and 'for ever' is only the first step towards ascertaining what is meant to be prefigured by the lake of fire, and all that is said about it. Our opponents have a perfect right

---

* Letter from Rev. Dr. Leask, editor of the *Rainbow*, to Mr. James Grant.

to press the word 'torment' in support of their view; and we have an equal right to press all those considerations which we believe incalculably outweigh it. If anyone maintained, from Jude verse 7, that the cities of Sodom and Gomorrah must still be a blazing mass of ruins, and their inhabitants be still writhing in the flames, whatever unbelieving or mistaken travellers may say to the contrary, we should scarcely admit that he had advanced very far towards establishing his position when he had proved the meanings ordinarily attached in Scripture to the words 'suffer,' 'vengeance,' 'eternal,' and 'fire.' We should still feel at liberty to consider whether the statement might not mean something more easily reconcileable with the evidence of our senses. They are, no doubt, liable sometimes to deceive us; but we must be able to place *some* dependence on them, or there could be no certainty about anything. Not less violently opposed to our moral sense is the interpretation that we are asked to put upon what is said of the 'lake of fire;' an interpretation, too, which directly contradicts the uniform teaching of the whole Bible from beginning to end. If Scripture is to be its own interpreter, there is an end of the question. That awful, but majestic, scene represents the final *destruction* of evil, and not the eternal perpetuation of it in its most aggravated and malignant forms. There is no 'lake of fire' in the 'new earth;' it has 'passed away' with the 'first earth,' upon which it was seen. The 'ages of ages' have elapsed, the 'smoke of their torment' has ceased to ascend, and in the eternal state 'there shall be no more death, neither sorrow nor crying, neither shall there be any more pain, for the former things have passed away.'

The two judgments by fire, the one before, the other after, the Millennium, are in exact accordance with the general teaching of Scripture on the same subject. The former is exclusively a judgment upon the living. The beast, the false prophet, and their adherents, being cast into the lake of fire, represents the destruction from off the face of the earth of all who are found in opposition to Christ at His coming—the gathering out of His kingdom all things that offend and them that do iniquity, and their being cast into a furnace of fire. The latter is the final judgment upon all evil doers, living and dead, wicked men and wicked spirits; together with the termination of all evil, physical as well as moral, represented by Death and Hades being cast into the lake of fire. In this judgment the wicked not only perish from off the earth, but are blotted out of creation; they are 'destroyed *soul* and body,' they ' lose *themselves*,' and perish everlastingly.

'From this stand-point we contemplate the final scene of retribution. There is heaven and there is hell. There is eternal life and there is eternal death. The redeemed enjoy the one: the lost are the subjects of the other. The Book of Revelation describes the latter—" Death and Hades were cast into the lake of fire. This is the second death." (Rev. xx. 14.) All that has been and continued to be evil: the fallen angels who now move in earth and air; the spirits who are kept in chains of darkness; the multitudes who have died without God and without hope; the multitudes whom the last day will find impenitent and unholy; have all been consigned to one common scene of punishment. According to their deserving is their chastisement. The time for each one's suffering over, he is wrapped in the slumber of eternal death. Gradually life dies out in that fearful prison until unbroken silence reigns throughout it. They who would not find life have found death. *But the scene remains for ever*. As Sodom and Gomorrha have exhibited to every succeeding generation of men the divine vengeance upon full-blown iniquity, so will the charred and burnt-out furnace of hell afford its eternal lesson to the intelligences of the future. As angels wing their way from world to world: as the redeemed touch with fresh delight their harps of gold: as new orders of spiritual life are called into existence by the Creator's hand: so the nature and the end of sin are always remembered in that scene where so many of the inhabitants of heaven and earth had bid an eternal farewell to the life which is so full of joy. That lesson of awe is read and pondered on by all. Doubtless it will be a lesson of mercy to myriads of whom we know nought as yet. But it will be a lesson read without the shudder of anguish. The dead know not anything. They have drunk the waters of Lethe, and forgotten long ago their misery. There is no eternal antagonism of good and evil: no eternal jarring of the notes of praise and wailing. Evil has died out, and with it sorrow. Throughout God's world of life all is joy, and peace, and love.'—*Rev. H. Constable.*

ETERNAL EVIL.

It has been objected to this expression that it is the punishment of evil, and not evil itself, that will be eternal. But punishment *is* an evil, however it may be overruled for good. Besides, one argument used to prove the certainty of endless punishment is that the condemned will be continually sinning, and therefore must be continually suffering. This was what I meant by saying that, according to the popular doctrine, 'the works of the devil will never be destroyed, but a portion of the universe be set apart for the eternal exhibition of them in their fullest maturity;' to which the writer in the *Bible Treasury* replies, in his usual style, 'It is a gross blunder; the punishment of the wicked is not the work of the devil; he is in the punishment himself.'

A striking illustration of the tendency of error to grow is afforded by a theory which Mr. Waller, tutor of St. John's Hall, Highbury, has propounded, to show the moral necessity for eternal evil: 'An incurably evil man is an agent far too powerful to be annihilated, if he can be employed;' which he explains to mean, that the wicked will be used to tempt other orders of beings yet to be created—the victims of their wiles being added to the number of the condemned, and 'perhaps' of the tempters; so that evil will be not only eternal, but eternally and indefinitely extending. Oh, blessed eternity to look forward to! It will scarcely have begun, when the hosts of immortal beings, waging eternal war with their Creator, writhing in agony under His mighty hand, yet defying Him to His face, and ever encouraged by repeated successes to fresh assaults upon His fair creation, will immeasurably exceed in number anything of which our finite minds can form the slightest conception. What loving heart can fail, in view of such a prospect, to 'rejoice with joy unspeakable and full of glory?'

This view harmonises remarkably well with that of President Edwards, and other thorough-going advocates of the popular doctrine, namely, that the sufferings of the condemned will enhance the joy and excite the hallelujahs of the redeemed. For here is a prospect of ever-fresh joy and ever-new hallelujahs opened up before them. Their love can never grow cold, or their praises languish; they will never need to hang their harps upon the willows, while multitudes are being constantly added to the number of the condemned, and the smoke of their torment ascends in ever denser and denser volume. As the wail of despair booms more heavily through the universe, it will only awaken louder shouts of triumph: the responsive echoes will reverberate from one to the other with ever-increasing power, until God's creation becomes—oh, what? Lord, open The eyes of thy servants to see the horror of horrors that their imagination has substituted for the glorious future set before us in Thy Word—of a universe reconciled to Thee, and Thyself 'all in all'!

Many of my opponents will repudiate this view; and therefore, to do them the utmost justice, I quote a passage of a very different kind from Delitzsch's ' Biblical Psychology ' (Clark's Library), which, they will readily admit, puts their case with consummate ability :—

'If the whole of creation were one being, it would indeed have to be perfected in such a manner as that the darkness should be in this one nature abolished in light. But, as the entire creation is an infinite number of beings, that triumph is then already perfected when those beings which have taken their stand in the principle of wrath are capable of nothing further in opposition to the Holy One, whose hereditary portion is in light, and which have become the footstool of God and of His Christ, i.e. the dark ground on which is enhanced the glory of the divine dominion. God is thus, moreover, "all in all." He who, in respect of His triune nature, is Love, embraces all who have laid themselves open to this love with the light of His glory; and all who have shut their hearts to this love He encircles with the darkness and the fire of His glory. Love has conquered. Evil is placed under bonds. There needs not its absolute annihilation that the six days of the world's history may close, as did that of the world's creation, with "everything very good." . . . Everything that redeeming love repelled to self-induration is for ever absorbed into the wrathful aspects of the glory, and there leads a life self-consuming, and, as it were, non-existent.'

The following brief observations are submitted :—

1. 'Capable of nothing further in opposition to the Holy One.'—Yes; they will be capable of hating Him, which, of all things, Love can least endure.

2. 'All [things] in all [persons].'—No; to some He will be only an object of terror.

3. 'He encircles with the darkness and the fire of His glory.'—How, then, can Christ 'reconcile all things to God?'

4. 'Love has conquered.'—No; it will be suffering an eternal defeat, and be eternally avenged by the triumph of Power.

5. 'Evil is placed under bonds.'—Not at all. It will merely be confined—though Mr. Waller will not even admit that—within a certain locality. And, to compensate for the restriction, it will be allowed to reign supreme, and to effect the highest conceivable triumph, without let or hindrance, in its own kingdom.

M

6. 'Everything very good.'—What is this but directly to 'call evil good'?

7. 'A life self-consuming, and, as it were, non-existent.'—How irrepressible the moral instinct which leads him unconsciously to acknowledge the self-contradiction of his hypothesis! An eternal 'self-consuming life' would be not 'as it were,' but really and truly 'non-existent.' It is an inherent impossibility, as well as in direct contradiction to God's own revelation.

To the direct Scriptural evidence already adduced against the eternity of evil, should be added St. Paul's declaration in 1 Cor. xv. 26, 'The last enemy that shall be destroyed is death.' Does not this imply that every enemy shall ultimately be destroyed—the victory being consummated by the destruction of death? And how can that be true, if the wicked are raised up to an everlasting life of sin and misery —if sin, the great 'enemy,' is to continue for ever? But, to borrow the language of the late Rev. W. de Burgh:—

'We believe, and we are well assured, that the time will come when we may traverse the whole of God's creation from the one end to the other, and not find a trace of sin or evil—not see the curse in any form —not hear a sigh or groan—not meet with an enemy of God; but when every heart that beats shall respond to His will, and every voice that sounds shall swell the chorus of His praise.'

If we may trust the *Paradise Lost*, it would appear that Milton was no believer in either the eternity of sin or the immortality of Satan. In Book II., line 734, Sin is represented as warning Satan and Death of

'His wrath, which one day will destroy ye both';

and, a little farther on, as addressing Satan thus:—

'Before mine eyes in opposition sits
Grim Death, my son and foe, who sets them on,
And me, his parent, would full soon devour,

> For want of other prey, but that he knows
> His end with mine involved; and knows that I
> Should prove a bitter morsel and his bane,
> Whenever that shall be: so Fate pronounced.
> But thou, O Father! I forewarn thee, shun
> His deadly arrow; neither vainly hope
> To be invulnerable in those bright arms,
> Though tempered heavenly; for that mortal dint,
> Save He who reigns above, none can resist.'

PS.—While these pages are passing through the press, the June number of the *Rainbow* has appeared. It contains a reply by Mr. Leonard Strong, of Torquay, to the admirable article on immortality by Mr. Maude, of Birkenhead, which was contained in the March number of the same magazine. In his rejoinder, Mr. Maude makes the following important remarks:—

'Mr. Strong thinks it is to be regretted that when I was led to bring the popular belief in the eternal duration of evil to the test of Scripture, I did not allow my thoughts to carry me back a little further, namely, to the original permission of evil; and endeavour to fathom that mystery also. To this it might suffice to reply that, whereas the 'mystery' in the one case is real, in the other it is only suppositive. That evil does actually exist is a fact which, however mysterious, cannot be questioned; but that it must and will necessarily exist to all eternity, is an inference which the Scriptures, as I read them, in nowise sanction. The objection, nevertheless, is a plausible one, and as it has been urged by much greater men than Mr. Strong, it may be worth while to consider it for a moment. Stated in the briefest form, it stands thus: "Seeing that God's goodness does permit so much evil to exist at present, may it not also permit still greater evil to exist through eternal ages?" I answer, that the premiss is by no means equal to the conclusion. Because God, not only without impeachment, but to the transcendent manifestation, of His divine goodness, permitted His only begotten Son to endure the temporary agony of the cross, it by no means follows that His goodness would have remained unimpeachable had He (*horresco referens*) permitted the Son of His love to endure that agony *to all eternity*! As a means to an end, the sufferings of Christ were not only consistent with, but most gloriously manifested, the Divine wisdom and love; and, in like manner, the temporal existence of evil, also as a means to an end, is quite consistent with those divine attributes; whereas its supposed eternal existence—which would make it an end as well as a means—cannot possibly be shown to be so. I do not, of course, intend to say that the recognition of its non-eternity completely solves the original mystery of the existence of evil; but I do unhesitatingly assert that it at least plucks the heart out of it. For, not only does it eliminate the portentous element of *infinity*, but it at the same time reduces it, in a great measure, from a moral to an intellectual difficulty. In a word, evil is to be regarded not as an end, but as the means employed by God for the attainment of an end, and only by a perfect acquaintance with the greatness and blessedness of that end can we justly estimate the wisdom and fitness of the means employed. It is no reflection on the skill of the human architect of some magnificent building, that *during its erection* he should find it expedient to use an unsightly scaffolding; but if, when the building was completed, it were found impossible to dispense with the scaffolding, would it not remain a monument of the architect's incapacity? In like manner, while the temporary permission of evil is at least conceivable, its supposed eternal existence is an insoluble problem.'

* * * * * *

'As regards my opponent's mode of dealing with those grand passages which so plainly assert the final deliverance of God's creation from all sin and sorrow, the matter simply amounts to this: that while such texts as appear to teach the hideous dogma of eternal torment are to be interpreted in the largest, most literal, and most offensive sense; such texts as, quite as strongly, teach this worthy and blessed consummation of the Creator's work, are to be explained, softened down, frittered away, lest, haply, they should be found to quench the fiery glories of an eternal hell. I must content myself with noticing only one specimen of Mr. Strong's exegesis, and its results. In reference to the sublime declaration of Rev. xxi. 1–5, that, in the new heavens and new earth, there shall be " no more death, neither sorrow, nor crying, neither shall there be any more pain (nor 'curse,' xxii. 3), because the former things have passed away, and all things are made new," he asserts that, while this will be true as far as the redeemed are concerned, the lost are nevertheless to be consigned to eternal torments in the lake of fire " in the centre of this globe." In other words, while the text distinctly declares that, in the "new earth," there shall be no more death, Mr. Strong asserts that *within it* death, in its most terrific form, shall eternally reign; while the text declares that there shall be no more pain, Mr. Strong holds that there will be eternal torment; and while the promise of the text is that there shall be "neither sorrow nor crying," Mr. Strong presumptuously asserts that there shall be unending "weeping, and wailing, and gnashing of teeth." Oh, but all this is to be covered up, and kept decently out of sight! As the murderer hides away the damning evidence of his guilt, so God is to hide away the terrible results of His sublime experiment in moral government from the eyes of His shuddering universe. But no, even this miserable relief cannot be conceded; for if in every other particular the language of Rev. xiv. 10, 11, is to be literally interpreted, so also must this, that those cast into the lake of fire are to be tormented for ever and ever "*in the presence of the holy angels, and in the presence of the Lamb.*" Never can the eyes of the redeemed be averted from the spectacle of their appalling misery; never shall the ears of the redeemed be closed to the hearing of their lamentable groans: the smoke of their torment will for ever and ever darken the new heavens, and their yells of agony to all eternity mingle with the music of celestial harps. *Can it be true?* And if it be, is not this a heaven only less to be dreaded than the fiery pit itself? But enough. With the moral argument Mr. Strong, very prudently, will have nothing to do. He simply casts dust into the air, and cries out— "The flesh! The flesh!" That is to say, in plain language, he dares not interrogate that moral consciousness—those innate convictions of truth and righteousness—which GOD (not the devil, as my opponent seems to imagine) has implanted in his spirit; because he knows what the response would surely be. Yet let him remember that the very apostle whose words he quotes, was not afraid to make such an appeal (Rom. iii. 4-6); and that when Abraham, in his sublime expostulation in behalf of the righteous inhabitants of Sodom, took upon himself to say to the Almighty, " That be far from Thee to do after this manner, *Shall not the judge of all the earth do right?*" the patriarch's appeal to his own moral consciousness was not only allowed by the Lord, but received from Him the most gracious answer.'

Though somewhat out of place here, I cannot forbear transcribing, without undertaking absolutely to endorse, the following thoughtful observations, from the same paper, on a very difficult branch of the subject:—

'The next point which it seems well to notice, is Mr. Strong's unhesitating assertion, "That death nowhere in the word of God means non-existence, but everywhere means a certain condition of existence." This somewhat bold statement raises the important and long-debated question, "What was the death threatened to and incurred by Adam?" In proceeding to answer it, I must first enquire, Whence was the literal and proper idea of death originally derived? *Beyond all doubt, it was from the death of the lower animals.* Science teaches us that many ages before the appearing of man upon this planet, death was the condition of animal existence, and the death of the inferior animals, a phenomenon with which he was acquainted, was the only kind of death of which Adam could have any conception. When, therefore, he was told, "In the day that thou eatest of the tree of the knowledge of good and evil, dying thou shalt die," he must necessarily have understood the punishment threatened to be death such as befell the lower animals; in other words, the extinction of his creaturely existence; and if this be not what was really intended, then the terms of the threatening were calculated only to deceive him—a supposition altogether repugnant to our ideas of the Divine veracity and benevolence. The death, therefore, which Adam was threatened with, in case of disobedience, and which he actually incurred, was death in the proper and ordinary acceptation of the word; that is, the absolute termination of that creaturely existence which God, at his creation, had conferred upon him. The only distinction between death in the case of a man, and death in the case of the mere animal, being that, while the animal dies once for all, the death of the body involving the termination of its existence, man dies by a double death, the first affecting only the body, but the second involving the extinction of the entire being. And this distinction, which, important as it is, does not at all affect the true definition of death, is only in necessary accordance with the peculiar constitution of man's nature. Had man possessed a *merely* animal existence, death would have been to him precisely what it is to any of the lower animals; but inasmuch as his nature was created *tripartite*, consisting of body, soul, and spirit (1 Thess. v. 23); and not, like the lower animals, *duplex*, consisting of soul and body (Gen. i. 30, *margin*), it follows of necessity that death in his case, in order to be final and entire, involves, not only that separation of the soul from the body, which constitutes death in the mere animal, but also the further separation of the soul from the spirit,* which latter might,

---

* 'The soul, which man has in common with the brute, would perish with the body, but for the spirit. It is the spirit which sustains the soul's consciousness after death, and supported by it, it arrests that dissolution to which it would otherwise tend.'—*Heard's Tripartite Nature of Man*, p. 177.

of course, as in fact it does, constitute a subsequent stage in the process of his dissolution.'

* * * * * *

'Further on, Mr. Strong writes, "Our Lord, when He died under judgment and wrath for our sins, was verily dead, but *never out of existence (of course I mean as man).*" I am not prepared to grant this in the sense intended. We stand here on the brink of a great and divine mystery. If the punishment threatened to, and incurred by, Adam was, as I have shown, the termination of his existence as a human being, and *if that punishment was really borne by Christ*, then I see not how we are to escape the conclusion that the death of Christ involved nothing less than the separation (for how long or how short a time I venture not to enquire) of His human soul from His human spirit, as well as of both of these from His human body.* In the light of this thought how significant and *definite* becomes the Messianic language of the Psalms. "I am counted with them that go down into the pit; I am as a man that hath no strength; free among the dead, like the slain that lie in the grave, whom Thou rememberest no more, and they are cut off by Thy hand. Thou hast laid me in the lowest pit, in darkness, in the deeps. Thy wrath lieth hard upon me, and Thou hast afflicted me with all Thy waves." (Ps. lxxxviii. 4–7.) "Save me, O God, for the waters are come in unto my soul. I sink in deep mire, where there is no standing; I am come into deep waters, where the floods overflow me. . . . . Deliver me out of the mire, and let me not sink; let me be delivered from them that hate me, and out of the deep waters. Let not the waterflood overflow me, neither let the deep swallow me up, and let not the pit shut her mouth upon me." (Ps. lxix. 1, 2, 14, 15.) So, in the gospels: "And He took with Him Peter and the two sons of Zebedee, and began to be sorrowful and very heavy. Then said He unto them, My soul is exceeding sorrowful, even unto death; tarry ye here, and watch with Me. And He went a little farther, and prayed, saying, O My Father, if it be possible, let this cup pass from Me; nevertheless, not as I will, but as Thou wilt. . . . . . And being in an agony, He prayed more earnestly, and His sweat was as it were great drops of blood falling down to the ground." (Matt. xxvi. 37–39; Luke xxii. 44.) In connection with these solemn passages, Heb. v. 7, demands our

---

* The great German commentator *Oldshausen* not only holds that there was such a separation of our Lord's soul and spirit, but that they were only reunited in the resurrection. See *Biblical Commentary on the Gospels.*

earnest attention: "Who, in the days of His flesh, when he had offered up prayers and supplications with strong crying and tears unto Him that was able to save Him *out of death* (ἐκ θανάτου), and was heard in that He feared." What means this strange and awful agony? What object had these prayers and supplications? That Christ so prayed to be delivered from the mere act of physical death, which many a martyr has borne with unflinching fortitude, cannot be supposed. These passages taken together, and considered in connection with the divine personality of the Lord Jesus, convey the idea of an anguish such as no mere man ever yet endured, and such as into the heart of any mere man it has never yet entered thoroughly to comprehend. And while it is easy and orthodox to say that it was the hiding of His Father's countenance which thus appalled Him, it is plain from the last quoted passage that what Christ really prayed to be saved out of was *death*, not simply wrath; yet not the death of the body alone, for in that, if He prayed concerning *it*, He was not heard. But it may be said if this be indeed the sense in which we are to understand the nature of Christ's atoning death; if His humanity was thus—even for a moment—utterly dissolved and broken up; then, awful thought! Christ has perished, His personal identity has come to an end, and the dark waters of death have indeed gone over His soul! No: for here the grand fundamental doctrine of the incarnation comes in. That this must indeed have been the case had Christ been a mere man is perfectly true; but, be it ever remembered, He was God as well as man; the personality appertained to the Divine nature, not to the human, and, therefore, though the union between the elements—body, soul, and spirit—of His most true humanity was suspended, the union between each one of those elements and His divine nature never was, the divine nature constituting a still abiding, all comprehending element, in which they were held together, and in which they were re-united for ever. And thus, in a far deeper and truer sense than Mr. Strong contemplates, was the soul-man brought to nought in the death of Christ, and we are new created, begotten again into a new life by the resurrection of Jesus Christ from the dead.'

MORAL EFFECTS OF THE POPULAR DOCTRINE UPON CHRISTIANS.

'EVEN on the best of men its influence has always been *heart-hardening*. "The Fathers" must have been *petrified* before they could teach that "*infants* departing from the body without baptism are certainly in damnation;"* that "the bliss of the saved will be greatly enhanced *by their being permitted to gaze* upon the punishment of the wicked;" † and that "the elect, while they see the unspeakable sufferings of the ungodly, *intoxicated with joy*, will thank God for their own salvation." ‡ And what an *indurating* process must have gone on, before, in later days, so good a man as Dr. Hopkins could have brought himself, in common with thousands of others, to affirm that "should eternal punishment cease, and the fire (of hell) be extinguished, it would in great measure obscure the light of heaven, and *put an end to a great part* of the happiness and glory of the blessed;" § or before, in our own, a Christian minister, editing a magazine devoted to the promotion of Christian union and benevolent effort, could bring himself to say that "the tender mercies of those who would throw down some of the pavement of heaven to cover over the pit of hell are cruel (to the saved!)"

'It seems *impossible* that any divine truth could ever occasion a state of mind so utterly *unchristian* as is indicated in sentiments like these.

* * * * * *

'*Intolerance* in relation to this subject can, in a free country like our own, scarcely go farther than it has done, since it has issued in a *terrorism* so abject, that the lips of thousands are now sealed by the mere fear of consequences. Well do those who have evoked this demon know, that few men *can afford to discuss*, and that most men will dread to examine, a topic so fenced by social penalties as is the doctrine under consideration. Mr. Barlow says, "I have scarcely ever seen a clergyman who could hear eternal punishment doubted without complimenting his opponent as an infidel or an atheist." Surely this temper of mind, *utterly unchristian* as it is, indicates a secret consciousness that the point in question can only retain its hold on men by the force of constant and vehement assertion.

'The *practical result* of such pressure may be seen in a state of things described by John Foster as *existing* even in his day, but which since then has become so common as scarcely to excite notice. He says, "A number, not large, but *of great piety and intelligence*, of ministers within my acquaintance have been disbelievers of the doctrine of eternal punishment; at the same time, *not feeling themselves imperatively called upon to make a public disavowal*, they content themselves with employing in their ministrations strong general terms in denouncing the doom of impenitent sinners." Recent avowals made in more than one of our most orthodox religious magazines are equally painful.

---

* Augustine.   † Aquinas.
‡ Peter Lombard.   § Works, ii. 457, 458.

'Tried, therefore, by the tone of mind it has fostered, and by the perversions of Scripture to which the necessity for defending it has given rise, no less than by its effects on the community at large, the doctrine fails to establish its divinity—*the tree does not bring forth good fruit.*

* * * * * *

'But a *third* test may be applied. *All truth*, before it can be influential, *must be realized*. But this doctrine is, from its very nature, and by the admission of its warmest defenders, incapable of being realized.

'Dr. Archer Butler does not scruple to say, that "were it possible for man's imagination to conceive the horrors of such a doom, all reasoning about it were at an end; it would scorch and wither all the powers of human thought. Human life were at a stand, could these things be really felt as they deserve. It is God's mercy," he adds, "that we can *believe* what adequately to conceive of were death." Surely the question may be put, Is it reasonable to suppose that God calls upon us to believe (even if it were possible to do so) *anything* which, if realized in the mind, would produce death or madness, and which, if true, "*ought* to separate the two sexes in monasteries and nunneries, so that at all events the accursed race should increase no more?"'—*Tracts for Thoughtful Christians.* By Henry Dunn.

As a specimen of the uncharitable dogmatism referred to above, take the following extract from a recent tract by 'An Old Soldier'—

'But how any clergyman of the Church of England, holding such views, can stand up before God and man and unhesitatingly lead his congregation in repeating the portions of the three Creeds above referred to, and then teach another gospel, is both lamentable and inexplicable.'

Observe, first, how he denounces those who differ from his interpretation of Scripture on future punishment, as teaching ' *another gospel*; ' which, according to St. Paul, renders any-one 'accursed.' And, secondly, how he assumes that every-one must necessarily understand the creeds in the same sense that he does; although the highest ecclesiastical court in this realm has formally condemned that assumption, and decided that the language is ambiguous.

So, another anonymous writer asks, 'How can Mr. Minton pray every Sunday, "From Thy wrath, and from everlasting damnation, good Lord deliver us," when he believes damnation is not everlasting?' The answer to which is, that damnation, like the 'eternal fire' that destroyed Sodom and Gomorrah, is everlasting *in its effects;* the condemned will 'perish everlastingly.'

THE DIVINE CHARACTER AND THE HUMAN CONSCIENCE.

SOME of our opponents express themselves rather strongly upon this point. Take the following, from Mr. Grant:—

'I speak with a thorough conviction of the truth of what I say, when I affirm that those who have come to the conclusion that future punishments will not be eternal, do assume, in almost every instance, that conclusion, not from the statements of Scripture, but from the substitution of their own feelings for what the law and testimony say on the subject. Instead of submitting with humility to the utterances of the Word of God, in relation to the destiny and duration of the wicked in the world to come, and bringing their own feelings into subjection to the volume of inspiration, they first of all resign themselves to the dictates of their own feelings, and then so interpret the holy oracles as to make them accord with the conclusions to which they have come. They presumptuously erect themselves into judges, guided only by their own feelings, as to what God may or may not do in His dealings, in a future state, with those who have lived and died in their sins; and then resolutely refuse to listen to the plain teachings of the Bible on the subject. They thus deliberately incur the awful guilt of deciding what must be the principles on which God will administer His moral government, so far as relates to the wicked, in that state of being which succeeds the present. This is practically setting themselves up as above God—as being wiser than God. *They* are, in effect, to be—not Jehovah—the arbiters of the destiny of the ungodly in the world to come.'

Yet this is the writer who complains that I show no 'charity' towards my opponents, that I 'make no allowance for them,' and 'load them with condemnation;' charges which are as purely fictitious as the opening statement in the preceding paragraph.

In a similar strain writes an excellent clergyman, whose name I withhold from personal regard:—

'We are at God's bar, and not God at our bar. Men talk as if they must needs vindicate and clear the character of God from the suspicion cast on it by His poor erring short-sighted creatures. Men talk as if the Eternal Jehovah were to be summoned to the judgment bar of their finite consciousness in order to be tried on these questions, Why was sin permitted? How can its existence be consistent with love? must there not be an end to the punishment even of the lost? And they talk as if they would wish to dismiss Jehovah from their judgment bar, with a certificate of His character being freed from suspicion. O proud man, when wilt thou learn to *beware* instead of judging? when wilt thou learn that thou must stand before the bar of God, and not venture in thy arrogance to summon God to the bar of thy judgment? when wilt thou learn to submit thy reason to Omniscient love, and in child-like faith and implicit trust rest on Him who is too wise to err and too good to be unkind, and who teaches respecting all mysteries, "What I do, thou knowest not now, but thou shalt know hereafter."'

All this is merely an unworthy caricaturing of those who seek to justify the ways of God to man, and remove the veil which human infirmity and Satanic craft have cast over the revelation that He has been pleased to make of His own righteousness and love. The fallacy of it will become apparent if we apply such reasoning to another of the Divine attributes—that of Truth. Suppose some one admitted the Bible to be the Word of God, but at the same time avowed that he had no confidence in either its threatenings or its promises, because, although God was perfect truth and it was impossible for Him to lie, yet our finite minds were incompetent to judge what course of action was consistent or inconsistent with truth *in Him*. If His promises were to fail, it might *seem* like lying, according to the 'finite consciousness' of us 'poor erring short-sighted creatures;' and, no doubt, for *us* to beguile one another by holding out deceptive allurements would be highly immoral. But who would dare to incur 'the awful guilt of deciding what must be the principles on which God will administer His moral government?' Wilt thou ' venture in thy arrogance to summon God to the bar of thy judgment,' and decide that He must necessarily keep His word, on pain of being made a liar? ' O proud man, when wilt thou learn to beware, instead of judging?'

Would not our opponents think that such reasoning was in the highest degree dishonouring to God's character, and that it turned His revelation of Himself into a mockery? Would they not endeavour to ' vindicate and clear the character of God from the suspicion cast on it by His poor erring shortsighted creatures,' and, as far as reason and argument could do it, ' wish to dismiss Jehovah from their judgment bar with a certificate of His character being free from suspicion'? Would they not urge that any revelation of Himself which God is pleased to make to us *can only* be addressed to 'our ideas,' and that if we are unable to form any opinion, from those ideas, of what He will or will not do, in consequence of such revelation, it cannot be of the slightest use to us?

Then why do they denounce us for making the same reply to them? We say that ' God is not unrighteous' to keep any of His creatures alive for ever in a state of hopeless misery. The whole Bible declares that He will do no such thing; and even we, ' short-sighted' as we are, can yet see how utterly inconsistent it would be with all that He Himself has revealed of His own justice and love. We are quite willing to weigh any arguments that may be brought against either of these positions; but when our brethren call us ' proud,' and accuse us of ' awful guilt,' ' apostacy,' ' infidelity,' and ' blasphemy,' because we maintain them, they do us a grievous wrong and sin against Christ.

Let it be observed too, in this connection, that the popular argument, derived from our alleged absolute inability to form the least idea as to what would or would not be an act of love or justice in the Divine Being, deprives the Gospel of all its power. For that power consists in the revelation which it makes of God's righteous love; not merely by a miraculously attested *declaration* of it, but by such a *manifestation* of it as is calculated to reach the human heart and conscience, and make us love Him whom *we see* to have first loved us. But if our moral incapacity to apprehend such matters be as complete as some of our opponents contend, there is nothing left in us to which the Gospel can appeal. Besides, St. John tells us that God's love is begotten in those who are born of Him, so that, whatever may be thought of the unregenerate, it is hard to believe that God's own children can understand nothing whatever of the 'Divine nature,' of which they themselves are made 'partakers.'

The following observations of Mr. Birks may be read with profit:—

'But if the thought would revolt us in the dealings of an earthly ruler, what is there, in the Almighty Power of God, to erase those moral outlines, which His own hand has engraven upon the consciences of men? "Far be it from God that He should do wickedness, and from the Almighty that He should commit iniquity."'

And again—

'In this case the sin of the Pharisees, with respect to the ceremonies of the law, has been transferred to the deeper mysteries of the Gospel; and heavy burdens, grievous to be borne, have been laid upon the natural conscience, which the imposers have not cared to lighten with one of their fingers. A strange notion seems almost to have been entertained, that faith was magnified, in proportion as the truths of revelation were presented in a shape repulsive to the moral instincts of thoughtful men. When conscience has been disposed to revolt against the burden, it has been sought to silence it by an appeal to the authority of the Bible, without any answering efforts to enlighten it on the ways of Divine Providence. The great enemy of souls has seized the advantage given him by a misdirected championship of truth.'

And again—

'Now it is not enough to say that the facts are revealed, and that God is just and holy, good and wise, and therefore all farther inquiry is presumptuous and dangerous. The conscience of man is too mighty a power to be set at rest by theological evasions. We may not, without folly, expect in this life to see all the reasons of the Divine counsels: but when we build up laboriously a human system on the basis of revealed facts, we are bound to inquire that the results shall not clash violently with the consenting voice of Scripture and reason, concerning the fundamental attributes of the Most High. We are not at liberty to call that conduct justice and wisdom in the Almighty, which we should charge with folly or cruelty in a human governor, nor to silence doubts which may have arisen from our own unskilful handling of the Word of Life, by a bare appeal to the Divine Sovereignty, as if the Most High were exalted above those eternal laws of justice and goodness which are binding on all the reasonable creatures He has made. This is nothing else than that sin of accepting persons, which the God of truth and holiness has so sternly and repeatedly condemned. Such erring advocates of Divine truth, however sincere in their mischievous course, must expect to hear from Him the reproof which Job addressed to his friends —" Will ye speak wickedly for God? and talk deceitfully for Him? Will ye accept His person? Will ye contend for God? Is it good that He should search you out? He will surely reprove you, if ye do secretly accept persons."'—*Difficulties of Belief.*

I am not claiming Mr. Birks as an advocate of my view; but the principles, so forcibly expressed above, are the strongest possible condemnation of the popular doctrine.

The remarks of another writer, also differing (apparently) from my conclusion, are well worthy of consideration:—

'If after a candid examination of Scripture, we remain in doubt whether or not the old dogmatic position is untenable, we ought carefully to weigh the arguments which proceed on moral and intellectual grounds, and to seek in them the supplementary aid we need. It can scarcely be denied, indeed some of the most strenuous maintainers of the dogma of an everlasting hell have admitted, that the dogma strains our faith in God to the utmost, and is quite at variance with what the sense of fitness, order, and justice demands. Sin and disorder may prevail largely in this temporary and transition state, but reason and piety bid us cherish the expectation that in the future and eternal state, sin and disorder will be alleviated, and at length made to cease. To imagine (without necessity laid upon us by perspicuous revelation) the imperfections, iniquities, wrongs, and woes of the present life, carried onward, aggravated, and immortalised, is to indulge in conjectures which border on blasphemy, which double most difficulties, relieve none, and go far to render faith in the High and Holy One an impossibility.

'If God is in truth our Almighty Creator, how can there be in us, His creatures, moral disorders which He will *never* be able to rectify or subdue? The resistance to the Divine will which the eternity of penal sufferings implies, is no limited or temporary resistance, but an unlimited, infinite resistance, which baffles all the resources of Omnipotence, and leaves the Creator no choice, but to smite and harass in vindictive anger, the creatures He has tried in vain to conquer. For we must bear in mind, that unless Christianity is a cunningly devised fable, the Almighty has taken the field against moral evil, and declared Himself to be its eternal unchanging foe. He has shown that there is nothing so truly opposed to His nature, nothing which He is so determined to overcome, as sin; but an everlasting hell, crowded with hosts of tortured sinners, would be an everlasting witness that He is unable to effect His purpose, and that, in spite of His utmost efforts, sin will hold its own. If redemption, when rightly understood, attests the hatefulness, does it not also, when rightly understood, predict the ultimate conquest of human sin? Has perfect wisdom united to Omnipotence, employed means so costly, to win a final result of doubtful victory, and incomplete success?

* * * * * *

'These are questions which the maintainers of the traditional dogma dare not face. They take refuge in emphatic avowals of human ignorance, and against appeals to reason, conscience, and the broad features of God's revealed character, they adopt a tone of protest and rebuke which there is nothing to justify or excuse. It is easy to exclaim, "Who are we that we should ask whether this or that is consistent with the wisdom, the justice, or the love of God? We, who take these liberties with the attributes of God, who are we but criminals? What right have we to murmur against our Lord, accusing His justice or mercy in punishing?" We can, perhaps, imagine circumstances in which language of this kind might be applicable. Hopeless, never ending misery for the lost, might have been revealed so distinctly and indubitably, as to make objections on moral grounds defiant and presumptuous. But it has not been so revealed, and, therefore, objections on moral grounds have a claim to a patient hearing, and are, in fact, a part of the evidence on which our conclusions must be built. They are not murmurings against our God, but against misapprehensions about God; they do not accuse His justice or mercy, but vindicate His justice and mercy against the defamations of human systems and errors. And no reasonable man, unfettered by the requirements of a theory, will venture to affirm that, because we are criminals, we have lost our moral nature, and are incapacitated from estimating the justice or injustice of our sentence.

* * * * * *

'The discretion which shuns being "wise above what is written," has been grievously violated, and with no good results, in proclaiming an eternity of future penalties. The fear of an eternal hell has not preserved the world from sin, and made men just, and temperate and holy, in a sufficient degree to encourage us to cling to it as more effective than the fear of a certain, righteous, retribution. The sense of the heinousness of sin is not deepened in sane minds by denouncing against sin an unspeakably awful vengeance, repugnant alike to God's character, and man's conceptions of justice and mercy. What is thought to be unjust and cruel soon ceases to be dreaded, and becomes practically impotent for the purposes of restraint. The most persistent assertions will not make efficient, threatenings which men do not in their hearts believe an Almighty, redeeming, and gracious God will execute. The very awfulness of the penalty discredits its reality; belief in a future retribution of any kind is weakened; and moral influence is lost, just in proportion as an eternity of torment is proclaimed. Unless our moral and intellectual constitution is changed—unless the broad features of justice and love which mark God's revelation in Christ Jesus our Saviour are swept away, sound and educated minds will shrink from the faith that endless misery is the *certain* doom of sinners. Whatever the lips may profess, the heart and intellect will revolt; doubts, which at least seem to rest on the surest moral and intellectual grounds, will intrude themselves, and in the presence of these the threatened penalty can have but slight deterring power. It has, I am aware, been suggested that such doubts have their source in a perversely rebellious heart, and in the secret dreads of an accusing conscience. The suggestion is uncharitable and insolent. The sentiments which Christianity itself inspires take up and intensify all the reasons which the understanding and natural affections set in array against the doctrine of endless life in endless pain. Men who love in their inmost hearts the God whose moral glory shines in the character of the Lord Jesus Christ, find in the strength of their love, the measure of their repugnance to the hideous thought, that vast multitudes of their fellow-creatures are to mourn for ever, beneath the merciless abandonment, or the still more merciless visitations, of their Creator and Redeemer. And a doctrine which cannot establish itself in the minds of numbers of cultivated, earnest, and pious men, is not likely to be so taught or so received as to be practically a restraint on the ignorant, the careless, and the ungodly. A fictitious, easy way of escape is contrived against a danger which is too frightful to be other than fictitious, and the consequence is that the standard of holiness is lowered, and the requirements of the Gospel pared down, to meet the supposition that Christians of frivolous and unfaithful, though not of scandalously sinful lives, are in peril of sinking into the agonies of utterly hopeless damnation. Whatever our theories may be, we dare not unflinchingly avow that such persons have, by missing salvation, fallen within the grasp of the horrible, everlasting alternative—and so, we talk as if salvation were an arbitrary and sudden act of mercy—we use freely the language of hope, and practically, though not intentionally, build each other up in the delusion that Christ came to save us in our sins, and not to cleanse us from our sins. Observation and experience bear no doubtful witness that this is one evil into which the commonly professed belief in the everlasting misery of the lost has betrayed us.'—*Rev. J. Burton.*

THE DESERT OF SIN.

What a contrast between the unnatural exaggerated representation of Sin's desert, given by popular theology, and the plain, simple, intelligible, yet tremendous declaration of God's word—' The soul that sinneth, it shall *die* !' How the one violates all our moral instincts; how the other commends itself to the universal conscience of mankind ! How impossible really to feel that the sins of a finite being during a limited period can deserve an eternity of suffering; how easy to recognise ' the judgment of God, that they which commit such things are worthy of *death* !'

Every moral creature is indebted solely to the good pleasure of God for calling him into existence, and is dependent upon Him each moment for the continuance of his life. If, therefore, he refuses to use his life in his Maker's service, is it likely that he will be allowed to retain possession of it? Life is the all-comprehensive trust committed to him by the Creator. If he abuses it, the trust is withdrawn. What can be more righteous, more God-like? What can be farther removed at once from weakness or from cruelty? How perfectly every object is attained by this act of justice! What possible gain could accrue from leaving him in possession of the life that he has misused, and allowing him to continue in sin and misery for ever? Absolutely none. While the loss would be enormous; for it would keep the universe in eternal discord.

What amount of suffering the sinner may have to undergo while life remains to him, is another question. On that point we only know, and only need to know, that in every case the stripes will be exactly proportioned to the heinousness of the offence, which the Judge of all the earth is alone competent to estimate. When, however, God resolves to spare the rebel no longer, but to inflict upon him the extreme penalty of the law, the righteousness of the sentence is patent to all. The conscience of the universe is satisfied, and all creation can say —Amen.

THE DOOM OF JUDAS.

The following remarks occurred in a leading article of the *Rock*:—

'Again, Mr. Minton's theory of destruction reduces the Divine threatenings to a sinner to the very extreme of absurdity, as in the case of the sinner whose future doom will be so intolerable that it would have been better for him if he had not been born. (See Matt. xxvi. 24.) This single text goes to the very root of the whole question, and utterly annihilates Mr. Minton's annihilation theory. In that solemn and awful declaration *two alternative conditions* were present to the mind of our blessed Redeemer—a condition of continued *existence* after *death in torment*, and a condition of *non-existence* before the life of the traitor Judas began. Here our Lord pointedly and positively *contrasts* the terrors and the torments that await Judas in a future state of suffering with the "better" lot that would have been his had he never been born—that is, to put it briefly, our Lord contrasts the *existence* of the wicked in a future state with their *non-existence* before their birth, and thus *totidem verbis* not only asserts what Mr. Minton denies, the continued existence of the wicked in a future state, but shows it forth in the strongest of all terms by contrasting it expressly with its *opposite—non-existence*. If a painter (who is presumed to be the best judge of colours) tells us to use *white* as a colour, and points to it expressly as the very opposite of *black*, by way of contrast, what are we to think of the amateur who persists in advising us to use *black* because *white* is a colour he cannot reconcile to his reason and notion of art? Equally absurd, we contend, is Mr. Minton's theory in the case of Judas, if he will persist in interpreting future punishment as non-existence, which punishment our Lord Himself not only asserts to be existence, but actually contrasts with non-existence.'

Observe, first, how the writer misrepresents my view of future punishment to be mere 'non-existence.'* Secondly, how he begs the whole question, as to *what* was 'present to the mind of our blessed Redeemer.' Thirdly, how entirely his own statement of it would fail to touch the question whether the 'continued existence after death in torment' was to be *endless* or not. Fourthly, how he assumes that anyone who declines to accept his dictum as to what was present to our Lord's mind, when He darkly but awfully spoke of some terrible doom awaiting the traitor, can only be influenced to act with such 'absurd' perverseness, by not being able to 'reconcile it with his reason.' And lastly, how triumphantly he believes himself to have made out by such a chain of reasoning that 'this passage goes to the root of the whole question,'—which it literally does not touch.

* Similarly the editor of the *Achill Herald* confounds everlasting destruction with disbelief in any future state. 'St. Paul does indeed mention the doctrine of annihilation, but only to condemn it. There were some who used it to make themselves easy in the indulgence of their lusts. They said, "Let us eat and drink, for to-morrow we die."'

It is certainly fatal to Universalism, even on Mr. Birks' ingenious view of the word 'good.' But upon Destructionism it has absolutely no bearing whatever; unless the editor maintains that Judas enjoyed during his lifetime such a wonderful amount of happiness, that neither the remorse which drove him to suicide, nor any mental anguish that he has since undergone, nor any suffering he may yet have to endure, if it be short of *endless* suffering, nor all of them together, could so overbalance it, that it would have been better for him never to have been born.

The above extract, if thoroughly digested, may be of invaluable service to those who are apt to be frightened by bold assertion, and to suppose that where there is so much smoke there must be some fire. It will be of special use in reading Mr. Grant's book.

PLATO AND THE NEW TESTAMENT.

'WE have brought forward a variety of phrases from the New Testament. We have now to consider the mighty bearing on their meaning of the fact that this New Testament *is written in the Greek tongue.* In that tongue all these phrases are to be found. Before the Gospel was preached, their meaning was fully established in the cultivated and the common mind of the human race. What is more—they were all in common use, and applied to, and their sense established, *with reference to this very point now under discussion.* The immortality of the soul was not a question for Jewish and Christian thought alone; it was the question of questions for the universal human mind. In particular it was the question of questions in the various schools of Grecian Philosophy. One of the noblest specimens of human reasoning, building its lofty superstructure on uncertain data, that has ever charmed, exalted, and, for our part we must add, bewildered the human intellect, is found in the dying discourse of Socrates to his friends, handed down to a deathless fame in the "Phædo" of Plato. Its object was to prove the immortality of the soul—that it could never cease to be—that through whatever changes it might pass, whatever pollutions it might suffer, whatever fearful torments it might endure, there was the deathless principle of the human soul which asserted an eternal life and utterly refused to die. It could never be, according to Plato, a thing of yesterday, an existence of the past but not of the present, a figure once jotted down in the book of life and then blotted out of it for ever. In what terms is the denial of its mortality conveyed? In the very terms in which the punishment of the wicked is asserted in the New Testament. Where this latter says the soul shall die, Plato says it shall not die; where this latter says it shall be destroyed, Plato says it shall not be destroyed; where this latter says it shall perish and suffer corruption, Plato says it shall not perish, and is incorruptible. The phrases are the very same, only that what Plato denies of all souls alike, the New Testament asserts of some of the souls of men. But the discussion of the question was not confined to the school of Plato or to his times. Every school of philosophy took it up, whether to confirm Plato's view, or to deny it, or to heap ridicule upon it. All the phrases we have been discussing from the New Testament had been explained, turned over and over, handled with all the power of the masters of language, presented in every phase, so that of their sense there could be no doubt, nor could there be anyone ignorant of their sense, before Jesus spoke, or an Evangelist or Apostle wrote. The subject had not died out before the days of Christ. It never could and never will die out. In every city of the Roman world were schools of Grecian thought in the days of the Apostles. In every school the question before us was discussed in the phrases and language of the New Testament. In Jerusalem and Rome, and Corinth, and Philippi, and Ephesus, and Thessalonica—wherever a Christian preacher opened his mouth to speak to man of his future destiny—were Platonists, or Epicureans, or Stoics, or Alexandrians, to whom the question of the soul's immortality was a question of constant thought, with whom the phrases in which the preacher addressed them as to their solemn future were familiar household words. Their language was his language, whether he spoke or wrote; their terms were his terms, and their meaning his meaning, else there were perplexities without a clue, logomachies without an end. And what did the Christian preacher declare, and the Christian writer write to that world-wide community which was ruled and bound together, not merely by the power of Roman will, but by the sceptre of the Grecian tongue? In Sermon and Disputation, in Gospel and History and Epistle and Revelation, the propagators of the new religion asserted of the persons of the wicked—i.e. of souls and bodies reunited at the resurrection—that which Plato had denied could happen to any soul. The cultivated intellect of the world, as well as the popular mind, read in the words of Christ, of Paul, of John, of Peter, of James, that what one of its sects of philosophy taught could happen to no soul; and what another taught should happen to all souls, the rising school of the Nazarene taught would happen to those whom its phraseology described as "unjust," "wicked," "unbelievers." Plato's noble conception, itself but the utterance of the longing of the human heart for its original inheritance, was taken up by the New Testament, only that it had here given to it its true direction, and had the eternal life after which it yearned connected with the God of Life manifested in His Son. In Jesus Christ was that "Life" which Plato fancied to exist in the soul itself. This Life He would bestow upon His people, realising more than the conception of Plato. But away from Him there was no life. On those who would not come to Him there would come finally—after stripes few or many—the end pictured for all by Epicurus. The Gospel brought together the fragments of truth scattered throughout human systems. Those who would soar it raised to God; those who would revel in the sty of sensuality it sunk to the state of the beasts that perish.'—*Rev. H. Constable.*

ARCHBISHOP WHATELY ON FUTURE PUNISHMENT.

The Scriptures do not, I think, afford us any ground for expecting that those who shall be condemned at the last day as having wilfully rejected or rebelled against their Lord will be finally delivered; that their doom, and that of the evil angels, will ever be reversed.

What that doom will be—whether the terms in which it is commonly spoken of in Scripture—'death,' 'destruction,' 'perishing,' &c., are to be understood figuratively, as denoting immortal life in a state of misery, or, more literally, as denoting a final extinction of existence—this is quite a different question. It is certain that the words, 'life,' 'eternal life,' 'immortality,' &c., are always applied to the condition of those, and of those only, who shall at the last day be approved as 'good and faithful servants,' who are to 'enter into the joy of their Lord.'

'Life,' as applied to their condition, is usually understood to mean 'happy life.' And that theirs will *be* a happy life, we are indeed plainly taught; but I do not think we are anywhere taught that the word 'life' does of itself necessarily imply happiness. If so, indeed, it would be a mere tautology to speak of a 'happy life,' and a contradiction to speak of a 'miserable life,' which we know is not the case, according to the usage of any language. In all ages and countries, 'life,' and the words answering to it in other languages, have always been applied, in ordinary discourse, to a wretched life, no less properly than to a happy one. Life, therefore, in the received sense of the word, would apply equally to the condition of the blest and of the condemned, supposing these last to be destined to continue for ever, living in a state of misery. And yet to *their* condition the words 'life' and 'immortality' never are applied in Scripture. If, therefore, we suppose the hearers of Jesus and His Apostles to have understood, as nearly as possible in the ordinary sense, the words employed, they must naturally have conceived them to mean (if they were taught nothing to the contrary) that the condemned were really and literally to be 'destroyed,' and cease to exist; not that they were to exist for ever in a state of wretchedness. For they are never spoken of as being kept alive, but as *forfeiting* life; as, for instance, 'Ye will not come to Me that ye might *have life*;' 'He that hath the Son hath life; and he that hath not the Son of God hath *not* life.' And again, 'perdition,' 'death,' 'destruction,' are employed in numerous passages to express the doom of the condemned; all which expressions would, as I have said, be naturally taken in their usual and obvious sense, if nothing were taught to the contrary.

That these expressions, however, are to be understood not in their ordinary sense, but figuratively, to signify an immortality of suffering, is inferred by a large proportion of

Christians from some other passages; as, where our Lord speaks of 'everlasting punishment,' 'everlasting fire,' and of being 'cast into hell, where their worm dieth not, and the fire is not quenched.'

This last expression of His is taken from the book of the prophet Isaiah (lxvi. 24), who speaks of 'the carcases of the men that have transgressed, whose worm shall not die, neither shall their fire be quenched; and they shall be an abhorring unto all flesh;' describing evidently the kind of doom inflicted by the eastern nations on the vilest offenders, who were not only slain, but their bodies deprived of the rites of burial, and either burned to ashes (which among them was considered a great indignity), or left to moulder above ground, and be devoured by worms.

From such passages as these, it has been inferred that the sufferings—and, consequently, the life—of the condemned is never to have an end. And the expressions will certainly bear that sense, which would, perhaps, be their most obvious and natural meaning, if these expressions were the only ones on the subject that are to be found in Scripture. But they will also bear another sense, which, if not more probable in itself, is certainly more reconcileable with the ordinary meaning of the words 'destruction,' etc., which so often occur. The expressions of 'eternal punishment,' 'unquenchable fire,' etc., may mean merely that there is to be *no deliverance*—no revival, no restoration—of the condemned. 'Death,' simply, does not shut out the hope of being brought to life again; 'eternal death' does. 'Fire' may be *quenched* before it has entirely consumed what it is burning; 'unquenchable fire' would seem most naturally to mean that which destroys it utterly.

It may be said, indeed, that supposing man's soul to be an immaterial being, it cannot be consumed and *destroyed* by literal *material* fire or worms. That is true; but no more can it *suffer* from these. We all know that no fire, literally so called, can give us any pain unless it reach our bodies. The 'fire,' therefore, and the 'worm' that are spoken of, must, at any rate, it would seem, be something figuratively so called—something that is to the soul what worms and fire are to a body. And as the effect of worms or fire is *not* to *preserve* the body they prey upon, but to consume, destroy, and put an end to it, it would follow, if the correspondence hold good, that the fire, figuratively so called, which is prepared for the condemned, is something that is really to destroy and put an end to them; and is called 'everlasting' or 'unquenchable' fire to denote that they are not to be saved from it, but that their destruction is to be *final*. So in the parable of the tares, our Lord describes Himself as saying, 'Gather ye first the tares, and bind them in bundles to *burn them*; but gather the wheat *into My garner*'—as if to denote that the one is to be (as we know is the practice of the husbandman) carefully preserved, and the other completely put an end to.

We must not, indeed, venture to conclude at once, from our conviction of the divine goodness and power, that evil will ever cease to exist, since we know not how to explain the existence of any evil at all. We can only say there is some *unknown cause* for it, and that it is a foolish presumption to think of assigning a limit to the effects of an unknown cause, except where revelation guides us. But when we are told that Christ is to 'reign till He shall have put all things under His feet,' and that 'the last enemy that shall be destroyed is *death*,' this does afford some ground for expecting the ultimate extinction of evil and of suffering by the total destruction of such as are incapable of good and of happiness. If 'eternal death' means *final* death—death without any revival—we can understand what is meant by 'Death being the last enemy *destroyed*,' viz. that none henceforth are to be subjected to it. But if 'death' be understood to mean everlasting life in misery, then it would appear that death is never to be destroyed at all, since, although no one should be henceforth *sentenced* to it, it would still be going on as a continual *infliction* for ever.

On the whole, therefore, I think we are not warranted in concluding (as some have done) so positively concerning this question as to make it a point of Christian faith to interpret figuratively and not literally the 'death' and 'destruction' spoken of in Scripture as the doom of the condemned; and to insist on the belief that they are to be kept alive for ever. —*Scripture Revelations of a Future State.**

'THE RESTITUTION OF ALL THINGS.'

BY THE REV. ANDREW JUKES.

This is a remarkable book. A more ingenious and attractive plea for Universalism has perhaps never appeared. And although, in my judgment, it fails to prove the endless existence of every form of human life that reaches some (undefined) stage of development, or to shake the direct evidence from Scripture that the ultimate reconciliation of all things, including the salvation of the human race, will be accomplished only after a vast destruction; yet no intelligent Christian can peruse its pages without receiving instruction. So comprehensive a knowledge of Scripture, combined with such a spiritual penetration into some of its depths, is rarely ex-

* It is somewhat remarkable that, after the publication of such views by so eminent a prelate, the author of this volume should be described, in reference to the present controversy, as 'one solitary clergyman,' and be taunted by the editor of the *Rock* with supposing himself to have 'made a great discovery,' and to be 'the only true prophet.'

hibited within the same compass. It is especially valuable upon the inspired revelations with reference to the 'ages,' which, in consequence of our mistranslation of certain Greek words, is almost entirely concealed from the English reader. I take the liberty of transcribing some of the most important passages; without in the least committing myself to all the writer's inferences from the numerous texts which, on the whole, he so ably expounds. In particular, I must again express my conviction that his belief in universal salvation is absolutely irreconcileable both with the general tenour of Scripture, and with many of its plainest statements. Still, we all need to have our views of the future enlarged by such considerations as Mr. Jukes adduces; and I cannot refrain from enriching these pages with some of his remarks, though totally dissenting from his opinion on the point referred to, and doubting upon one or two others.

'The language of the New Testament, in its use of the word which our translators have rendered "for ever" and "for ever and ever,"* but which is literally "for the age," or "for the ages of ages," points not uncertainly to the same solution of the great riddle, though as yet the glad tidings of the "ages to come" have been but little opened out. The epistles of St. Paul will prove that the "ages" are periods in which God is gradually working out a purpose of grace, which was ordained in Christ before the fall, and before those "age-times,"† in and through which the fall is being remedied. So we read that "God's wisdom was ordained before the ages to our glory" ‡—that is, that God had a purpose before the ages out of the very fall to bring greater glory both to Himself and to His fallen creature. Then we are told distinctly of "the purpose of the ages," § showing that the work of renewal would only be accomplished through successive ages.

*   *   *   *   *   *

---

* εἰς αἰῶνα, and εἰς αἰῶνας αἰώνων.

† χρόνοι αἰώνιοι (2 Tim. i. 9; Tit. i. 2).

‡ 1 Cor. ii. 7: πρὸ τῶν αἰώνων.

§ Eph. iii. 11 : κατὰ πρόθεσιν τῶν αἰώνων—translated, in our Authorised Version, 'the eternal purpose.'

'Now, what is this "purpose of the ages" which St. Paul speaks of, but of which the Church in these days seems to know, or at least says, next to nothing? I have already anticipated the answer. The "ages" are the fulfilment or substance of the "times and seasons" of the Sabbatic year and Jubilee under the old law. They are those "times of refreshment from the presence of the Lord when He shall send Jesus Christ, who before was preached;"* and when, in due order, liberty and cleansing will be obtained by those who are now in bondage and unclean, and rest be gained by those who now are without their rightful inheritance. In the "ages," and in no other mystery of the gospel, do we find those "good things to come," of which the legal times and seasons were the "shadow." † Of course, as some of these "ages" are "to come," being indeed the "times and seasons which the Father hath put in His own power,"‡ we can as yet know little of their distinctive character, except that, as being the ages in which God is fulfilling His purpose in Christ, we may be assured their issue must be glorious. Yet they are constantly referred to in the New Testament, and the book of the Revelation more than any other speaks of them,§ for this book opens out the processes and stages of the great redemption, which make up the Revelation of Jesus Christ which God gives Him; and this Revelation is not accomplished in one act, but through the "ages" and "ages of ages" foreshadowed by the "times" and "times of times" of the old law, the "age-times," again to use the language of St. Paul, in which the Lord is revealed as meeting the ruin of the creature. And the reason why we sometimes read of "ages," and sometimes of "the age," when both seem to refer to and speak of the same one great consummation, is that the various "ages" are but the component parts of a still greater "age," as the seven Sabbatic years only made up one Jubilee.

'At any rate, and whatever the future "ages" may be, those past (and St. Paul speaks of "the ends" of some) are clearly not endless; and the language of Scripture as to those to come seems to teach that they are limited, since Christ's mediatorial kingdom, which is "for the ages of ages," must yet be "delivered up to the Father, that God may be all in all." ||

* * * * * *

---

* Acts iii. 19. † Heb. x. 1. ‡ Acts i. 7.
§ Rev. i. 6, 18; iv. 9, 10; v. 13, 14; vii. 12; x. 6; xi. 15; xiv. 11; xv. 7; xix. 3; xx. 10; xxii. 5.
|| Compare Rev. xi. 15, and 1 Cor. xv. 24.

'The "ages," therefore, are periods in which God works, because there is evil and His rest is broken by it, but which have an end and pass away, when the work appointed to be done in them has been accomplished. The "ages," like the "days" of creation, speak of a prior fall: they are the "times" in which God works, because He cannot rest in sin and misery. His perfect rest is not in the "ages," but beyond them, when the mediatorial kingdom, which is "for the ages of ages,"* is "delivered up,"† and Christ, by whom all things are wrought in the ages, goes back to the glory which He had "before the age-times,"‡ "that God may be all in all."§ The words "Jesus Christ (that is, Anointed Saviour), the same yesterday, to-day, and for the ages,"‖ imply that through these "ages" a Saviour is needed, and will be found, as much as "to-day" and "yesterday." It will, I think too, be found that the adjective ¶ founded on this word, whether applied to "life," "punishment," "redemption," "covenant," "times," or even "God" Himself, is always connected with remedial labour, and with the idea of "ages" as periods in which God is working to meet and correct some awful fall. Thus the "æonial covenant"** (I must coin a word, to show what is the term used in the original) is that which comprehends "the ages" during which "Jesus Christ is the same"—that is, a Saviour; an office only needed for the fallen, for "they that are whole need not a physician." The "æonial God" (language found but once in the New Testament††) refers, as the context shows, to God as

---

* Rev. xi. 15. † 1 Cor. xv. 24.

‡ 2 Tim. i. 9, and Tit. i. 2 : πρὸ χρόνων αἰωνίων—translated, in our Version, 'before the world began.' The Vulgate translation here is, 'Ante sæcularia tempora,' which is as literal a rendering as possible.

§ 1 Cor. xv. 28. ‖ Heb. xiii. 8 : εἰς τοὺς αἰῶνας.
¶ αἰώνιος. ** Heb. xiii. 20.

†† Rom. xvi. 25, 26. In this passage we read, first, of 'the mystery kept secret from *the æonial times*,' μυστήριον χρόνοις αἰωνίοις σεσιγημένον (translated, in our English version, 'Since the world began'); and then of '*the æonial God*,' αἰωνίου Θεοῦ, 'by whose command this mystery is now made manifest.' In the Septuagint version of the Old Testament, the epithet αἰώνιος is only applied to God four times, in one of which the corresponding עוֹלָם of the Hebrew is not to be found, though in all the reference is direct, either to 'the age of ages,' or to God's redeeming work as wrought through 'the ages.' The passages are Gen. xxi. 33, where, after the birth of Isaac, the type of Christ, God is known by this name, אֵל עוֹלָם; then Isa. xxvi. 4, and xl. 28, in both which the

working His secret of grace through "æonial times"—that is, successive worlds or "ages," in some of which "the mystery has been hid, but now is made manifest by the commandment of the æonial God"—that is (if I err not), the God who works through these "ages." And so of the rest, whether "redemption,"* "salvation,"† "spirit," ‡ "fire," § or "inheritance," ‖ all of which in certain texts are called "æonial," the epithet seems to refer to the same remedial plan, wrought out by God through "worlds" or "ages." And does not our Lord refer to this in the well-known words, "This is life eternal ¶ (that is, the life of the age or of the ages), that they may know Thee, the only true God, and Jesus Christ whom Thou hast sent?"** Does He not say here, that to know the only true God, as the sender of His Son to be a Saviour, and to know that Son as a Saviour and Redeemer, mark and constitute the renewed life which is peculiar to the ages? Æonial or eternal life therefore is not, as so many think, the living on and on for ever and ever. It is rather, as our Lord defines it, a life, the distinctive peculiarity of which is, that it has to do with a Saviour, and so is part of a remedial plan. This, as being our Lord's own explanation of the word, is surely conclusive as to its meaning. But even had we not this key, the word carries with it in itself its own solution; for "æonial" is simply "of the ages," and the "ages," like the days of creation, as being periods in which God works, witness not only that there is some fall to be remedied, but that God through these days or ages is working to remedy it.††

---

context shows the reason for the epithet; and, lastly, Job xxiii. 12, in which passage the LXX. have given us αἰώνιος for אֱלֹהִים, or Elohim, in the original, which name, as we see from a comparison of Gen. i. and ii. (in the former of which God is always Elohim, in the latter Jehovah Elohim), refers to the One who is working through periods of labour to change a ruined world, until His image is seen ruling it—a title not lost when the day of rest is reached, but to which another name, showing what God is in Himself, is then added. In Exod. iii. 15, we read of God's ὄνομα αἰώνιον—that is, His name as connected with deliverance. I believe the word is never used but in this connection.

* Heb. ix. 12.   † Heb. v. 9.   ‡ Heb. ix. 14.
§ Jude 7.   ‖ Heb. ix. 15.   ¶ ἡ αἰώνιος ζωή.
** St. John xvii. 3.

†† As to the Old Testament use of the word 'age' or 'ages' (translated 'for ever' in the English version), a few words may be added here. We have, first, the unconditional promise of God that 'the seed of Abraham shall inherit the land for ever:' לְעוֹלָם—LXX., εἰς τὸν αἰῶνα

'Be this as it may, the adjective "æonial," or age-long, cannot carry a force or express a duration greater than that of the ages or "æons"

—(Exod. xxxii. 13). The same words are used of the Aaronic priesthood (Exod. xl. 15); of the office of the Levites (1 Chron. xv. 2); of the inheritance given to Caleb (Joshua xiv. 9) ; of Ai being a desolation (Joshua viii. 28); of the leprosy of Gehazi cleaving to his seed (2 Kings v. 27); of the heathen bondsmen whom Israel possessed, of whom it is said, 'They shall be their bondsmen for ever' (Lev. xxv. 46). The same words are also used of the curse to come on Israel for their disobedience: 'These curses shall come on thee, and pursue thee till thou be destroyed; and they shall be upon thee for a sign, and upon thy children for ever' (Deut. xxviii. 45, 46). So of Ammon and Moab it is said, 'Thou shalt not seek their peace for ever' (Deut. xxiii. 6); and again, 'They shall not come into the congregation of the Lord for ever' (Deut. xxiii. 3); here עַד עוֹלָם. In all these and other similar instances, עוֹלָם, and its equivalent αἰών, mean the age or dispensation. In Exod. xxi. 6, where the ear of the servant who will not go free is bored, and he becomes a 'servant for ever' (עוֹלָם; LXX., εἰς τὸν αἰῶνα), the sense must necessarily be much more limited; as also in 1 Sam. i. 22. It is to be observed also that not only the singular, עוֹלָם, as in 1 Kings ix. 3, and 2 Kings xxi. 7, but the plural, עוֹלָמִים, is used in 1 Kings viii. 13, and 2 Chron. vi. 2, in reference to the temple at Jerusalem. The double expression, לְעוֹלָם וָעֶד, is variously translated by the LXX.; sometimes εἰς τὸν αἰῶνα καὶ ἔτι, as in Dan. xii. 3, where it is used of those 'that turn many to righteousness;' sometimes τὸν αἰῶνα καὶ ἐπ' αἰῶνος καὶ ἔτι, as in Exod. xv. 18, where it is used of God; sometimes εἰς τὸν αἰῶνα τοῦ αἰῶνος, as in Psalm xlv. 2, where it is used of Christ and His kingdom; while in Micah iv. 7, the same Hebrew words, here עוֹלָם וָעֶד, are translated by the LXX., and here only, by the plural, ἕως εἰς τοὺς αἰῶνας. More commonly, however, עַד עוֹלָם is rendered simply ἕως τοῦ αἰῶνος by the LXX., as in Gen. xiii. 15; Joshua iv. 7, and elsewhere. Lastly, in Dan. vii. 18, we have both the singular and the plural form together, עַד עָלְמָא וְעַד עָלַם עָלְמַיָּא, rendered by the LXX. ἕως αἰῶνος τῶν αἰώνων. The adjective αἰώνιος is used continually by the LXX.—in reference to the Passover (Exod. xii. 14, 17), the tabernacle service (Exod. xxvii. 21), the priestly office of the sons of Aaron (Exod. xxviii. 43), the meat-offering (Lev. vi. 18), and other things of the Jewish dispensation—all of which are called νόμιμον αἰώνιον. So in Jer. xxiii. 40, we have αἰώνιον ὀνείδεισμον, and ἀτιμίαν αἰώνιον, used of the corrective judgments on Israel, whose restoration is also foretold.

which it speaks of. If, therefore, these "ages" are limited periods, some of which are already past, while others, we know not how many, are yet to come, the word "æonial" cannot mean strictly never-ending. Nor does this affect the true eternity of bliss of God's elect, or of the redeemed who are brought back to live in God's life, of whom it is said, "Neither can they die any more, for they are equal to the angels, and are the children of God, being the children of the resurrection;"* for this depends on a participation in the divine nature, and upon that power which can "change these vile bodies, that they may be fashioned like unto Christ's glorious body, according to the working whereby He is able even to subdue all things unto Himself."†

The following observations also, in their general spirit, are worthy of the deepest attention:—

'The writer feels the solemn responsibility of dissenting on such a question from the current creed of Christendom; and nothing but his most assured conviction that the popular notion of never-ending punishment is as thorough a misunderstanding of God's Word as the doctrine of Transubstantiation, and that the one as much as the other conduces directly to infidelity, though both equally claim to stand on the express words of Holy Scripture, would have led him to moot a subject which cannot even be questioned in some quarters without provoking the charge of heresy. Truth is worth all this, and much more. If we will not buy it at all cost, we are not worthy of it.

* * * * * *

'But is it possible that the Church should have been allowed to err on so important a point as the doctrine of future judgment? Would our Lord Himself have used, or permitted others to use, words which, if final restitution be true, might be understood as teaching the very opposite? I say again, look at the doctrine of Transubstantiation. Has, or has not, the Church been suffered to err as to the meaning of words which are at the very foundation of her highest act of worship? Did not our Lord, when He said, "Take, eat, this is my body," ‡ know how monstrously the words would be perverted? Yet, though a single sentence would have made any mistake almost impossible, He did not add another word. Why? Because the very form in which the Word

---

* St. Luke xx. 36.

† Phil. iii. 21. See also 1 Cor. xv. 53; Rom. viii. 29; Heb. vii. 16; xii. 28; 1 St. Peter i. 3, 4, 5; 1 St. John iii. 2.

‡ St. Matt. xxvi. 26.

is given is part of our discipline; and because, without His Spirit, let His words be what they may, we never really understand Him. Transubstantiation is a mistake built on Christ's very words; and the doctrine of endless torments is but another like misunderstanding, which not only directly contradicts many other Scriptures, but practically denies and falsifies the glorious revelation of Himself, which God has given us in the gospel, and in the face of Jesus Christ. Both show the Church's state. And though thousands of God's children have held, not these only, but many other errors, the fact, instead of approving their errors, only proves the grace of Him, who, spite of such errors, can yet bless and make His children a blessing.

* * * * * *

'Such then, I believe, is the testimony of Scripture as to the purpose and way of God our Saviour. That it will be judged as false doctrine by those who, like Israel of old, can see no purpose of God beyond their own dispensation, is as certain as that Israel slew the prophets, and rejected the counsel of God toward sinners of the Gentiles; that it will be hateful also to fallen spirits may be seen from the way in which proud souls in every age rebel against the gospel. Their thought is that they shall continue for ever. Very humbling is it to think that all their pride and rebellion must be overthrown. Even with true souls, who have been teaching another doctrine, there must be special difficulties in receiving a truth which proves them to have been in error. Now, therefore, as of old, Samaritans know Christ as "Saviour of the world," * while masters of Israel reject Him in this character. For teachers to learn is to unlearn; and that is not easy. Nor can we expect that those who occupy the chief seats in the synagogue will readily descend from them and humble themselves, not only to take the place of learners, but to be reproached for doing so. How can masters of Israel eat their own words? All these things, and, still more, our natural hard thoughts of God, are against the spread of the doctrine set forth in these pages. But if it be God's purpose, it shall stand, and each succeeding age shall make it more manifest. Meanwhile He says, "He that hath my word, let him speak my word faithfully. What is the chaff to the wheat? saith the Lord." † I do not fear, therefore, that the declaration of God's righteousness and love will lead men, as some suppose, to think less of Him. "We are saved by hope," ‡ not by fear. It is the lie, that He is a destroyer and does not love us,

---

* St. John iv. 42.

† Jer. xxiii. 28. ‡ Rom. viii. 24.

which has kept and yet keeps souls from Him. And though some argue that the doctrine of final restitution, even supposing it to be true, ought not to be whispered, except with great reserve, because men will abuse it, I cannot but think their prudence unwise, and that the truth, when God has revealed it, may be trusted to do its own work. Of course this truth, like every other, may be abused. What good thing is there which may not be perverted? The Bible and the gospel itself may be wrested to men's destruction, and Christ Himself be made a savour of death to those He died for. But surely this is no reason for locking up the Bible or the gospel, or for keeping back or denying any truth which God has graciously revealed to us. And when I think of past objections to the gospel, that if grace is preached, men will abuse it, and sin that grace may more abound—when I remember how the doctrine of justification by faith has been opposed, on the ground that it must undermine all practical godliness—when I see how God's election, clearly as it is revealed in Holy Scripture, is denied by some, who, wiser than God, think that such a doctrine must be perilous to man and opposed to God's love and truth—I have less faith in the supposed consequences of any doctrine, assured that if it be only true, its truth must in the end justify it. I rather believe that if the exactness of final retribution were understood, if men saw that so long as they continue in sin they must be under judgment, and that only by death to sin are they delivered, they could not pervert the gospel as they now do, nor abuse that preaching of the Cross which is indeed salvation.

'I cannot but think too that this doctrine of final restitution would meet much of the hopeless scepticism which is certainly increased by this dogma of never-ending punishment. Men turn from the gospel and from the Scriptures, not knowing what they contain, offended at the announcement, which shocks them, that God who is Love consigns all but a "little flock," the "few who find the narrow way," to endless misery. Even true believers groan under the burden which this doctrine, as it is commonly received, must lay on all thoughtful and unselfish minds. "For my part," says Henry Rogers, "I fancy I should not grieve if the whole race of mankind died in its fourth year. As far as we can see, I do not know that it would be a thing much to be lamented."* "The same gospel," says Isaac Taylor, "which penetrates our souls with warm emotions, dispersive of selfishness, brings in upon

---

* Professor Henry Rogers, in *Greyson's Letters*. Letter vii. to C. Mason, Esq., vol. i, p. 34.

the heart a sympathy that tempts us often to wish that itself were not true, or that it had not taught us so to feel."* Even more affecting are the words of Albert Barnes, as a witness to the darkness of the ordinary orthodox theology: "These and a hundred difficulties meet the mind, when we think on this great subject; and they meet us when we endeavour to urge our fellow-sinners to be reconciled to God, and to put confidence in Him. I confess for one that I feel these, and feel them more sensibly and powerfully the more I look at them, and the longer I live. I do not know that I have a ray of light on this subject which I had not when the subject first flashed across my soul. I have read to some extent what wise and good men have written. I have looked at their theories and explanations. I have endeavoured to weigh their arguments, for my whole soul pants for light and relief on these questions. But I get neither; and in the distress and anguish of my own spirit, I confess that I see no light whatever. I see not one ray to disclose to me the reason why sin came into the world, why the earth is strewed with the dying and the dead, and why man must suffer to all eternity."†

'Such confessions are surely sad enough; but they do not and cannot express one thousandth part of the horror which the idea of never-ending misery should produce in every loving heart. As Archer Butler says, "Were it possible for man's imagination to conceive the horrors of such a doom as this, all reasoning about it would be at an end; it would scorch and wither all the powers of human thought."‡ Indeed, human life would be at a stand, could this doctrine of eternal punishment be realised. Can such a doctrine then be true? If it be, let men declare it always and in every place. But if it be simply the result of a misconception of God's Word, it is high time that the Church awake to truer readings of it.

'It is not for me to judge God's saints who have gone before. Their judgment is with the Lord, and their work with their God. But when I think of the words, not of the carnal and profane, but even of some of God's dear children in that long night, when "the beast," which looked "like a lamb, but spake as a dragon," had dominion §—when I find Augustine saying, that "though infants departing from the body without baptism will be in the mildest damnation of all, yet he greatly

---

* Isaac Taylor's *Restoration of Belief*, p. 367.
† Albert Barnes's *Practical Sermons*, p. 123.
‡ *Sermons*, second series, p. 383.
§ Rev. xiii. 11.

deceives and is deceived who preaches that they will not be in damnation," meaning thereby unending punishment; or Thomas Aquinas, that "the bliss of the saved may please them more, and they may render more abundant thanks to God for it, that they are permitted to gaze on the punishment of the wicked;" or Peter Lombard, that "the elect, while they see the unspeakable sufferings of the ungodly, shall not be affected with grief, but rather satiated with joy at the sight, and give thanks to God for their own salvation;" or Luther, that "it is the highest degree of faith to believe that God is merciful, who saves so few and damns so many; to believe Him just, who of His own will makes us necessarily damnable"—when I remember that such men have said such things, and that words like these have been approved by Christians, I can only fall down and pray that such a night may not return, and that where it yet weighs on men's hearts the Lord may scatter it.'

'RELIGIOUS TENDENCIES OF THE TIMES.'

BY MR. JAMES GRANT.

My subject has already led me to mention this book. There are several personal references in it, to which, on its first appearance, I wrote full replies. But I prefer to pass them over in silence, and to let them fall by their own weight. Anyone with the two volumes before him can easily judge between us.

The writer's direct defence of Eternal Evil is grounded on those old traditional arguments, with which we are all familiar, and which had been already considered in the preceding sermons. But as he publicly declared his belief that he had ' entered *fully* into the question,' and as the *Christian Advocate* recommends his book to anyone who wishes to see ' how full and varied' are the proofs of the popular doctrine, it may be useful to give the following list of arguments against it, or replies to arguments in favour of it, with which Mr. Grant has not even attempted to grapple :—

1. That when Adam was threatened with death, as the

penalty of sin, he could not possibly understand it to mean eternal life in misery.

2. That the typical sacrifices taught death, and not endless suffering, to be the penalty of sin.

3. That the ever recurring alternative of Life or Death, set before us in Scripture, teaches the same.

4. That our interpretation of these words is confirmed by Christ's warning, that if we try to save our life by unfaithfulness to Him in this world, we shall 'lose *it*,' that is the same thing which we tried to save, in the world to come.

5. That the final destruction of the wicked being compared to that of 'natural brute beasts,' precludes its consisting of eternal torture.

6. That our being urged to seek for 'immortality,' as well as 'glory and honour,' by 'patient continuance in well-doing,' precludes the idea of all men alike possessing immortality.

7. That the promise 'Whoso doeth the will of God abideth for ever' leans strongly to the same side.

8. That the contrast between the natural man perishing like the grass, and the regenerate man being born of incorruptible seed, namely the word of the Lord which abideth for ever, precludes the idea of equal duration.

9. That the way of Holiness could not be called 'the way everlasting,' in contrast to every 'wicked way,' if the two ways were equally everlasting.

10. That the doctrine of endless suffering being the wages of sin is inconsistent with the vicarious sacrifice of Christ, inasmuch as He did not endure it.

11. That the metaphysical argument in favour of every sin incurring infinite guilt, because it is committed against an infinite being, could only hold good if it were committed *by* an infinite being.

12. That the argument drawn from Matt. xxv. 46 to prove that if the wicked do not live for ever, neither will the righteous, could only prove at the very utmost, that the endless bliss of the righteous was not asserted *in that passage*, and would leave all the other assertions of it quite untouched.

13. That the word rendered 'contempt,' to which we are told in Dan. xii. the wicked will awake, is the same that is rendered 'abhorring' in Isa. lxvi., and is there predicted of 'carcases;' so that it does not necessarily describe the wicked as awaking to become everlastingly *conscious* of contempt, but may describe them as awaking to become *objects* of 'everlasting contempt.'

14. That the word rendered 'unquenchable,' when applied to fire, does not mean that it will burn on for ever; as is shown by Homer's saying that an unquenchable fire broke out in one of the ships of Troy, which was extinguished by Patroclus,—and also by many passages in the Old Testament.

15. That the 'torment' in 'the lake of fire' toward the end of Revelation, is part of a dramatic scene, so highly figurative that there is hardly another incident in it which anyone expects to be literally fulfilled; and that the casting of Death and Hell into the lake of fire indicates its representing destruction rather than torture.

16. That the doctrine of Eternal Evil is totally at variance with any reasonable understanding of the predicted reconciliation of all things to God by Christ, so that 'God may be all in all.'

17. That it is inconsistent with the declaration, that 'The Son of God was manifested that He might destroy the works of the devil,' and 'that through death he might destroy him that had the power of death, that is the devil.'

18. Also with the revealed truth, that 'in Him (Christ) all things consist.' *

To the best of my belief there is not a word in Mr. Grant's 500 pages, from which it could be gathered that he had ever heard or thought of any of the foregoing points. In fact, like most other writers on the same side, he has altogether failed to perceive the magnitude of this great subject. The confident tone of his assertions, and his vehement denunciations of those who venture to differ from him in their interpretation of Scripture, may produce a considerable effect upon weak or ill-informed minds; but they will fall perfectly harmless upon those who have been enabled to penetrate into the heart of the whole matter, namely, Life and Immortality in Christ alone.†

* In a private letter, since published, Mr. Grant maintains that some of the arguments mentioned above *are* answered, directly or indirectly, in the course of his volume. But, after examining the passages he adduces, I cannot admit his plea even in a single case. Several of the *subjects* are treated of—such as 'unquenchable fire' and 'infinite guilt'—but no attempt is made to meet any of the specified points in connection with those subjects.

† 'On the second great point of agreement among "Annihilationists," the grand and blessed doctrine of *immortality only in Christ*, Mr. Grant presents us with—a blank! It is actually never mentioned. Not a reference, not an allusion, not a word about it is to be found in the whole book! Now, that it should be a truth quite beyond Mr. Grant's range of spiritual vision is only what might be expected; but how prominent, we might even say how supreme, a position it occupies in the system he is controverting, must surely have been well known to him from the perusal (if he really perused them) of the books he mentions. He was bound, therefore, to meet and disprove it: and the very significant fact that he has made no attempt to do so, can be accounted for only on the supposition, either that he had utterly failed to acquaint himself with the doctrine he denounces, or, as in the former case, that he felt himself unable to grapple with it..... To grapple with the profound and perilous questions connected with man's essential nature and eternal destiny, we hold him to be as incompetent as is the passing shower to melt the rock on which it falls, or as is a child to overthrow a giant by tilting against him with a bundle of straws. And it is a

Precisely analogous to his treatment of the Scripture evidences, is his treatment of the question relating to the respective consequences of preaching these opposing views. Two whole sermons in this volume are exclusively occupied with pointing out the disastrous results that follow the popular doctrine of Eternal Evil. Without attempting to answer any one of those allegations, and apparently without the slightest consciousness that there could be a second opinion on the subject, Mr. Grant just lays it down, that 'The conviction, if groundless, that future punishments will be only of limited, not of eternal duration, is an error so absolutely frightful that the human mind shrinks from its contemplation. On the other hand, should perchance, after all, the opposite belief —namely, that punishments in a future state will be of endless duration—be a mistaken faith, and that a period will be put, sooner or later, to the miseries of those who have died unsaved, the mistaken notion will involve no disastrous results. Not the slightest harm will come to anyone, because it was reserved for the light of eternity to dispel, on this point, the darkness which enveloped his mind in time.'

Where can a man have been living to utter such a sentiment as that? * Could anything betray more entire ignorance

lamentable indication of the low ebb of theology among us to find such a work as this receiving the warm commendation and eager suffrages of our religious newspapers and magazines. Throughout his book, it is quite obvious that Mr. Grant is destitute of even the rudiments of the theological learning essential in dealing with his subject; it is equally manifest that he is incapable of constructing a logical argument.'—*The Rainbow.*

* 'The doctrine of Eternal Punishment is now actively at work in undermining Christianity itself; it is—sometimes openly, but much oftener in secret—driving thousands into infidelity; and is, beyond all question, the great repulsive force which prevents the alien from entering within the Christian pale.'—*Eternal Punishment and Eternal Death,* by J. W. Barlow, M.A.

of what is going on in the Church and the world, and consequently more hopeless incompetence to deal with the 'Religious Tendencies of the Times'?

There is one other assertion, however, that perhaps exceeds even that; and is so thoroughly characteristic of the whole book, that it must not be omitted.

'Let me impress deeply and abidingly on their minds this great fact, that no one of those many learned and gifted men who have written in favour of the limited duration of future punishments, have been able to point to one *single* passage of Scripture, which can, by any amount of ingenuity, however great, be made to give even a seeming *positive* sanction to the doctrine that there will be an end to the misery in a future state, of those who have perished in their sins in the present world.'

Not one single text, even apparently, to sanction the belief that the wages of sin is death, that the finally impenitent will be destroyed soul and body in Hell, that they will be consumed, devoured, burnt up, and perish for ever!* I should be sorry to speak with undue severity of Mr. Grant's book, especially when it has been recommended by the *Christian Advocate*, as 'on the whole, with a little caution here and there, a safe and comprehensive guide.' But it is only the simple truth to say that it abounds in statements just as sweeping

---

* Mr. Grant says 'The brutes, we are elsewhere told, are destined to perish, *that is, when they die there is nothing more of them.*' Yet when Scripture declares that the wicked will perish for ever, no amount of ingenuity can make it lend even a seeming positive sanction to the doctrine that there will be 'nothing more of them!'

Another specimen of this writer's consistency may be found by comparing what he says (p. 91) on the text, 'Many of them that sleep in the dust of the earth shall awake,' namely that 'the word *many* means *all*, just as the expression "By one man's disobedience *many* were made sinners," demonstrably means *all*,' with what he says (p. 254) on the words 'many sons,' in Heb. ii. 8, namely that they are fatal to the theory of ultimate universal salvation, inasmuch as '*many* cannot be regarded as equivalent to *all*.'

and just as reliable. The word 'positive' is printed in italics; and therefore Mr. Grant may understand his own assertion in some sense not obvious to the ordinary reader. But the fact is, that there are literally *hundreds* of texts, which not only *seem* to afford the most 'positive sanction' that could be expressed in human language to the view Mr. Grant impugns, but which require the utmost 'ingenuity' of the subtlest casuists to rationalise away, so as to make them sanction anything else!

If anyone thinks that this is an exaggeration, let him look out in his Concordance the words, live, die, destroy, perish, with their cognate forms, and words of similar import; and then, setting aside the traditions of men, disregarding party anathemas, and, if he pleases, waiving all consideration of what may be consistent or inconsistent with the revelation which has been made to us of the Divine nature and character, let him honestly, as in the sight of God, ask himself this one question—

WHAT SAITH THE SCRIPTURE?

PS.—While these pages are passing through the press, another volume of 'Religious Tendencies' has appeared from Mr. Grant's prolific pen. There is nothing in it, in the way of argument, that requires any further answer. Indeed, upon Mr. Grant himself argument seems to be thrown away. For, on p. 144, he says, 'It is a significant fact, that I have never met with an Annihilationist, either in print or in private, who undertook to answer the argument in question (from Dan. xii. 2) against their hypothesis'; though on p. 4 he had himself actually put 'in print' the 'answer' which I 'undertook' to give to that very 'argument' in my published sermons, and which, as my letter to him shows, I had 'in private' pressed upon his attention.

In this volume he has taken Mr. Garbett's judicious advice to avoid the Scriptural word 'destruction,' which expresses what we *do* believe, and persists in fastening upon us the unscriptural word 'annihilation,' which expresses what we have repeatedly declared that we do *not* believe. This is all the more unpardonable, inasmuch as a scientific argument is brought against our belief in the *destruction* of the wicked 'soul and body in hell,' grounded upon the opinion commonly entertained, that even God Himself never *annihilates* a single particle of matter.

He has also followed the example of many others on that side, in assuming the impossibility of his opponents understanding language in any sense different from his own, and thereupon denouncing them as dishonest lying hypocrites. Witness the following:—

'I regret to learn that, notwithstanding the vehemence with which the doctrine of everlasting punishments is denounced by him, as "horrible," "monstrous," "revolting," and so forth, he still continues to make a practical profession of his faith in it, by reading that part of the Litany in which the prayer occurs, that God would be pleased to deliver those using the prayer from everlasting damnation. The prayer stands thus: "From Thy wrath and from everlasting damnation, good Lord deliver us"; the latter four words of response being said by all the congregation. To me there is something inexpressibly awful in the fact, that any man holding up, both in the pulpit and through the press, the doctrine of eternal punishments, as one which is absolutely frightful, and deeply dishonourable to God, could bring himself to proclaim publicly, Sunday after Sunday, his belief in that "dreadful doctrine," by praying himself, and asking his people to pray, for deliverance from "everlasting damnation."'

Now, there could of course be nothing 'inexpressibly awful' even to his mind 'in the fact' of my interpreting those words differently from himself; nor would my use of them, in that case, constitute any 'practical profession' of what *he* understands by them. Unless the whole paragraph is 'sound and fury, signifying nothing,' it can only be a direct charge of wilful hypocrisy. His horror is excited by the fact—not that I can 'bring myself' to regard 'everlasting damnation' as meaning condemnation to the everlasting punishment of irremediable destruction,* but—that I can 'bring myself to *proclaim publicly,* Sunday after Sunday, *my belief"* in a doctrine which I elsewhere repudiate. And this, let it be observed, after abundant material had been supplied in 'The Glory of Christ' for a right understanding of the sense in which I take the words; after I had publicly replied to the same attack from other quarters; and after the Church of England had formally decided, in her highest court of appeal, that not a single word in her formularies teaches the doctrine of endless suffering.

Mr. Grant closes his first chapter in so kindly, and even complimentary, a tone towards myself, that hostile criticism is almost disarmed. Yet it would be ungenerous to Dr. Leask, who has incurred such sacrifices for the truth's sake, if I were to pass over in silence the unwarranted attack which is made upon him in this last volume. It is precisely the same as that made upon me in the former volume. Persons of Mr. Grant's temperament seem to think it a necessary part of common honesty that, whenever a doubt arises in anyone's mind, it should be at once proclaimed to the world. That neither Dr. Leask nor myself acted on such a principle is the whole gravamen of our opponent's furious assaults upon us. It may be necessary to inform him that, after a view has been long under consideration, it is not always easy to know the precise moment when it becomes sufficiently matured to justify its

* Just as the fire which consumed Sodom and Gomorrah is called 'eternal fire,' although it has long since ceased to burn, and those cities have long since ceased to exist.

publication. It is often something which looks like a mere accident, that at last, to borrow Mr. Grant's mild language, 'tears the mask from the face.' For myself, I am thankful to feel perfectly satisfied with the crisis, when I was enabled to see the truth distinctly and to proclaim it fearlessly. For Dr. Leask, I have his own assurance that, during the greater portion of the time referred to, it would not have been easy for him to preach 'his universalist or annihilationist creed' (which Mr. Grant seems unable to distinguish), inasmuch as he was then a 'blind follower of the blind' in believing the popular creed.

There is another point which I cannot refrain from noticing, as strikingly illustrative of the spirit too apt to be engendered by a cordial acceptance of the doctrine of eternal torment; and that is, the encouragement given by Mr. Grant to certain members of the Evangelical Alliance in their present attempt to expel from that body the ablest man that ever belonged to it, and who is still one of its honorary secretaries. Mr. Birks believes that an irreversible sentence of condemnation will be passed upon the wicked, and that they will live for ever to bear the consequences of it. One might have thought that this would have been enough to satisfy the most determined advocate of 'eternal punishment.' But, no. Unhappily for his own comfort, from a party point of view, he holds that this punishment will help to work a salutary change in their moral condition, so that hell will not continue for ever to be the frightful scene that it is usually painted. This deviation from the strict line of orthodoxy Mr. Grant and his friends cannot endure; it is 'vital error.' They can no more tolerate any mitigation of the sufferings of the lost than any termination of them.* So the Evangelical Alliance, which was formed

* 'Mr. Birks' hypothesis as to the nature of the punishment does not involve anything resembling those intense agonies, that writhing of

to promote brotherly love amongst Christians, must be purified from Mr. Birks; and, unless this can be effected, its members are solemnly warned, in the most authoritative manner, that they will 'seriously compromise their character as Christians,' that 'the Alliance cannot long exist,' that even its dissolution would be better than 'the flagrant inconsistency of conduct involved in maintaining external fellowship with one whose creed on points of momentous importance they privately condemn in the strongest terms,'* that 'not only the Divine blessing will be withheld from the labours of the Alliance, but none of their members, however much their hearts may otherwise be right with God, can enjoy real peace of conscience.'

And this is the writer who, a few pages later, speaks with severe, though richly-deserved, censure of the bigotry, intolerance, and more than papal assumption, of an extreme section of Plymouth Brethren! Could Mr. Darby himself out-Herod the above?

Not long ago a series of meetings was held in Freemasons' Hall for confession of sin with reference to the divisions amongst Christians, and for special prayer that they might exhibit more of the unity of the spirit in the bond of peace.

body as well as anguish of mind, with which the Scriptures uniformly associate the doom of the ungodly in the world to come, when they speak of the worm that never dies, the fire that is never quenched, the weeping, and wailing, and gnashing of teeth, and the smoke of their torments, which ascendeth up for ever and ever.'—P. 209.

For a graphic description of these agonies, by the powerful pen of President Edwards, see p. xxxii. of this volume.

* These 'points of momentous importance'—these 'vital errors'—all resolving themselves into an attempt to render the doctrine of eternal misery less violently opposed to the revelation which God has made of His own character, and to the moral instincts which He has implanted in our nature, by eliminating some of the most frightful of the horrors associated with it by Dante, President Edwards, and Mr. James Grant.

Two persons of long-established Christian character, who believe that life and immortality are in Christ alone, and consequently that all out of Christ will 'perish everlastingly,' attended the first and second meetings as silent worshippers. On the third occasion, when presenting themselves at the door they were refused admission, on the ground that they were unbelievers in eternal punishment. They pleaded that they had not yet opened their lips at any of the meetings, and had no intention of doing so. But all in vain. They were told that their 'presence was an offence to the brethren,' who 'could not recognise them as Christians at all,' and they were turned away; one of them, an American, from whose lips I received the account, saying that he little thought when coming to London, of the honour that would be put upon him in being counted worthy to suffer shame, and to have his name cast out as evil, for the truth's sake. Mr. Grant will, no doubt, say—The perpetrators of that act must have been Darbyites. Very likely indeed; but was their conduct one particle worse than that which he himself is urging upon the Evangelical Alliance?

What a bitter satire upon the glorious word 'evangelical' is involved in its application to the doctrine of eternal torture! Evangelium—gospel—good news. The *good news*— that sin and misery will last *for ever*; and that, not only without the slightest mitigation, but with an aggravated intensity of horror far beyond our present power of conception! Let it not be said that the good news consists in the offer of salvation, and the prospect of eternal glory that is set before the believer; for in all that we are entirely agreed. The only difference between us relates to the destiny of those who finally reject the offer. So that, if the doctrine of eternal torment is 'evangelical,' and the doctrine of destruction *not* 'evangelical,' it can only be that 'those intense agonies, that writhing of body as well as anguish of mind' to all eternity, which Mr. Grant so peremptorily requires us to believe in, are themselves regarded as an essential part of the good news. And, according to the view of President Edwards, this is strictly logical. For he evidently believes that the happiness of the redeemed would not be complete without a continued view of the misery of the condemned:—

'When they (the saints) shall see how miserable others of their fellow creatures are, who were naturally in the same circumstances with themselves; when they shall see the smoke of their torment, and the raging of the flames of their burning, and hear their dolorous shrieks and cries, and consider that they, in the meantime, are in the most blissful state, and shall surely be in it to all eternity, *how will they rejoice!* . . . *How joyfully will they sing to God and the Lamb* WHEN THEY BEHOLD THIS!'—*Works*, vol. ii. p. 209, edit. 1840.

If this be true, then an '*Evangelical* Alliance' is right in refusing to bate one jot of all the horrors of the Augustinian theory, and Mr. Grant is its most faithful and outspoken representative.

The following remarks, however,—extracted from a Leaflet entitled 'Sectarianism,' published by Mr. Kellaway, of Weymouth,—are earnestly commended to the attention of all whom they may concern:—

'A very apt writer on the subject of sectarianism once said,—" I learned long ago that it is not with men we are at war, but with doctrines and sentiments. I do not therefore see any reason why we should act like the sons of Ishmael toward each other. A man embraces a false sentiment—what then? Is he therefore a hypocrite, a scoundrel, or a liar? Who of us do not hold *some* sentiments which may be wrong? Shall we therefore all fall on each other with words and acts of cruelty? What little Pope amongst us will start up and say, " I am right—you are all wrong?" Is not every man entitled to respect, love, kindness, and consideration? Will it reform any man to look at him with a countenance fraught with wrath and thunder? But the man is in a fatal error—what then? What will save him from his error? Will it make him see *his* error and *our* truth by appearing toward him unkind, vinegar-faced, and cloudy? Will turning him out of doors by treating him with such cold contempt that he cannot remain in our company, draw him any nearer to the truth and to Christ? This was not the policy of the Galilean. The enemies of Christ said before Him, "This man receiveth *sinners* and eateth with them." Hear the reply of the Son of God to this charge: "They that are whole need no physician; but they that are sick."

'One of the primary laws of reformation, both in doctrine and in practice, is association. Jesus came down from heaven that He might associate with men and reform them. It does not make us sinners to talk with, walk with, eat with, worship with, sinners, of necessity. It does not make them saints to let them see us all shun them, and treat them with contempt. When will men learn that bigotry, sectarianism, coldness, contempt, stiffness, and reserve, are not attractive elements? When will men learn that they cannot scold, drive, frighten, or *repulse* human beings into truth? When shall we learn, if men are brought into truth at all, it will be done by association, love, plainness, frankness, kindness, and argument?'

THE POWER OF PRAYER.

ABOUT twenty years ago, a Christian in Philadelphia was asked to give a course of lectures, in answer to a book that had lately appeared in favour of Universalism. After delivering the first lecture, he felt so deeply the responsibility of his position that he besought the Lord with all earnestness to show him clearly the whole truth of the matter, *whatever it might be*, and whatever consequences his acknowledgment of it might involve. His eyes were opened almost immediately, and he saw that he and his opponent were *both* wrong. He saw the glorious truth of life and immortality in Christ alone; and from that day to this he has seen it, with ever-increasing clearness, to be the grand revelation which God has made to us in His Word. He has rejoiced in being counted worthy to suffer shame, and obloquy, and persecution for the truth as it is in Jesus, esteeming the reproach of Christ greater riches than popular applause, the smiles of party, or even the approbation of the best of men. 'If ever,' were his own words to me, 'the Spirit of God alone taught any man any truth out of the Word, against all his own prejudices, He taught me that.'

Reader, will you try the same experiment, and ask God, not to confirm you in your present opinions, but 'to show you the whole truth of the matter, *whatever it may be*'? If you have sufficient distrust of your own infallibility to enable you to do this *honestly*, and sufficient love of truth for its own sake to make you do it *earnestly*, I shall have no fear of the result.

With great reluctance, and at the last moment, I am induced to mention an incident in my own experience, hoping that it may gain from some of my friends a more dispassionate consideration for the arguments contained in this volume. When entering the pulpit to deliver one of the foregoing discourses, I felt oppressed with a sense of my own unworthiness of the honour which God had put upon me, in calling me to bear witness to His truth, and probably to have my name cast out as evil for its sake. I wondered why He could have enrolled me among the small band of men, who have been given light to see and courage to proclaim the two great truths of revelation, namely, that life and immortality are in Christ alone, and that at length God will be 'all in all.' At that moment, for the first time during many years, was recalled to my mind a petition that formed part of the *first* prayer ever taught me, and which the mother of my children was also urged to embody in theirs,—'Give me Thy Holy Spirit *to guide me into all truth.*' The mystery was at once explained; the seed sown near half a century before was sending up a fresh shoot; and though I was almost incapacitated for proceeding with the sermon, I have never since doubted the Divine call, grudged the sacrifices that it has cost me, or quailed before the storm of opposition that I knew full well would be evoked. Some have thought they were doing God service by the most unscrupulous efforts to alienate my flock, while others have believed themselves to be proving their faithfulness by refusing to support any public or private benevolent enterprise with which my name might be connected. But none of these things move me; I know the truth, and the truth has set me free; it has set free many others also; and it will yet deliver many more from that dark shadow, out of which even some of Christ's most honoured servants appear so strangely unwilling to emerge.

BE TRUE.

'Speak thou the truth. Let others fence
  And trim their words for pay;
In pleasant sunshine of pretence
  Let others bask their day.

'Guard thou the fact; though clouds of night
  Down on thy watch-tower stoop;
Though thou should'st see thine heart's delight
  Borne from thee by their swoop.

'Face thou the wind; though safer seem
  In shelter to abide,
We were not made to sit and dream;
  The safe must first be tried.

'Where God hath set His thorns about,
  Cry not, "The way is plain;"
His path within for those without
  Is paved with toil and pain.

'One fragment of His blessed word
  Into thy spirit burned,
Is better than the whole, half-heard,
  And by thine interest turned.

'Show thou the light. If conscience gleam,
  Set not the bushel down;
The smallest spark may send his beam
  O'er hamlet, tower, and town.

'Woe, woe to him, on safety bent,
  Who creeps to age from youth,
Failing to grasp his life's intent,
  Because he fears the truth.

'Be true to every inmost thought,
  And as thy thought, thy speech:
What thou hast not by suffering bought,
  Presume thou not to teach.

'Hold on! Hold on! thou hast the rock;
  The foes are on the sand:
The first world-tempest's ruthless shock
  Scatters their shifting strand.

'While each wild gust the mist shall clear
  We now see darkly through;
And justified, at last appear
  The true in Him that's TRUE.'—*Dean Alford*

BY THE SAME AUTHOR.

'The MERCHANTS of TARSHISH; ' or, England, America, and Russia in the Last War. Ezekiel, Chapter XXXVIII. A Lecture delivered during the Crimean Campaign. Now first published. Price 6d.

OUR PRESENT POSITION. The 1260 Years of Papal Domination just expiring, and 'The Time of the End' commencing. Price 9d.

The CENTRAL SUPERSTITION of CHRISTENDOM. A Sermon on the Perversion of the Lord's Supper. Second Edition. Price 3d.

The PHILOSOPHY of PRAYER; or, The Power of Faith one of the 'Immutable Laws of the Universe.' Price 6d.

A LETTER to the BISHOP of LONDON on LITURGICAL REVISION. Second Edition. Price 6d.

LECTURES on UNITARIANISM. Second Thousand. Price 2s.

The ROMISH DOCTRINE of INTENTION; or, Has the Church of Rome, on her own showing, any Pope, Priest, Sacraments, or Rule of Faith? Third Edition. Price 3d.

The FOUNDATIONS of the EARTH. An Ancient Record, interpreted by the light of Modern Science. Price 6d.

The FIRST RESURRECTION. Reprinted from the 'Quarterly Journal of Prophecy.' Second Edition. Price 6d.

CHRISTIAN UNION. Reprinted from the 'Christian Observer.' Price 2d.

'FORBID HIM NOT.' A Sermon on Schism. Second Edition. Price 2d.

The SAVING POWER of the GOSPEL. Second Thousand. Price 1d.

RIGHTEOUSNESS and REDEMPTION. Second Edition. Price 1d.

The BELIEVER'S COMPLETENESS in CHRIST. Sixth Edition. Price 1d.

The ETERNITY of EVIL. Eighth Thousand (exclusive of American Editions). Price 6d. per dozen, or 3s. per 100.

LETTER to a CHRISTIAN MINISTER on FUTURE PUNISHMENT. Third Thousand. Price 1d. or 6s. per 100.

TRUTH and LOVE. Price 6d. per dozen, or 3s. per 100.

DEATH and DESTRUCTION. Notes on an Address delivered at a Clerical Meeting in defence of the Doctrine that the end of the wicked will be an everlasting life of misery in the world to come. Price 1d. or 6s. per 100.

IMMORTALITY. An appeal to Evangelists. With a Letter from the Rev. Dr. MORTIMER, late Head Master of the City of London School. Price 6d. per dozen, or 3s. per 100.

'WHOSE END IS DESTRUCTION.' Price 6d. per dozen, or 3s. per 100.

'The WAY EVERLASTING.' A Review of the Controversy upon Eternal Evil. Price 1s.

The DESTINY of the ELECT CHURCH. Rom. viii. 29, 30. Price 3d.

*** *Most of the above may be obtained at a reduced price from S. Lynch, 57 Coleshill Street, Eaton Square.*

The following Works may be consulted upon the main subject treated of in this volume.

REVELATIONS of a FUTURE STATE.
ARCHBISHOP WHATELY. Longmans.

ESSAYS in ECCLESIASTICAL BIOGRAPHY
(The Epilogue). Sir JAMES STEPHEN. Longmans.

LIFE in CHRIST; or, Immortality peculiar to the Regenerate.
Rev. E. WHITE. Jackson & Walford.

LIFE or DEATH.
E. F. LITTON, M.A., Barrister-at-Law. Longmans.

CHRIST our LIFE. Price 1s. 6d.
A CLERGYMAN of the ESTABLISHED CHURCH (the late Rev. W. de Burgh). Simpkin, Marshall, & Co.

POPULAR IDEAS of IMMORTALITY.
Rev. W. KER, M.A., Incumbent of Tipton, Staffordshire. Laxton, Dudley.

ENDLESS SUFFERINGS not the DOCTRINE of SCRIPTURE.
Rev. T. DAVIS, M.A., Incumbent of Roundhay, Yorkshire. Longmans.

The DURATION and NATURE of FUTURE PUNISHMENT. Price 2s.
Rev. H. CONSTABLE, M.A., Prebendary of Cork. Longmans.

The TRIPARTITE NATURE of MAN.
Rev. J. B. HEARD, M.A. Hamilton, Adams, & Co.

LIFE and DEATH, as TAUGHT in SCRIPTURE.
Elliot Stock.

EVERLASTING PUNISHMENT not EVERLASTING PAIN.
Rev. R. REYNOLDSON, for nearly 40 years Minister of Upper Hill Street Chapel, Wisbeach. Elliot Stock.

ETERNAL PUNISHMENT and ETERNAL DEATH.
Rev. J. W. BARLOW, M.A., Fellow and Tutor of Trinity College, Dublin. Longmans.

SCRIPTURE DOCTRINE of FUTURE PUNISHMENT.
Rev. H. H. DOBNEY. Ward & Co.

The KINGDOM of GOD.
HENRY DUNN. Simpkin, Marshall, & Co.

The DURATION of EVIL. Simpkin, Marshall, & Co.

The QUESTION of AGES. W. MORRIS, M.D., Philadelphia.

DEBT and GRACE. Professor HUDSON, New York.

The ENTIRE EVIDENCE of EVANGELISTS and APOSTLES on FUTURE PUNISHMENT. Price 1s. 6d.
Rev. W. GRIFFITH. Elliot Stock.

The RESTITUTION of ALL THINGS. Price 8d.
Rev. H. CONSTABLE, M.A., Prebendary of Cork. James Clarke & Co.

LIFE in CHRIST ONLY. Price 6d.
Rev. E. WHITE. James Clarke & Co.

PAULINE THEOLOGY. Price 1s.
W. H. HASTINGS, Boston, U.S. Elliot Stock.

FORGOTTEN THEMES, or FACTS for FAITH. Price 1s.
G. A. BREWER, Plymouth, U.S. Elliot Stock.

The MOMENTOUS QUESTION—Who shall Live for Ever?
Price 3d. W. MORRIS. Elliot Stock.

A DIALOGUE on LIFE in CHRIST. Price 4d.
S. WRIGHT. Elliot Stock.

FOR GOD and the TRUTH. A Reply to Dr. Angus.
Price 2d. Elliot Stock.

FUTURE PUNISHMENT. Letter to a Lady. Price 1d.
HENRY CONSTABLE, M.A. Prebendary of Cork. Elliot Stock.

WILL SIN and SUFFERING be EVERLASTING?
Price 3d. JOSEPH STRATFORD. Elliot Stock.

REV. S. MINTON RIGHT, and the *RECORD* WRONG,
on the Question of Endless Miseries.
Rev. H. SMITH WARLEIGH, Rector of Abchurch. Elliot Stock.

The RAINBOW. 6d. monthly. Kent & Co.

OLD TRUTHS in NEW FORMS. Price 1s.
Rev. JOSEPH PARKER, D.D. Hurren, Poultry Chapel House, Cheapside.

www.ingramcontent.com/pod-product-compliance
Lightning Source LLC
Chambersburg PA
CBHW031936230426
43672CB00010B/1946